# GENRE KNOWLEDGE IN
# DISCIPLINARY COMMUNICATION:
## COGNITION/CULTURE/POWER

# GENRE KNOWLEDGE IN DISCIPLINARY COMMUNICATION:

## COGNITION/CULTURE/POWER

**Carol Berkenkotter**
*Michigan Technological University*

**Thomas N. Huckin**
*University of Utah*

**LEA** LAWRENCE ERLBAUM ASSOCIATES, PUBLISHERS
1995   Hillsdale, New Jersey                    Hove, UK

Lawrence Erlbaum Associates, Inc., Publishers
365 Broadway
Hillsdale, New Jersey 07642

Cover design by Jan Melchior

**Library of Congress Cataloging-in-Publication Data**

Berkenkotter, Carol.
  Genre knowledge in disciplinary communication : cognition,
culture, power / Carol Berkenkotter, Thomas N. Huckin.
      p.    cm.
  Includes bibliographical references and index.
  ISBN 0-8058-1611-9 (alk. paper).—ISBN 0-8058-1612-7 (pbk. :
alk.paper)
  1. Rhetoric.  2. Discourse analysis.  3. Register (Linguistics)
4. Sublanguage.  I. Huckin, Thomas N.  II. Title.
P301.B47  1994
401'.41—dc20                                      94-16549
                                                      CIP

Books published by Lawrence Erlbaum Associates are printed on acid-free
paper, and their bindings are chosen for strength and durability.

Printed in the United States of America
10  9  8  7  6  5  4  3  2

*For Jim and Christiane*

# CONTENTS

# PREFACE

A writer's development of genre knowledge has not only a sociocultural dimension, but a systemic dimension as well. Language users are situated artful actors whose acts of communication occur within semiotic systems. In the course of our studies of disciplinary communication conducted since the mid 1980s, we have perceived the operations of systems as diverse as peer review in scientific publication and language in a first-grade science classroom.

We use the term *genre knowledge* to refer to an individual's repertoire of situationally appropriate responses to recurrent situations—from immediate encounters to distanced communication through the medium of print, and more recently, the electronic media. One way to study the textual character of disciplinary communication is to examine both the situated actions of writers, and the communicative systems in which disciplinary actors participate. It is these two perspectives that we present in this book.

A word about our methodology is relevant here. We have used a variety of research techniques in these studies, which, given the differences in our training, has proven to be a genuine asset over the years we have worked together. These techniques include case study and ethnographic techniques, and rhetorical and discourse analyses of changing features in large corpuses and in the texts of individual writers. Our use of these techniques has enabled us to engage in both microlevel and macrolevel analyses and to develop a perspective that reflects both foci. From this perspective we propose that what microlevel studies of actors' situated actions frequently depict as *individual processes*, can also be interpreted (from the macrolevel) as *communicative acts within a discursive network or system*. Genre is the concept that enables us to envision the interpenetration of process and system in disciplinary communication. We have come a long way from our notions of genre in graduate school.

Although studies of genre have been until recently the province of literary scholars, this scholarship has been generally concerned with the formal features of literary texts. In contrast, rhetorical studies of genre have focused more on the social dynamics and social constitution of nonliterary forms of writing and speaking. During the 1980s, within a number of fields one could see a burgeoning interest in the history and sociocultural functions of disciplinary genres. Some of this work grew out of the work of European and American linguists in Language for Specific Purposes and English for Specific Purposes interested in legal and scientific communication. Another group of linguists, the critical discourse analysts, have been concerned from the perspective of social semiotics with the ideological character of professional discourse. Within the fields of rhetoric and communication, scholars interested in the textual dynamics of scientific and scholarly communities have focused on such genres as the experimental article and literature review in the natural sciences and the literary critic's interpretive essay. Much of this work has been influenced by studies of the social dimension of science conducted by sociologists of science in England and elsewhere in Europe. These scholars in the 1970s and early 1980s conducted pioneering laboratory studies that focused from a social constructionist perspective on the "manufacture of knowledge" in scientific communities. In particular, the interest of sociologists of science in the social construction of scientific discourse has had considerable impact on American rhetoric of science.

In 1992, an international conference on genre at Carleton University in Ottawa, Canada, brought together linguists, rhetoricians, educational researchers, literary theorists, and composition scholars to present recent work and to articulate the central issues and concerns growing out of the various fields engaged in genre scholarship. It is in the context and the intellectual traditions of the work described here that we offer our studies of the genres of disciplinary communication.

We have combined our respective expertise in the fields of discourse analysis and cognitively based rhetorical research to develop what we are calling a *sociocognitive theory of genre*. We describe this theory as *grounded* because it is based on the empirical findings of our 8 years of case study research. We have also drawn from such sources as our reading of structuration theory in sociology, activity theory in developmental psychology, and historical rhetorical studies. The five principles that constitute the theory are described in the first chapter of this book. Through the research that we present in the subsequent chapters we further develop and comment on the principles we present in chapter 1. Thus, chapter 2 illustrates the dynamic nature of genres by showing how a well established genre, the scientific journal article, changes over time. Chapters 3 and 4 are concerned with the textual dynamics of scientific publication both from the perspective of the scientist who must revise a manuscript and from an examination of peer review correspondence between scientist, editor, and reviewers. Chapters

5 and 6 examine the relationship between disciplinary formation and the features of evolving genres in disciplinary communities. Chapter 7 presents a socialization study of a doctoral student's acquisition of the registers and genre conventions of social science expository prose and essayist prose in the humanities. In the last chapter we move away from our own research to consider the pedagogical implications of a sociocognitive theory of genre. Specifically we raise a number of questions concerning the explicit teaching of "classroom" or "curriculum" genres.

It is our hope and ambition that the research methods and the theoretical framework presented in these chapters will raise provocative questions for scholars, researchers, and teachers in a number of fields: linguists who teach and conduct research in ESP and LSP and are interested in methods for studying professional communication; scholars in the fields of communication, rhetoric, and sociology of science with an interest in the textual dynamics of scientific and scholarly communities; educational researchers interested in cognition in context; and composition scholars interested in writing in the disciplines.

*Carol Berkenkotter*
*Thomas N. Huckin*

# ACKNOWLEDGMENTS

Our awareness of the conventions of acknowledgment sections requires that we be mercifully brief. However, a book is the fruit of many minds interacting and much supportive labor, and thus we need considerable space to acknowledge the intellectual and personal debts we owe to colleagues, friends, and family. There would be no book without the invaluable information provided by John Ackerman, Eunice Carlson, Elizabeth Flynn, John Weis, Barbara Araneo, Keith Bishop, Robert Kraemer, John Woolford, William Brown, Michael Widom, Robert Suter, and William McClure. In acting as informants and specialist consultants, these colleagues provided us with some of the most important insights we present in the various chapters. In particular we would like to thank John Ackerman and Eunice Carlson for their candor in describing their respective experiences as writers. We owe them an enormous debt for allowing us to make public their private thoughts and utterances.

There are also a number of colleagues with whom we have discussed a number of ideas that appear in chapter 1. Many of them were kind enough to read and comment on various chapters in the book. Carolyn Miller, Martin Nystrand, John Swales, Charles Bazerman, Greg Myers, David Russell, Donald Rubin, Cindy Selfe, Marilyn Cooper, Trent Batson, Richard Lee Enos, and Alan Gross read and commented on drafts of these chapters. Aviva Freedman and Peter Medway provided us with a forum for presenting the theoretical material in chapter 1 by inviting us to give a paper at the Ottawa Conference on Rethinking Genre. Special thanks goes to Charles Bazerman, whose work on the development of the experimental article and whose thinking about genre has served as a catalyst for much of the recent work in this area, including our own.

We owe as well a debt to the many graduate students who have thought with us in seminars and over messy tables in restaurants. Bill Jabusch, Edith Peschke, Jerry Savage, Sean Clancey, Terry McNinch, Scott Oates, Louise Rehling, Brenton Faber, and Kate Remlinger discussed many of the concepts in chapter 1 and elsewhere. Jerry Savage, Kate Remlinger, and Bill Jabusch are using genre approaches in their own studies, and we have profited from discussing their work with them. Mark Hagen's knowledge of computer graphics has been indispensable to us, and Margaret Olsen and Melanie Stoddard helped us by proofreading and typing.

There has been considerable support for this project, which came from various sources. Hollis Heimbouch, our editor at Lawrence Erlbaum Associates, showed support for the project at a time when she could only see a portion of the manuscript. She has provided sound advice throughout the project. Teresa Faella, our production editor, made editing and proofreading a less arduous task. Two sabbatical leaves and release time from Michigan Technological University made it possible to begin the project and bring it to completion. A grant from the National Council of Teachers of English to study discourse patterns in classroom conversation enabled us to think about speech genres in relation to activities conducted in time and space. And finally there has been the support of our families. To Jim and Christiane who have made it possible for us to juggle the demands of our academic careers with those of conducting the research and writing, no amount of gratitude could possibly suffice—at least not in this incarnation.

Grateful acknowledgment is made to the following for permission to reprint previously published material, which has been updated and revised for this volume:

Berkenkotter, C. (1990). Evolution of a scholarly forum: *Reader*, 1977–1988. In G. Kirsch & D. H. Roen (Eds.), *A sense of audience in written communication.* Newbury Park, CA: Sage Publications. Copyright 1990 by Sage Publications, Inc. Reprinted by permission of Sage Publications, Inc.

Berkenkotter, C., & Huckin, T. N. (1993). Rethinking genre from a sociocognitive perspective. *Written Communication, 10*(4), 475–509. Copyright 1993 by Sage Publications, Inc. Reprinted by permission of Sage Publications, Inc.

Berkenkotter, C., & Huckin, T. N. (1993). You are what you cite: Novelty and intertextuality in a biologist's experimental article. In N. R. Blyler & C. Thralls (Eds.), *Professional communication: The social perspective.* Newbury Park, CA: Sage Publications. Copyright 1993 by Sage Publications, Inc. Reprinted by permission of Sage Publications, Inc.

Berkenkotter, C., Huckin, T. N., & Ackerman, J. (1988). Conventions, conversations, and the writer: Case study of a student in a rhetoric Ph.D. program. *Research in the Teaching of English, 22*(1), 9–44. Copyright 1988 by the National Council of Teachers of English. Reprinted with permission.

# 1

# RETHINKING GENRE FROM A SOCIOCOGNITIVE PERSPECTIVE

*The significance of generic categories ... resides in their cognitive and cultural value, and the purpose of genre theory is to lay out the implicit knowledge of the users of genres.*

—Ryan (1981, p. 112)

*... the shapes of knowledge are ineluctably local, indivisible from their instruments and their encasements.*

—Geertz (1983, p. 4)

Written communication functions within disciplinary cultures to facilitate the multiple social interactions that are instrumental in the production of knowledge. In the sciences and humanities, maintaining the production of knowledge is crucial for institutional recognition, the development of subspecialities, and the advancement of scientists' and scholars' research programs. Scientific and scholarly productivity are also the criteria by which careers are assessed, tenure given, and grants awarded. Knowledge production is carried out and codified largely through generic forms of writing: lab reports, working papers, reviews, grant proposals, technical reports, conference papers, journal articles, monographs, and so on. Genres are the media through which scholars and scientists communicate with their peers. Genres are intimately linked to a discipline's methodology, and they package information in ways that conform to a discipline's norms, values, and ideology. Understanding the genres of written communication in one's field is, therefore, essential to professional success.

A great deal has been written about the literary genres, and in rhetorical studies, genre theory has had a healthy resurgence since the late 1970s. Much of this material can be seen as various attempts to develop taxonomies or classificatory schemes or to set forth hierarchical models of the constitutive elements of genre (for reviews, see Campbell & Jamieson, 1978; Miller, 1984; Swales, 1990). This taxonomical scholarship and theory building has been based largely on analyses of the features of written or oral texts. Although such an approach enables one to make generalizations about what some writers refer to as a genre's *form, substance, and context* (see, e.g., Yates & Orlikowski, 1992), it does not enable us to determine anything about the ways in which genre is embedded in the communicative activities of the members of a discipline. Nor does a traditional rhetorical approach enable us to understand the functions of genre from the perspective of the actor who must draw upon genre knowledge to perform effectively.

Bakhtin (1981) argued that genres and other forms of verbal communication are sites of tension between unifying ("centripetal") forces and stratifying ("centrifugal") forces. "The authentic environment of an utterance, the environment in which it lives and takes shape, is dialogized heteroglossia, anonymous and social as language, but simultaneously concrete, filled with specific content and accented as an individual utterance" (p. 272). Genres are "typical forms of utterances" (Bakhtin, 1986, p. 63), and as such, they should be studied in their actual social contexts of use. In particular, analysts should pay attention to ways in which genre users manipulate genres for particular rhetorical purposes. Bakhtin (1981) argued that this "intentional dimension" can only be fully understood and appreciated by observing "insiders":

> For the speakers of the language themselves, these generic languages and professional jargons are directly intentional—they denote and express directly and fully, and are capable of expressing themselves without mediation; but outside, that is, for those not participating in the given purview, these languages may be treated as objects, as typifactions, as local color. For such outsiders, the intentions permeating these languages become *things*, limited in their meaning and expression. (p. 289)

To date, very little work on genre in rhetorical studies has been informed by actual case research with *insiders*. Instead, there has long been a tendency among genre scholars to reify genres, to see them as linguistic abstractions, and to understate their "changeable, flexible and plastic" (Bakhtin, 1986, p. 80) nature.[1]

---

[1]This is so even in cases where the theorist cites some case-study research. For example, Swales (1990) briefly mentioned the anthropological research of Knorr-Cetina, Latour, and Woolgar, and Gilbert and Mulkay, but otherwise relied heavily on her own text-based analyses. Schryer's (1993) description of a veterinary medical record system draws heavily on her own ethnographic research, but not in a way that enables her to capture the rhetorical dynamism posited by Bakhtinian theory; instead of showing how insiders manipulate and modify the genre for rhetorical purposes, her account emphasizes its more stable and normalizing aspects.

A noticeable exception is Myers (1990), who tapped substantial insider knowledge in depicting the struggles of practicing biologists to make the best use of certain scientific genres.

In this chapter we argue for an alternative way of looking at the genres of academic cultures, focusing on the ways in which writers use genre knowledge (or fail to use such knowledge) as they engage in such disciplinary activities as writing up laboratory experiments, judging conference proposals, negotiating with reviewers over the revisions of a research report, reading the drafts of a scientific article, or creating a new forum for scholarly publication. Our thinking is based on 8 years of rhetorical and linguistic analyses of case study data that foreground individual writers' language-in-use; this approach has led to our present view that writers acquire and strategically deploy genre knowledge as they participate in their field's or profession's knowledge-producing activities.

Our thesis is that genres are inherently dynamic rhetorical structures that can be manipulated according to the conditions of use, and that genre knowledge is therefore best conceptualized as a form of situated cognition embedded in disciplinary activities. For writers to make things happen (i.e., to publish, to exert an influence on the field, to be cited), they must know how to strategically utilize their understanding of genre. Their work must always appear to be on the cutting edge. This means that they must understand the directions in which a field is developing at any given time and possess the rhetorical savvy necessary for positioning their work within it. An academic writer needs to possess a highly developed sense of timing: At this moment, what are the compelling issues, questions, and problems with which knowledgeable peers are concerned? What is the history of these issues in the field? In the humanities, and the social and natural sciences especially, knowing what winds are blowing in the intellectual zeitgeist is essential to good timing (Miller, 1992).

The theoretical view we espouse here is *grounded* (Glaser & Strauss, 1967; Lincoln & Guba, 1985) in our observations of the professional activities of individual writers, specifically in the data that we have been collecting since 1984 on adult writers in disciplinary communities. Our method, however, has not been purely inductive. Over the last several years our perspective has been informed by a number of disciplines and by various writers' theoretical constructs. These include structuration theory in sociology,[2] rhetorical studies,[3] interpretive anthropology,[4] ethnomethodology,[5] Bakhtin's theory of speech genres (1986), Vygotsky's theory of ontogenesis,[6] and Russian activity theory[7] as it has shaped the movement in U.S. psychology called *situated* or *everyday cognition*.[8] From our research and from this literature we have developed five principles that constitute a theoretical framework:

---

[2]See Giddens (1984), Bourdieu (1987), and Bryant and Jary (1991).

[3]See Bitzer (1968), Miller (1984), Yates and Orlikowski (1992), and especially the rhetoric of science (Bazerman, 1988; Swales, 1990).

[4]See Geertz (1973, 1983), Clifford (1983), and Clifford and Marcus (1986).

[5]See Garfinkel (1967).

[6]See Vygotsky (1978, 1986).

[7]See Wertsch (1981, 1991).

[8]See Brown, Collins, and Duguid (1989) and Rogoff and Lave (1984).

- *Dynamism.* Genres are dynamic rhetorical forms that are developed from actors' responses to recurrent situations and that serve to stabilize experience and give it coherence and meaning. Genres change over time in response to their users' sociocognitive needs.
- *Situatedness.* Our knowledge of genres is derived from and embedded in our participation in the communicative activities of daily and professional life. As such, genre knowledge is a form of "situated cognition" that continues to develop as we participate in the activities of the ambient culture.
- *Form and Content.* Genre knowledge embraces both form and content, including a sense of what content is appropriate to a particular purpose in a particular situation at a particular point in time.
- *Duality of Structure.* As we draw on genre rules to engage in professional activities, we *constitute* social structures (in professional, institutional, and organizational contexts) and simultaneously *reproduce* these structures.
- *Community Ownership.* Genre conventions signal a discourse community's norms, epistemology, ideology, and social ontology.

In the sections that follow we explicate each of these principles in detail, referring to a number of constructs in the literature mentioned earlier. We are not so much articulating a fully developed sociocognitive theory of genre as we are *working toward one* by integrating concepts from a number of fields. Thus we present a synthesis of perspectives and constructs from which a sociocognitive theory of genre can be developed.

## DYNAMISM

Genres are dynamic rhetorical forms that are developed from actors' responses to recurrent situations and that serve to stabilize experience and give it coherence and meaning. Genres change over time in response to their users' sociocognitive needs.

This principle is derived from contemporary rhetorical examinations of genre (as reviewed by Campbell & Jamieson, 1978; Miller, 1984) and is perhaps best exemplified by Bitzer's (1968) discussion of recurrent rhetorical situations:

> From day to day, year to year, comparable situations occur, prompting comparable responses; hence rhetorical forms are born, and a special vocabulary, grammar, and style are established. ... The situations recur and, because we experience situations and the rhetorical responses to them, a form of discourse is not only established but comes to have a power of its own—the tradition itself tends to function as a constraint upon any new response in the form. (p. 13)

Although Bitzer did not use the term *genre*, his notion of rhetorical forms emerging in response to recurrent situations sparked several scholarly discussions of rhetorical genres. A number of scholars invoked Bitzer's notion of recurring rhetorical responses to situational exigencies to characterize genre (Campbell & Jamieson, 1978; Harrell & Linkugel, 1978; Miller, 1984; Simons, 1978). And recently in an essay that examines the genres of organizational communication, Yates and Orlikowski (1992) treated Bitzer's claim as a concept symbol (Small, 1978) to mean that "genres emerge within a particular sociohistorical context and are reinforced over time as a situation recurs. . . . These genres, in turn, shape future responses to similar situations" (p. 305).

In a widely cited essay that reconceptualizes rhetorical views of genre from a sociological perspective, Miller (1984) proposed that "recurrence" does not refer to external conditions (a realist view) but rather, is socially constructed: "What recurs cannot be a material configuration of objects, events, and people, nor can it be a subjective configuration, a 'perception,' for these too are unique from moment to moment and person to person. Recurrence is an intersubjective phenomenon, a social occurrence, and cannot be understood on materialist terms" (p. 156).

Miller's major contribution to the discussion of genre was to take the notion of genre as recurrent response to a rhetorical situation and link it to Schutz and Luckmann's (1973) construct of "typification" as a socially construed meaning-making process. Our "stock of knowledge," Miller (1984) argued, following Schutz and Luckmann, is based on types:

> useful only insofar as [this knowledge] can be brought to bear on new experience: the new is made familiar through the recognition of relevant similarities; those similarities become constituted as a type. . . . It is through the process of typification that we create recurrence, analogies, similarities. What recurs is not a material situation (a real objective factual event) but our construal of a type. The typified situation, including typifications of participants, underlies typification in rhetoric. Successful communication would require that the participants share common types; this is possible insofar as types are socially created. (pp. 156–157)

Miller's social constructionist view of genre, which incorporates Schutz and Luckman's notion of typification, has been significant to rhetorical studies of genre for a number of reasons. First, it has influenced scholarship in the rhetoric of science (e.g., Bazerman, 1988; Swales, 1990). Second, it has provided scholars with an interpretive framework for dealing with the thorny issue of the relationship between socially determined human communicative activity and agency.[9] Finally,

---

[9]For example, Bazerman (1994) extended Miller's notion of typification in some important ways, rescuing agency from an overly deterministic reading of typification as socialization into categories of response independent of individuality:

> . . . such typification of moments goes hand in hand with learning genres of responses: this is the time for such-and-such kind of comment. Moreover, this typification helps us develop our set of characteristic social actions. We are learning how to recognize not only categories of social moments and what works rhetorically in such moments but also how we can act and respond . . .

Miller's application of the construct of typification—grounded as it is in Schutz's sociological perspective of actors' behaviors in the life-world, in contrast to previous rhetorical and literary notions of genre—extricates the concept from its moorings in Aristotelian and literary classification systems, relocating it in a more microlevel understanding of the generic communicative behaviors of actors in everyday life. As she stated:

> To consider as potential genres such homely discourse as the letter of recommendation, the user manual, the progress report, the ransom note, the lecture, and the white paper, as well as the eulogy, the apologia, the inaugural, the public proceeding, and the sermon, is not to trivialize the study of genres; it is to take seriously the rhetoric in which we are immersed and the situations in which we find ourselves. (Miller, 1984, p. 155)

Miller's insistence that considerations of genre encompass the typifications of the agora as well as those of the senate has been important to studies in technical and organizational communication (see e.g., Devitt, 1991; Herndl, Fennell, & Miller, 1991; Miller & Selzer, 1985; Yates & Orlikowski, 1992). And in locating genre in the social actions and practices of everyday life (in the professions and other social institutions such as the school), Miller's essay anticipates the interest in Bakhtin's construct of *speech genres*, which will figure importantly later in this discussion.

But just as language itself has to accommodate both stability and change, genres must do more than encapsulate intersubjective perceptions of recurring situations. They must also try to deal with the fact that recurring situations resemble each other only in certain ways and only to a certain degree. As the world changes, both in material conditions and in actors' collective and individual perceptions of it, the types produced by typification must themselves undergo constant incremental change. Furthermore, individual actors have their own uniquely formed knowledge of the world; and socially induced perceptions of commonality do not eradicate subjective perceptions of difference. Genres, therefore, are always sites of contention between stability and change. They are inherently dynamic, constantly (if gradually) changing over time in response to the sociocognitive needs of individual users. This dynamism resembles that found in other aspects of language acquisition, including, for example, the negotiated learning and use of individual words (cf. Huckin, Haynes, & Coady, 1993; Pinker, 1984), and to a lesser extent, the construction of sentences via "emergent" grammar (Goodwin, 1979; Hopper, 1988).

---

*Nonetheless given the great variety of our biographies, we develop different constructs of moments and appropriate responses* [italics added]. . . . Each [of us] perceives the moment as a different kind of occasion, calling on a different repertoire of responses. Each individual's characteristic sense-making and action patterns contribute to what we call *personality*. (p. 178)

An example of this internal dynamism can be found in Huckin's study of 350 scientific journal articles published between 1944 and 1989 (chap. 2). In this study, Huckin analyzed formal patterns and interviewed a number of working scientists who regularly read and contribute to the literature. The scientific journal article has long been thought of as a conservative, relatively static genre, especially on the formal level, yet Huckin found that it had actually undergone significant changes over this 45-year period. For example, he found experimental results increasingly being foregrounded in titles, abstracts, introductions, and section headings, but methods and procedures sections increasingly being relegated to secondary status. The interviews with scientists revealed perhaps the main reason for these changes, namely, that in this age of information explosion, readers of scientific journals cannot keep up with the literature and are forced to skim journal articles the way many newspaper readers skim newspapers. These scientist readers are also writers, and their individual reading behavior affects their writing strategies. Inasmuch as they also belong to a scientific community, they find themselves responding in similar ways to similar communicative pressures. Thus, on both a communal and individual (i.e., sociocognitive) level, scientists shape the genre to better serve their needs. The result is a continually evolving, not static, genre.

## SITUATEDNESS

Our knowledge of genres is derived from and embedded in our participation in the communicative activities of daily and professional life. As such, genre knowledge is a form of "situated cognition" (Brown, Collins, & Duguid, 1989) that continues to develop as we participate in the activities of the culture.

From a sociocognitive perspective, genre knowledge of academic discourse entails an understanding of both oral and written forms of appropriate communicative behaviors. This knowledge, rather than being explicitly taught, is transmitted through enculturation as apprentices become socialized to the ways of speaking in particular disciplinary communities. Because it is impossible for us to dwell in the social world without repertoires of typified social responses in recurrent situations—from greetings and thank yous to acceptance speeches and full-blown, written expositions of scientific or scholarly investigations—we use genres to package our speech and make of it a recognizable response to the exigencies of the situation.

Bakhtin's (1986) distinction between "primary" and "secondary" speech genres is a useful framework for helping us to distinguish between those forms of response that we use in daily communicative activities (greeting our children after school, making love, calling a colleague to ask for a favor) and those that are removed from the contexts of activities in which "primary genres" are embedded (e.g., scholarly and scientific articles, written forms of organizational communication, summons, subpoenas, patents). These "secondary genres" codify activity in situations occurring over time and in distant locales.[10] For this reason Bakhtin called the secondary speech genres "complex." The primary speech genres, in contrast, are "simple"; it is not the formal characteristics that are foregrounded but rather the particular communicative activities in which these genres are embedded. For example, young children, when they enter public school (or even preschool programs), learn the ways in which space and time in the classroom are configured during the school day and year and by association they learn the various forms of talk appropriate to a particular time of day and spacial configuration (e.g., sharing circle, reading groups, drawing and painting, etc.). Thus, children's accumulation of *school* genre knowledge begins very early in public school as they learn the patterned responses or "participation structures" (Cazden, 1986) associated with various school temporal/spatial activities, such as "sharing time"—which take place in the sharing circle.[11]

The sharing circle or "show and tell," like every other classroom language event, is governed by rules of interaction. Children leave their desks or tables and go to an open area in the classroom where they sit on the floor as a group. In the center of this group is the teacher, who most often sits on a child's chair. In this setting children make presentations to the group about some experience they have had outside of school. When a child's language behavior is not appropriate—interrupting while other children or the teacher is talking, taking the floor without raising a hand—the teacher gives strong negative cues (verbal and nonverbal) to child and peers. Time and space configurations are, therefore, an intrinsic part of primary speech genres. From this perspective, school days in school classrooms can be seen to consist of series of contiguous time/space/speech events: reading time, storytime, writing time, sharing circle, and so forth, as can be seen in Fig. 1.1. Through repeatedly carrying out these activities, children come to learn what are situationally appropriate generic behaviors. Although Bakhtin does not elaborate his concept of primary speech genres in such detail, we would argue that the given characterization is entirely consistent with Bakhtin's view that the primary genres are to be found in the local communicative activities of everyday life.

---

[10]Although he did not use the term *genre*, Giddens' (1984) concept of the reciprocal, reflexive character of structuration possesses an interesting resemblance to Bakhtin's notion of the textual dynamics involved in actors' creation of secondary genres:

> Repetitive activities located in one context of time and space have regularized consequences unintended by those who engage in those activities, in more or less "distant" time–space contexts. What happens in this second series of contexts then, directly or indirectly, influences the further conditions of action in the original context. To understand what is going on no explanatory variables are needed other than those which explain why individuals are motivated to engage in regularized social practices across time and space, and what consequences ensue. ( p. 14)

[11]For studies of the ways in which teacher–student interactions are controlled through the teacher's contextualization cues, see McHoul (1978) and Dorr-Bremme (1990).

*Speech acts as primary genres?*

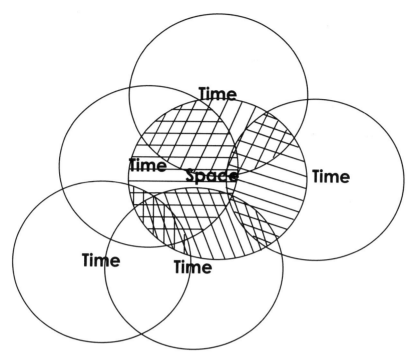

FIG. 1.1.  Structuration of school days through recurrent events (e.g., "show and tell time," "spelling time," "nap time").

Whereas primary genres are embedded in the milieu in which they occur, secondary speech genres are removed from their instantiation. Bakhtin (1986) put the matter this way:

> Secondary (complex) speech genres—novels, dramas, all kinds of scientific research, major genres of commentary and so forth—arise in more complex and comparatively highly developed and organized cultural communication (primarily written) that is artistic, scientific, sociopolitical, and so on. During the process of their formation they absorb and digest various primary (simple) genres that have taken form in unmediated speech communion. These primary genres are altered and assume a special character when they enter into complex ones. They lose their immediate relation to actual reality and to the real utterances of others. For example rejoinders of everyday dialogue or letters found in a novel retain their form and their everyday significance on the plane of the novel's content. They enter into actual reality only via the novel as a whole, that is, as a literary, artistic event and not as everyday life. (p. 62)

Bakhtin's theoretical formulation seems prescient in light of recent research in the sociology of science (Gilbert & Mulkay, 1984; Latour, 1987; Latour & Woolgar, 1986) that suggests that the experimental article reifies archetypal experiential activities (such as scientists' lab experiments) by transforming them into seamless accounts of scientific activity. Thus Bakhtin's notion of secondary genres as forms of organized cultural communication helps us to see a basic and major difference between the genres of everyday life and their more culturally complex cousins. It is not possible in these latter forms to discern the embedding of tangible activities in the genre as we are able to in the case of the genre-in-activity of the elementary school classroom. Yet Bakhtin maintained that even though the secondary speech genres reflect complex cultural communication, it is the primary genres that "legislate permissible locutions in lived life and secondary genres made up out of these . . . constitute not only literary but all other text types (legal, scientific, journalistic) as well. In fact, what distinguishes one human undertaking from another, one science from another is the roster of genres each has appropriated as its own" (Holquist, 1986, pp. xv–xvi).

Bakhtin's perspective, grounded as it is in his concept of the dialogical nature of *all* oral and written communication, is one way of resolving the thorny issue of what kinds of communicative acts should be accorded "genre status," as Swales (1990) put it. This latter view is most often espoused by scholars in literary studies, rhetorical studies, and discourse analysis who focus on the formal characteristics of texts (written and oral) rather than on the activities or practices in which genres are embedded.[12] Their view rests on what Brandt (1990) called "strong text" (formalist) assumptions rather than a dialogical view of language-in-interaction (see also Nystrand & Wiemelt, 1991). This latter perspective is more common among sociolinguists and educational psychologists who share Bakhtin's (and Vygotsky's) view that social interaction is at the center of language and concept learning.

For Bakhtin (1986) the "responsive utterance" is the basic unit of analysis of human communication. The utterance is a rejoinder made in response to the other (which may also be internalized). Thus communication, oral *or* written, is constituted by a series of turns:

> Sooner or later what is heard and actively understood will find its response in the subsequent speech or behavior of the listener. In most cases, genres of complex cultural communication are intended precisely for this kind of actively responsive understanding with delayed action. . . . Any utterance—from a short, single-word rejoinder in everyday dialogue to the large novel or scientific treatise—has, so to speak, an absolute beginning and absolute end: its beginning is preceded by the utterance of others, and its end is followed by the responsive utterances of others. (pp. 68–69, 71)

From a Bakhtinian dialogical perspective, academic—or any other institutional—discourse can be seen to take place on a "conversational continuum" that

---

[12]For discussions of criteria that should be applied to determine which typifications can be considered genres, as opposed to pre-genres, forms, or appropriate level of abstraction, see Miller (1984), Swales (1991), and Yates and Orlikowski (1992). For critiques of this approach, see Derrida on the law of genre (1981) and Bennett (1990).

inevitably for the language user involves a transition from naturalistic conversational turns to turns that are extended and monological. Along similar lines, Bergvall (1992) argued that:

> Academic discourse takes place on a variety of levels: casual hallway chats, lectures, conversations between teachers and students in and out of class, e-mail, memos, scholarly papers, books. Each of these is a form of academic "conversation," with a variety of levels of formality, personal involvement, number of participants, etc. The length of turns ranges from the quick exchanges of informal, intense conversation to the extended monologues of writing. Usually conversation is a natural pattern learned in childhood, but the appropriate use of the voice in academic conversation, particularly the monologic style, requires extensive training, and enculturation into the modes of conversation sanctioned by academic discourse communities. New members must learn style, vocabulary, citation format, organization and length of texts or talk, etc. (p. 1)[13]

This view that actors' knowledge of academic discourse in its various permutations grows out of their enculturation to the oral and written "forms of talk" of the academy brings us to our next point—that genre knowledge is a form of *situated cognition*, in other words, knowledge that is indexical, "inextricably a product of the activity and situations in which it [is] produced" (Brown, Collins, & Duguid, 1989, p. 33). Learning the genres of academic discourse, like other forms of concept learning, evolves "with each new occasion of use because new situations, negotiations, and activities inevitably recast it in a new, more densely textured form" (Brown, Collins, & Duguid, 1989, p. 33).[14] As we have seen in our own research and that of others dealing with "cognitive apprenticeship" (Collins, Brown, & Newman, 1989), generally the enculturation into the practices of disciplinary communities is "picked up" in the local milieu of the culture rather than being explicitly taught. As Brown, Collins, and Duguid (1989) suggested:

---

[13]A number of linguists whose work is associated with the systemic–functional school of linguistics (pioneered by M. A. K. Halliday) have written extensively on the importance of making explicit to children the conventions of the primary and secondary speech genres found in different disciplinary settings, such as *talking science* (see Lemke, 1990). The best known of these neo-Hallidayans is Kress (1982, 1987, 1989, 1993a, 1993b), whose work on the social semiotics of school language learning calls attention to the ways in which childrens' and adolescents' social identities are situated in the multiple discourses they acquire through reading, writing, listening, and speaking. Other noted members of the "genre school" include Christie, Martin, and Rothery. This group's research and writing have provoked a heated debate in the United Kingdom over whether or not teachers should be trained to explicitly teach curriculum genres, that is, the genres of speaking and writing that are appropriate to different disciplinary contexts such as science, history, and literary study. The issues that this debate has raised can be found in Reid (1988).

[14]Learning the genres of academic discourse thus involves learning both spoken and written modes, as mediated by the technologies entering the culture such as e-mail and electronic conferences. Because technology alters genres, producing blurred genres (see, e.g., Ferrara, Brunner, & Whittemore, 1991; Yates & Orlikowski, 1992), part of one's apprenticeship involves becoming fluent in various communicative media.

Given the chance to observe and practice *in situ* the behavior of members of a culture, people pick up the relevant jargon, imitate behavior, and gradually start to act in accordance with its norms. These cultural practices are often recondite and extremely complex. Nevertheless, given the opportunity to observe and practice them, people adopt them with great success. Students, for instance, can quickly get an implicit sense of what is suitable diction, what makes a relevant question, what is legitimate or illegitimate behavior in a particular activity. (p. 34)

Brown, Collins, and Duguid's argument here is based on their own as well as other studies of situated or everyday cognition (Engstrom, 1987; Lave, 1977, 1988a, 1988b; Lave & Wegner, 1991; Rogoff, 1990; Rogoff & Lave, 1984; Scribner, 1984). These studies owe a debt to the work of Russian activity theorists such as Vygotsky, Leontiev, and others, which has also influenced recent educational research (see Cazden, 1989; Clay & Cazden, 1990; Cole, 1985, 1990; Daiute, 1989, 1990; Dyson, 1987, 1988, 1990; Gallimore & Tharp, 1990; Wertsch, 1991). We believe that these latter studies are also relevant to our inquiries concerning the nature of genre knowledge.

Wertsch (1991) observed that Bakhtin and Vygotsky held a number of ideas in common:

First [they shared] the assertion that to understand human mental action one must understand the semiotic devices [such as language] used to mediate such action. . . . Second [they held] the assumption that certain aspects of human mental functioning are fundamentally tied to communicative practices . . . that human communicative practices give rise to mental functioning in the individual. (pp. 12–13)

These views undergird much of what has recently been written about the situated nature of individual concept development. For example, Brown, Collins, and Duguid (1989) argued that acquiring conceptual knowledge, like learning the use of tools, is "both situated and progressively developed through activity" (p. 33):

People who use tools actively rather than just acquire them . . . build an increasingly rich, implicit understanding of the world in which they use the tools and of the tools themselves. The understanding, both of the world and of the tool, continually changes as a result of their interaction. . . . The culture and the use of a tool act together to determine the way that practitioners see the world; and the way the world appears to them determines the culture's understanding of the world and of the tools. Unfortunately, students are too often asked to use the tools of a discipline without being able to adopt its culture. To learn to use tools as practitioners use them, a student, like an apprentice, must enter the community and its culture. (p. 33)

An activity-based theory of genre knowledge would therefore locate our learning of academic genres in the processes that Vygotsky described as "socially distributed cognition," occurring in the situated activities of a practitioner-in-training. Genre knowledge, as we have seen in our own research, is very much a part of the conceptual tool kit of professional academic writers, linked to their knowledge of how to use the other tools of their trade: the biologist's lab assay, the literary historian's knowledge of how to synthesize information from archival microfiche, the psychologist's use of statistical procedures to determine degrees of freedom, the metallurgist's knowledge of the workings of the electron microscope. This is what we mean when we claim that genre knowledge is a form of situated cognition, inextricable from professional writers' procedural and social knowledge. *Social knowledge*, as we use the term here, refers to writers' familiarity with the research networks in their field (Kaufer & Geisler, 1989). It is the knowledge they draw on to create an appropriate rhetorical and conceptual context in which to position their own research and knowledge claims. Genre knowledge, procedural knowledge (which includes a knowledge of tools and their uses as well as of a discipline's methods and interpretive framework), and social knowledge are acquired incrementally as students progress through a period of apprenticeship, generally at the graduate level.

Learning the genres of disciplinary or professional discourse would therefore be similar to second language acquisition, requiring immersion into the culture and a lengthy period of apprenticeship and enculturation (cf. Freedman, 1993). In contrast, undergraduate university students, like secondary school students, learn many institutional, or curriculum, genres. Following Brown, Collins, and Duguid's (1989) line of reasoning, we would contend that many of these pedagogical genres contain *some* of the textual features and *some* of the conventions of disciplinary genres but that they are also linked to and instantiate classroom-based activities such as reading, writing, solving decontextualized math problems, or conducting simple experiments of the kind found in lab manuals. This view has a number of important implications for current notions of the teaching of disciplinary discourse. It may be the case, for example, that writing-across-the-curriculum programs should try to sensitize faculty in the disciplines to the fact that, in contrast to the specialized rhetorics they routinely use in their professional writing, the genres of the undergraduate curricula are characterized by quite different textual features and conventions, given their classroom-based contexts and rhetorical functions.

## FORM AND CONTENT

Genre knowledge embraces both form and content, including a sense of what content is appropriate to a particular purpose in a particular situation at a particular point in time.

If genres are dynamic rhetorical structures and genre knowledge a form of situated cognition, it follows that both genres and genre knowledge are more sharply and richly defined to the extent that they are *localized* (in both time and place). Traditional generic classifications are pitched at such a broad level of generality that they can describe only superficial parameters of form or content. For example, "the business letter," as discussed in traditional writing textbooks, is depicted in largely formal terms with only vague comments about content. By contrast, more localized genres like "a letter from a Utah bank promoting a new savings program" can be more fully described, with reference made to specific aspects of content (e.g., subtopics such as interest rates, security, tax benefits, etc. discussed in ways that are relevant to people from Utah). In the dynamic, grounded view of genre that we advocate here, what constitutes true genre knowledge is not just a knowledge of formal conventions but a knowledge of appropriate topics and relevant details as well.

Recent studies of academic discourse contain numerous examples of how deeply content is implicated in genre knowledge. For instance, Marshall and Barritt (1990), in their study of *American Educational Research Journal* articles, explained how this particular genre is strongly affected by philosophical considerations. They noted that "the forms of argument, in other words the rhetoric, used by scholars who publish in *AERJ* continue to be influenced by the objectivist tradition of research that owes so much to the analogy between natural and social events" (p. 605). They showed how this positivist stance manifests itself in particular textual features, such as the way in which reference is made to teachers, students, and parents. For example:

> Parents' decisions and opinions, when they are considered at all, are dismissed as economically motivated or as the result of intimidation rather than treated as genuine reflections of alternative beliefs about schools, education, or their own children. . . . It would be possible for the rhetoric of these articles to acknowledge parents as most often genuinely concerned about their children's well being. Parents could be constituted as adults who have perceptions different from those of teachers or researchers but whose views are no less accurate, complete, or complicated. . . . Yet such a shift in the rhetoric would necessitate attention to the role of the experience, common sense, reflection, relationship, perception, and motivation of parents as well as of researchers; a different rhetoric that would negate the authority of the researcher as expert knower. (p. 603)

The clear implication is that anyone wishing to publish in *AERJ* would do well to not give parents the same voice or status as researchers and, more generally, to avoid any methodology not adhering to positivistic norms. (For some other examples of how basic philosophical differences between social science research and humanistic scholarship reveal themselves in textual features, see Hansen, 1988; MacDonald, 1987, 1989, 1992.)

Another aspect of content that should be considered in defining a genre is background knowledge, that is, knowledge (of the world, of a particular community, of a discipline, etc.) that readers of that genre are assumed to have. A recent study by Giltrow (1992) provides a good example. Giltrow collected all newspaper reports of sentencing for violent crime that appeared in a major Canadian daily over a 2-month period in 1950 and over a 3-month period in 1990. She then analyzed and compared these two sets, focusing on how textual coherence is maintained via unstated assumptions of background knowledge. For example, in the following excerpt from a 1991 article about a child molester, a naive reader might wonder how the third sentence is related to the first two:

> The judge agreed with prosecutor Wendy Sabean that Blakemore, 31, of Georgetown "poses a real threat to the safety of others." The judge was told that Blakemore has confessed to sexually assaulting at least 17 boys and girls ranging in age from 6 to 10. Blakemore wants his mother, father, and Sunday school teacher charged for abusing him when he was a child, court was told. (*Toronto Star*, Jan. 3, 1991, p. A9)

Giltrow noted that the reporter who wrote this article was apparently assuming that a typical reader of this particular newspaper in 1991 would know (or believe, at least) that "a widely observed cause of adult violence is childhood experience of abuse by family members and/or respected members of the community" (p. 7). Indeed, as Giltrow showed, this assumption is embedded in the genre, enabling those readers who are familiar with the genre to move smoothly through the article. By contrast, such an assumption was apparently *not* part of the background knowledge expected of readers in 1950. The family was seen then, according to Giltrow, not as a corrupting influence but as a corrective one. Hence, in 1950 the excerpt quoted above would not have had the coherence it had in 1991. In addition to showing how background knowledge bears on genre knowledge, this example indicates how genres can, indeed must, change over time as community knowledge itself changes.

Closely related to background knowledge is the concept of surprise value or novelty, which can also play a role in definitions of genre and genre knowledge. In writing up news reports, for example, a journalist is expected to have a keen sense of what aspects of a story are most "newsworthy." Indeed, newsworthiness is the primary factor in the use of the so-called inverted-pyramid text schema (Van Dijk, 1986). An appreciation of novelty is also important in academic disciplines. Bazerman (1985), Huckin (1987), and Kaufer and Geisler (1989), among others, showed how scholarly articles are expected to be at the "cutting edge," to make an original and novel contribution to disciplinary knowledge. The two philosophers in Kaufer and Geisler's study, for example, based their composing strategies on proposing novel knowledge claims and showing how these claims went beyond the consensual knowledge, or "framework knowledge," of the field. Their rhetorical expertise contrasts sharply with the inexpert behavior of two undergraduate students, who merely summarized the framework knowledge in one case and ignored it in the other. Kaufer and Geisler (1989) observed that:

Despite significant differences between them, both freshmen, we submit, lacked the concept of novelty as a design strategy for academic argument. What exactly did they lack? They lacked the knowledge or skill to interplay two competing impulses: the impulse to account for the information one inherits from a cultural community (represented in sources) and the impulse to move beyond these givens by breaking a consensus within them (even if the consensus is only "As of yet, no one has"). Writers who successfully orchestrate both impulses design for newness. (p. 297)

In Berkenkotter and Huckin (1993a), we presented a case study showing how an experienced microbiologist uses the peer review process to orchestrate these two impulses.

Another aspect of content that should be taken into account in much academic writing (as well as in journalism and other fields) is that of *kairos*, or rhetorical timing. A good illustration of this strategy can be seen in the history of the discovery of DNA, as discussed in Miller (1992). DNA was first theorized by Avery and two colleagues in 1944. Nine years later its structural properties were described by Watson and Crick, who received much greater acclaim than did Avery, as well as the Nobel Prize. Halloran (1984) attributed these differences in reception partly to differences in the way the two teams wrote their reports. Avery's report of his discovery (published in the *Journal of Experimental Medicine*) is very cautious in style: long-winded, depersonalized, and dense with technical details; Watson and Crick's famous *Nature* report is short, elliptical, and coy. Halloran implied that Watson and Crick simply made better use of the genre than did Avery. In a strong counterargument, however, Miller observed that the rhetorical conditions for the two reports were vastly different. Avery was far ahead of his time, breaking new ground at a pace for which the scientific community was unprepared. Watson and Crick, by contrast, were riding the crest of a wave long in the making and well known to many observers. "Avery was working at one end of a nine-year 'revolution' in the understanding of genetic mechanisms, Watson and Crick at the other. The *kairos* in each case was quite different" (Miller, 1992, p. 311). In Giltrow's terms, the background knowledge that each writer could assume of his audience was very different. Thus, Avery was compelled to painstakingly lay out his methodology and findings and carefully situate his work in the larger body of scientific knowledge, whereas Watson and Crick could rush into print with only the sketchiest of details. Indeed, as Miller (1992) noted, "We might suspect that the two papers belong to quite different genres, which are defined in part by the rhetorical action achievable within the differing scientific situations" (p. 318).

In these examples, we can see how matters of content—epistemology, background knowledge, surprise value, kairos—influenced the selection and use of formal features in the instantiation of particular genres. Considerations of audience and situation are fundamental to these determinations, underscoring the rhetorical nature of genre knowledge and genre use. This is especially apparent in more "localized" cases where the characteristics of the audience and the situation are more sharply delineated. But this raises an interesting question: Is there some point at which a piece of communication becomes so localized that it ceases to be generic? In other words, is there some "threshold" of genericness? At the beginning of this section we suggested that "a letter from a Utah bank promoting a new savings program" could be considered a localized genre. But what if it is a new kind of savings program, and it is being promoted by only one bank via only one letter? Would such a letter constitute a genre? We feel that genericness is not an all-or-nothing proposition and that there is not a threshold as such. Instead, communicators engage in (and their texts reveal) various degrees of *generic activity.* No act of communication springs out of nothing. In one way or another, all acts of communication build on prior texts and text elements, elements that exist on different levels, including words, phrases, discourse patterns, illustrations, and so on. If texts arise out of discursive differences, as Bakhtin, Kress, and many others argued, such texts can be expected to embody different kinds of *recurring rhetorical responses* in different ways. Thus, rather than taking a holistic, normative approach to genre, as is done in traditional studies, we feel it makes more sense to take a more articulated approach in which individual texts are seen to contain heterogeneous mixtures of elements, some of which are recognizably more generic than others.[15]

## DUALITY OF STRUCTURE

In our use of organizational or disciplinary genres, we *constitute* social structures (in professional, institutional, and organizational contexts) and simultaneously *reproduce* these structures.

To make this principle clear, we need to introduce the concept of *duality of structure* that is at the center of structuration theory in sociology, as developed mainly by Giddens (1979, 1984). Traditional conceptions (Parsons, Althusser) maintain a clear separation between social structure and human action. Giddens (1984) noted that according to this view, "structure" is seen as "external to human action, as a source of constraint on the free initiative of the independently constituted subject" (pp. 6–17).

Such frameworks leave little conceptual space for a reflexive agent. Rather, the social actor is seen as something of a sociological dope who knows little of the institutions working in the background and whose values he or she is producing and reproducing. Giddens faults these schools of sociological thought

---

[15]Swales (1990) also argued against a definitional approach to genre in favor of a "family resemblance" approach according to which "exemplars or instances of genres vary in their prototypicality" (p. 49). We share Swales' endorsement of prototype theory, but we are using it somewhat differently, namely, to describe generic elements at all levels rather than just unitary texts.

because they discount people's reasons for their actions and assume that the only "real" stimuli for people's actions are institutional forces.

In contrast, Giddens (1984) argued that:

> The knowledge of social conventions, of oneself and of other human beings, presumed in being able to "go on" in the diversity of contexts of social life is detailed and dazzling. All competent members of society are vastly skilled in the practical accomplishments of sociology and are expert "sociologists." The knowledge they possess is not incidental to the persistent patterning of social life, but is integral to it. (p. 26)

According to this perspective, human agency and social structure can be seen to be implicated in each other rather than being opposed (Swales, 1993).

In place of dualisms such as the individual and society, or subject and object, Giddens (1979) proposed a single conceptual move, the *duality of structure*. Through this concept Giddens argued that social life was essentially recursive: "Structure is both medium and outcome of the reproduction of practices. Structure enters simultaneously into the constitution of the agent and social practices, and 'exists' in the generating moments of this constitution" (p. 5). Reproduction, it should be noted, does not mean simple replication; Giddens sees reproduction as allowing for changes and evolution within it. Duality of structure is akin to Bourdieu's (1987) concept of "double structuration," though Bourdieu put more emphasis on agents' struggle and on the use of strategies rather than rules.

As might be expected with the spread of such concepts through academic culture, a number of researchers and scholars in various fields have begun invoking Giddens' duality of structure concept to argue for a reciprocal relationship between social structure and rule-governed communicative activity. For example, in the field of conversation analysis, Wilson (1991) contended that:

> Traditionally, sociology seeks to describe and explain social phenomena in terms of notions such as status, role, class, religion, positionally determined interests, attitudes, beliefs, values, and so on. Although these may represent quite different substantive theoretical commitments, they share the fundamental Durkheimian assumption that social structure is exterior to and constraining on individuals and their actions and, consequently, *is an independent causal factor that can be adduced to explain social phenomena.* ... The actor is portrayed as a judgemental dope, whose sense-making activities, if any, are treated as epiphenomenal, since the relations between categories and rules, on the one hand, and their concrete instances, on the other, are assumed for theoretical purposes to be transparent and unproblematic. (pp. 26–27, italics added)

The problem with this formulation is, acccording to Wilson, that it does not account for actors selecting the social–structural contexts that are most relevant to their communicative activity in a particular setting at a particular time—what

*Competence to write one kind of argument (as accurate)*
*& competence to read (easily) many kinds — and to respond appropriately*

Giddens (1984) described as actors' monitoring of their behavior. "Consequently," Wilson suggests, "parties to a concrete interaction must address who they relevantly are and what it is they are about on any given occasion. . . . This is an irremediable circumstance facing the participants, and the [conversation] analyst cannot settle the issue on their behalf by invoking some theoretical scheme or interpretation of the situation" (p. 25).

In contrast to the conventional view of social structure, conversation analysts such as Garfinkel, Goffman, Zimmerman, Wilson, and Mehan, who subscribe to the principle of relevance as developed from ethnomethodological research on microlevel social interactions, depict social structure as consisting of:

> Matters that are described and oriented to by members of society on relevant occasions as essential resources for conducting their affairs and at the same time, reproduced as external and constraining social facts through that same interaction. Thus, we must abandon any standard Durkheimian conception of social structure that takes externality for granted as a methodological stipulation. Rather, externality and constraint are members' accomplishments, and social structure and social interaction are reflexively related rather than standing in causal or formal definitional relations to one another. (Wilson, 1991, p. 27)

*summary*

What does this alternative conception of social structure—derived from structuration theory and grounded in the findings of ethnomethodological research—have to do with rhetorical discussions of genre and, in particular, with our approach to genre from the perspective of actors' genre knowledge? Wilson's characterization of the reflexive, reciprocal relationship between social structure and social interaction is based on microlevel research on conversational interactions. Our perspective on genre, as we have indicated, is similarly based on several years of microlevel (although not ethnomethodological) investigations of academic researchers' meaning-making processes as they try to communicate with an audience of fellow professionals.[16] We have repeatedly observed such individuals drawing on genre knowledge to meet the requirements of a particular rhetorical moment. We would argue, with Wilson (1991), that "the fundamental justification for a classification of occasions must be that the participants orient to it [the occasion] as a type of situation, and moreover, orient to the present interaction as an instance of that type" (p. 39). People appear to orient to genre as situationally appropriate and relevant to a particular cultural framework.

A related perspective is taken by Mehan (1991), who, as a conversation analyst investigating oral classroom interactions, argued that:

---

[16]Our studies are not ethnomethodological in the sense that Garfinkel (1967) used the term in referring to studies of "the formal properties of commonplace, practical common sense actions 'from within' actual settings as ongoing accomplishments of those settings'" (p. viii). Although his definition is applicable to recent work on conversation analysis (see, e.g., Boden & Zimmerman, 1991), we think that we would be stretching a point to refer to case study data as ethnomethodological, although our research aims coincide.

A second position on macro-micro relationships denies that the phenomenal aspects of society are merely reflections of large scale institutional forces. Instead they are contingent outcomes of people's practical activity (Giddens, 1979). Researchers in this constructionist tradition attempt to locate social structure in social interaction. ... The constructionist line of investigation, as I see it, studies the situated artful practices of people and the ways in which these are employed to create an objectified everyday world without losing sight of institutional and cultural context. In this line of work, everyday practices are examined for the way in which they exhibit, *indeed, generate* social structure. The practices which generate the social structures are treated as endogenous to the work domains in which they occur and which they constitute. (p. 75, italics added)

To borrow from Mehan, then, our use of rhetorical genres is both constitutive of social structure (as it is instantiated through our observing a genre's rules-for-use or conventions) and generative as situated, artful practice.

Two researchers in the field of organizational communication, Yates and Orlikowski (1992), have attempted to capture this complex interrelationship in their discussion of the evolution of an institutional genre as a result of changing technological and demographic conditions.[17] They contended that social structures emerge from historical, institutional contexts constituted by the collaborative work of people adjusting to changing times and technologies. They suggested that one can best understand the development of organizational genres such as the business letter and the memo as "communicative action[s] situated in a stream of social practices which shape and are shaped by it" (p. 22). In their case history of the evolution of the office memo as a form of internal business correspondence away from the business letter genre of external correspondence, Yates and Orlikowski attempted to demonstrate that a reciprocal relationship exists between the changing textual features of a new genre and concomitant rules for use that are determined by people responding to a changing technological and demographic climate.

For example, the appearance of the typewriter and the vertical file (which dramatically increased the production and storage of inter- and intraoffice documents) can be seen to have led to the need for textual features and conventions that would help workers distinguish the office memo from formal business correspondence. With the appearance of the typewriter, which was adopted by businesses in response to the growth in correspondence and which increased the

---

[17]Yates and Orlikowski (1992) attempted to express the reciprocal relationship between social structure and human action in the following way:

> Structuration theory is centrally concerned with the reproduction and transformation of social structures, which are enacted through generalizable techniques or social rules. These rules shape the action taken by individuals in organizations, while at the same time by regularly drawing on the rules, individuals affirm and reproduce the social structures in an ongoing, recursive interaction.... The approach we develop ... draws on the notion of structuration to capture the reciprocal and recursive relationship between genre and organizational communication, and to position the role of communication media within it. (pp. 4–5)

production of all correspondence, there emerged conventions such as underlining, subheads, and the use of all capital letters to facilitate readability. When tab stops were added to typewriters at the outset of the 20th century, it became possible for the writer to easily make columns, including the columns comprising the typical To–From–Subject–Date heading. With the advent of typewriter technology there also appeared a need for a new occupational group, typists, to serve as operators of this new technology. Typists acted as agents of standardization and served to stabilize the document format within and across firms. Thus, according to Yates and Orlikowski's account of the evolution of the office memo, technological development acted in concert with demographic changes to influence the practices of a new population of office workers—all of which combined to influence the development of the genre's distinctive features and conventions. To paraphrase Giddens (1984) paraphrasing Marx, it is the social actors that are the agents of change (in this case, change in the structural features and conventions that come to distinguish internal correspondence from the business letter), but not through conditions of their own making.

In attempting to characterize the reciprocal character of the evolution of textual features and conventions of the interoffice memo, Yates and Orlikowski were among the first in organizational communication to draw on Giddens' (1984) structuration theory (see also Contractor & Eisenberg, 1990; Manning, 1989; Poole & DeSanctis, 1990). Their contribution to our understanding of the institutional dynamics of genre, building as it does on Bazerman's (1988) studies of the evolution of the experimental article, has important implications for scholars in rhetorical studies interested in the textual dynamics of the professions.

## COMMUNITY OWNERSHIP

Genre conventions signal a discourse community's norms, epistemology, ideology, and social ontology.

Asserting a relationship between the concept of genre and that of "discourse community" is a slippery proposition because neither concept refers to a static entity. Nevertheless, recent research in composition studies and discourse analysis supports our view that studying the genres of professional and disciplinary communication provides important information about the textual dynamics of discourse communities. For example, Swales' work on the conventions of the experimental article (Swales & Najjar, 1987) and more recently on the genres of academic writing (Swales, 1990) makes a strong case for understanding the functions of genre in terms of the discourse communities that "own" them (pp. 25–27).[18]

---

[18]Swales (1990) characterized a relationship between discourse communities and the generic forms of communication that they produce, suggesting that:

Similarly, Bazerman's (1988) study of the development of the experimental article in the natural sciences establishes an important connection between the formation of a scientific discourse community and the development of appropriate discursive strategies for making claims about experiments which, in turn, reveal the inner workings of the natural world. In examining the evolution of the experimental article in the natural sciences (in the first scientific journal, the *Philosophical Transactions of the Royal Society of London*), Bazerman demonstrated a fruitful historical methodology for understanding the emergence of a genre's textual features and rhetorical conventions in relation to disciplinary community formation. His study of the development of the features and conventions of scientific writing between 1665 and 1800 reveals how the increasingly complex interactions of an emergent argumentative community of natural scientists is tied to the appearance of genre conventions.

Our own research on discourse communities has led to our growing attention to the ways in which the genres of academic writing function to instantiate the norms, values, epistemologies, and ideological assumptions of academic cultures. Over the last several years we have had many opportunities to observe how writers and readers convey, through their textual practices, the beliefs and value systems of the disciplinary cultures in which they participate. In one study (Berkenkotter, Huckin, & Ackerman, 1988, 1991), for example, we observed a graduate student's socialization into a field of study and noted the extent to which his acquiring discipline-specific text conventions was connected to his learning a research methodology. Although the assumptions, norms, and values underlying the empirical methodology that he learned were not made fully explicit to this student during his training, he nonetheless assimilated the rationalist–realist epistemology that constitutes empiricist inquiry in the social sciences.

A study by Berkenkotter (1990) of the formation of a disciplinary subspecialty in literary studies, as seen through the evolution of a scholarly journal, reveals how disciplinary norms and values are codified as the forum becomes professionalized. In this case study, an emergent community of literary specialists interested in reader-response theory, criticism, and pedagogy organized a newsletter as a forum for exchanging ideas. The early issues of the newsletter contained a number of informal personal statements expressing the discontent of young professors with the norms of scholarly writing. These writers specifically inveighed against the elaborate style of professional discourse with its jargon, convoluted syntax, and pedantic authorial persona. A number of the contributors to the newsletter declared themselves to be members of a vanguard interested in

---

Discourse communities are sociorhetorical networks that form in order to work toward sets of common goals. One of the characteristics that established members of these discourse communities possess is familiarity with the particular genres that are used in the communicative furtherance of those sets of goals. In consequence, genres are the properties of discourse communities; that is to say, genres belong to discourse communities, not individuals, other kinds of grouping, or to wider speech communities. (p. 9)

transforming conventional academic writing with its underlying elitist, hegemonic value system. Despite this concern, as the newsletter evolved into a scholarly journal, it incorporated the formal textual features and conventions of literary scholarship and thereby demonstrated its movement into the disciplinary mainstream. The contributors' increasing use of the standard conventions of formal scholarly discourse with its overt intertextual mechanisms suggests that, despite a short period of rebellion, the textual instantiation of the values of the academy was an inevitable outcome of the institutionalization of the journal. What counted as knowledge had to be couched in the formal discourse of the literary scholar.

A third example of how genre conventions instantiate a discourse community's values and ideology can be seen in our study of a biologist's revisions of an experimental article (chap. 3 & 4). The biologist, who had published considerably in the field of immunology, submitted for review a paper with an underdeveloped introduction; instead of the standard literature review, she attempted to justify her present study by citing her own prior research, including an unpublished manuscript. Reviewers of the manuscript insisted that she position her study and her findings in the context of related scientific activity in the field. In the biologist's subsequent attempts to accommodate her reviewers, we see evidence of the ways in which genre conventions instantiate the scientific community's values and epistemology. In the final draft of the biologist's manuscript there appears a constructed narrative (what the biologist called a "phony story"), a chronology of events in other labs leading to, and therefore justifying, the present study. Such a narrative, which the reviewers agreed was essential for publishing local findings, reinforces a view of scientific activity as collective, inductive, and cumulative. As Lewontin (1991) suggested:

> Most natural scientists, and especially biologists, are really positivists. They rely heavily both on confirmation and falsification, and they believe that the gathering of facts, followed by inference rather than the testing of theories, is the primary enterprise of science. At times they speak highly of "strong inference," by which they mean something close to a Popperian falsification criterion, but this is not the modal form of biological work. . . . Whatever the popularity of notions about "normal science" and "paradigm shifts," the ideal of the "critical experiment" and "strong inference" remain the chief epistemological commitments of scientific ideology. (pp. 141–142)

This view of science is reinforced, Lewontin suggested, by scientists' daily reading and writing. The four-part structure of the scientific paper and the content within each of the four parts functions to reinforce the normative view just described of how science gets done. Learning the schema of the four-part structure of the scientific report (which for most students occurs at the graduate level as they write with their senior professors) means that young professionals assimilate the epistemology of their discipline as they learn the conventions of writing science. As we noted earlier, this was the case with the graduate student in educational research whom we observed learning the conventions of the social science research report (which is modeled on the the experimental article in the natural sciences). To the extent that epistemological assumptions are embedded in the conventions of a genre, it seems reasonable to infer that many of this student's assumptions regarding empirical research in education studies were linked to the formal means of communication in which he regularly engaged.

## CONCLUSION

When we speak of genre knowledge in disciplinary and professional cultures, we refer to knowledge that professionals need in order to communicate in disciplinary communities. Our perspective is both structurational, that is, based on our reading of Giddens (1979, 1984), and sociocognitive, compatible we believe with much recent research on language-in-activity coming from such diverse fields as sociolinguistics, cognitive psychology, educational anthropology, and conversation analysis. In our discussion of the five principles that undergird our understanding of genre, we have attempted to present a synthesis of some of this recent work. We then integrated these concepts with those that have emerged from our empirical studies to produce a framework for a sociocognitive theory of genre. We wish to underscore the relevance of structuration theory because we consider it a rich and exciting body of theory for insight regarding the relationship between available patterns for communicative utterances (Ongstad, 1992) and people's ability to alter or modify such patterns.

As social actors, we constantly monitor our actions and recognize the available patterns through which we might act at any given moment, yet we are capable of modifying those patterns to accommodate our reading of the rhetorical moment. We determine, for example, when a colleague offers a "Good morning. How are you?" those occasions when what is called for is a short, conventional reply, and those occasions (given our relation to that colleague), when it is appropriate for us to unburden ourselves of the rage we felt when we could not start the car because it was −10° outside. We have the linguistic and rhetorical repertoires to choose our comments *artfully* in light of our reading of the occasion and of our relation to our interlocutor as we conceive it through both retrospective and prospective structuring of other occasions. It is through our constitution of many such encounters as they are enacted across time and space that we construct our social worlds.

Full participation in disciplinary and professional cultures demands a similarly informed knowledge of written genres. Genres are the intellectual scaffolds on which community-based knowledge is constructed. To be fully effective in this role, genres must be flexible and dynamic, capable of modification according to the rhetorical exigencies of the situation. At the same time, though, they must be stable enough to capture those aspects of situations that tend to recur. This tension between stability and change lies at the heart of genre use and genre knowledge and is perhaps best seen in the work of those who are most deeply engaged in disciplinary activity. Fully invested disciplinary actors are typically well aware of the textual patterns and epistemological norms of their discourse community, but are also aware of the need to be at the cutting edge, to push for novelty and originality. As the intellectual content of a field changes over time, so must the forms used to discuss it; this is why genre knowledge involves both form *and* content. In using the genres customarily employed by other members of their discourse community, disciplinary actors help constitute the community and simultaneously reproduce it (though, as we noted earlier, not in a simple replicative way). Thus, genres themselves, when examined closely from the perspective of those who use them, reveal much about a discourse community's norms, epistemology, ideology, and social ontology.

# 2

# NEWS VALUE IN SCIENTIFIC JOURNAL ARTICLES

A good illustration of the principles laid out in the preceding chapter can be found in the recent evolution of the scientific journal article, the primary genre for the dissemination of new scientific knowledge. In his *Shaping Written Knowledge*, Bazerman (1988) provided extensive historical discussion of this genre, noting how textual features have changed in accordance with changes in the epistemological and social orientation of scientific disciplines. Surveying the first scientific journal (*The Philosophical Transactions of the Royal Society of London*) from its beginnings in 1665 until 1800, he observed that experimental reports occupied a relatively minor niche during this time, in contrast to simple observations of natural events. Toward the end of this period, however, experimental reports increased in frequency, constituting 39% of the articles published in 1800. The genre evolved in a number of ways, becoming more problem- and theory-oriented. Increasing attention was paid to testing and proof and to the precise description of methods and results. In short, nature began to be treated not as a given but, in Bazerman's words, as "a matter of contention" (p. 77).

In a separate chapter, Bazerman described how experimental reports in physics have changed during the 20th century. Analyzing a corpus of articles from *Physical Review* published between 1893 and 1980, he noted how the tremendous growth of the field has been reflected in the growth of the journal: In 1893 *PR* contained approximately 190,000 words or their equivalent, and in 1980 the figure was 30 million. Bazerman suggested that much of the field's growth can be attributed to the development of a common theory, and he argued that "common theory has become an extremely strong force in structuring articles and binding articles to each other" (p. 157). To support this observation, he pointed to various changes in the textual features characteristic of the experimental report genre. The average length of articles, for example, has steadily increased from about 4,500 words or their equivalent in 1900 to over 10,000 in 1980, reflecting a greater elaboration of theory, knowledge, and background information. Part of this increase is attributable to the use of references to prior literature. Although there were only about 1.5 references per article in 1910, in 1980 there were more than 25. Furthermore, the use of references has become more focused and more integrated into the argument, with the references themselves often being discussed in greater detail than before. Subject matter has become more abstract. In the 1890s, referring expressions (noun phrases) referred to concrete objects as often as they did to processes, qualities, or other abstract concepts, but by 1980 the ratio was 1:3. This increasing abstractness can also be seen in the nature of technical vocabulary and in the shift of visual aids from drawings of apparatus to extensive equations and schematized graphs. On the organizational level, Bazerman noted a shift of emphasis away from methods in favor of theory, discussion, and conclusion sections.

We wanted to extend Bazerman's pioneering studies in two ways, first by broadening and updating the scope of his textual analyses, and second by studying the discursive practices of actual users of the genre and thus linking generic change to situated cognition. Accordingly, we developed a stratified randomly selected corpus of 350 journal articles in physics, biology, and general science covering the period 1944–1989, and we conducted lengthy interviews with seven respected research scientists in the departments of physics and biology at Carnegie Mellon University. Related case studies of scientists' reading and writing behavior can be found in the scholarly literature of the past decade. Gilbert and Mulkay's *Pandora's Box* (1984), for example, draws on interviews with 34 British and U.S. biochemists to describe two different forms of social accounting: the *empiricist repertoire*, emphasizing fidelity to nature, and the *contingent repertoire*, based on personal or social circumstances. Myers' *Writing Biology* (1990) contains extensive case studies of two biologists, describing their composing strategies as they try to get their work funded and published. Myers pointed out in particular how these scientists had to alter their principal claims in order to have them accepted by the gatekeepers of the scientific community. Bazerman (1988, chap. 8) studied the reading behavior of three physicists. He observed that they drew on schema knowledge to read journal articles selectively and that they looked mainly for novel results. Rymer (1988) studied the composing processes of nine eminent biologists, noting among other things that these scientists used a wide variety of writing strategies and techniques in composing journal articles, that they revised their drafts extensively, and that they frequently discovered new interpretations of their results while going through the composing process.

We were intrigued by these studies and wanted to know more about how scientists' reading behavior might influence their writing behavior, both individually and collectively. In particular, we were interested in exploring the extent to which novelty, or "news value," exercised a role in these behaviors and whether or not it had any bearing on the evolution of the genre. As Bazerman (1988) noted, "scientific communities are by their nature committed to new formulations, new knowledge" (p. 308), and it seemed to us that all of the case studies already mentioned revealed a major interest in scientific news value on the part of virtually all the scientists involved.

More generally, we wanted to see what the evolution of the genre might indicate about the scientific community itself, especially from a structuration standpoint. Genre conventions are products of discourse communities and are thereby "windows" into the functioning of such communities. As Fairclough (1992) noted, "a genre implies not only a particular text type, but also particular processes of producing, distributing and consuming texts. . . . Changes in social practice are both manifested on the plane of language in changes in the system of genres, and in part brought about by such changes" (p. 126).

## METHODS AND MATERIALS

The seven scientists who served as consultants for this study are all active researchers who regularly read the journals we selected and frequently contribute to them; several serve on their editorial boards. Four are senior scientists, three of them heading large laboratory teams; another is close to that status; the other two are only a few years beyond the doctorate. Four are physicists, two being condensed matter theorists, another a medium-energy nuclear theorist, and the fourth a small-particle experimentalist. Three are biologists, two being molecular biologists, and the other a protein biochemist.

To maximize both the quality and quantity of information obtained, all interviews were conducted one-on-one in a relaxed, conversational fashion, without tape recorder, in the consultant's personal office (except for one, which took place in Huckin's office). Initial interviews took about 2 hours. Two of the consultants participated in follow-up interviews of about 1 hour each, and three of them provided lengthy written responses to a draft of this manuscript. Our purpose in conducting these interviews, we told them, was simply to "learn about how scientists read and write about science." We did not impose any hypotheses on them or ask any leading questions. Rather, we began with the simple question, "How do you select and read journal articles?" To help them answer this question, we had them operationalize the process for us. All of these scientists subscribed to 15 or 20 specialized journals, all published on a frequent basis. Thus, their desks contained piles of journals, some still unopened. We took advantage of this situation (which several of them made joking comments about) by asking them to randomly select one of these newly arrived journals and show us how they would find and read an article in it. As they did this, we observed and took notes, and invited them to comment on their strategies. Typically, this opened up a general monologue on "how scientists read," and in this context all informants made some kind of comment about how they always looked for something "new" and/or "interesting." This allowed us to gracefully switch to a second line of inquiry, namely, "Is there anything special you do as a *writer* to catch the reader's attention and promote your ideas?"

As part of these interviews, we asked our consultants to identify the most important journals in their field. This yielded the following list: *Biochemistry, Cell, Journal of Biological Chemistry, Journal of Cell Biology, Journal of Molecular Biology, Molecular/Cellular Biology, Nature, Nucleic Acids Research, Physical Review, Physical Review Letters, Proceedings of the National Academy of Sciences* (*PNAS*), and *Science*. Using these titles, we then developed a study corpus of 350 articles by selecting the first 10 articles of the third issue of each journal every 15th year from 1944 on (i.e., 1944, 1959, 1974, and 1989). Only 5 of the 12 journals were being published in 1944, 7 in 1959, and 11 in 1974, which accounts for a corpus of only 350 articles instead of the 480 there would be if all 12 journals had been published throughout this 45-year period.

## RESULTS

### The Search for New Information

All seven of these scientists displayed a scanning and reading pattern dominated by the search for interesting new information. They quickly scanned the table of contents looking for key words and noting names of authors. Often, the conjunction of a topic (as indicated by one or more key words) and a certain author's name would enable them to make a confident judgment about whether the article was worth reading. If it was, they typically read the article in the following manner: First they read the title and then the abstract. Then they looked for the most important data, usually in graphs, tables, drawings, and other visual aids. Next they typically read the Results section. At this point their reading patterns varied, depending on how well they knew the topic and how confident they were of the scientific methods used. Sometimes they read the Discussion section; sometimes they read a paragraph or two in the Introduction. Time permitting, some went back to the beginning and read the article straight through.

This variation in reading patterns is clearly related to subject matter, as Bazerman (1988) noted in his case studies of physicists reading physics articles (chap. 8). All seven of these scientists were quick to point out that certain topics are of central interest in their ongoing research, whereas other topics are only of general intellectual interest. For articles dealing with central topics, these scientists employed a highly selective, nonlinear reading strategy of searching for major findings and conclusions and ignoring methodology. For articles dealing with more general topics, they typically took a more linear approach, working through the Introduction, then (optionally) the Methods section, then the Results, and finally the Discussion. They were quite conscious of these different reading strategies and readily acknowledged that sometimes they read as specialists and at other times more as nonspecialists.[1]

## Analogous to Newspaper Reading

This reading pattern is strikingly similar to that displayed by newspaper readers. Newspaper readers typically look for the most surprising, most newsworthy information first (i.e., the headline statement). Then, if interested, they read further into an article, looking for other information generally according to its news value. Newspaper editors and reporters have long been aware of these preferences, of course, and have created a well-known text schema reflecting this pattern—the so-called *inverted pyramid*. This ordering schema accommodates the interests of typical readers, allowing them to proceed in top-down fashion. (A top-down schema also works to the advantage of editors, in that it allows them to meet last-minute demands for space by simply lopping off paragraphs at the end of articles rather than having to edit more selectively.)

Van Dijk (1986), after analyzing news reports from hundreds of newspapers around the world, described this schema as shown in Fig. 2.1. He noted that this is a strong tendency, not a strict rule of order.[2]

Now let us suppose that the text segments identified by Van Dijk for news reports serve functions that are roughly analogous to the main segments of scientific journal reports (i.e., headline = title, lead = abstract, main event = major findings, etc.). If the reading behavior of the seven scientists we interviewed is characteristic of scientists in general, there appears to be a correspondence between the textual layout of news reports and the reading pattern of scientists (see Fig. 2.2). Whereas the textual layout of news reports mirrors almost exactly the anticipated top-down reading pattern, the textual layout of scientific journal articles, of course, is quite different. The traditional sequence of Introduction–Method–Results–Discussion reflects the chronology of idealized Baconian scientific procedure (Gross 1990, chap. 6) or "narrative of science" (Myers 1990), not necessarily the chronology of reading.

This discrepancy between what we might call a narrative, writer-based text-schema on the one hand and a highly selective, purpose-driven reading schema on the other is not seriously dysfunctional. Because the text schema is quite standardized, experienced readers know where to look for certain information and can skip around quite efficiently. Furthermore, when reading articles out of their specialty, most of them read in more of a top-down manner, giving more

---

[1]This specialist–nonspecialist distinction corresponds to the esoteric-exoteric distinction discussed in Fleck (1981).

[2]Exceptions can be found, including a recent trend in U.S. journalism to have a human interest lead-in and a more narrative style of development.

Summary $\begin{cases} \text{Headline} \\ \text{Lead} \end{cases}$

News story $\begin{cases} \text{Main event} \\ \text{Details of main event} \\ \text{Background} \\ \text{Consequences} \\ \text{Comments} \\ \text{Etc.} \end{cases}$

FIG. 2.1.   Standard layout of newspaper reports (after Van Dijk, 1986).

attention to the Introduction. In this latter case there was no particular discrepancy between writing and reading approaches.

But the discrepancy between their specialist reading schema and the traditional writer-based text schema is clearly nonoptimal. After all, the reader has to *search* for information, rather than just proceeding top-down. The only text features that facilitate a top-down approach are the Title and Abstract, which appear first and are read first (but which, it should be noted, are often written last). Newspaper articles, by contrast, are noticeably reader based: Instead of recounting a narrative of events chronologically, they pick out the most surprising information and put it up front. This tactic not only helps catch the reader's attention, it also facilitates selective reading. If pressed for time or only mildly interested in a topic, readers can terminate their reading after only the first few paragraphs and still have the gist of a story.

## How Text Features Have Changed

In recent decades, science has become both increasingly specialized and increasingly caught up in the information explosion. This has been amply documented by historians of science, and our own consultants were quick to agree. Now according to the tenets of functionalism, whereby "form follows function," if there is a discrepancy between the form of a product and its intended or actual function, there will be pressure to *change* the form to better accommodate the function. In the case of scientific journal articles, this means that we would expect the journals to gradually modify their genre conventions so as to better accom-

| Newspaper report | | Scientific journal article |
|---|---|---|
| Headline | = | Title |
| Lead | = | Abstract |
| Main event | = | Major findings (including visual aids) |
| Details of main event | = | Results |
| Background | = | Introduction |
| Consequences | = | Discussion |
| Comments, etc. | = | Implications, etc. |

FIG. 2.2.   Typical reading sequences for newspaper reports and scientific journal articles, showing how they parallel each other.

modate the needs of specialist readers and readers pressed for time (who may, in many cases, be one and the same). In other words, we would expect to see the gradual emergence of a text schema that is more closely aligned with the news-oriented reading schema described in the preceding section.

Our analysis of the 350 journal articles in our corpus supports this hypothesis. The 12 scientific journals that we examined have all modified the genre conventions in a way that foregrounds the most important findings of an investigation, that is to say, promotes news value.

First, *titles* have become more informative. Twenty years ago, titles were almost strictly topical. Here is one, for example, from a 1967 issue of *Proceedings from the National Academy of Science*: "On the Specificity of DNA Polymerase." Today, one can expect the same journal to contain something like this: "Rho-dependent Transcription Termination of a Bacterial Operon Is Antagonized by an Extrachromosomal Gene Product." Not only is the newer title semantically richer, it also has the syntactic form of a full sentence. As recently as 20 years ago, full-sentence titles like this were rare; today they constitute more than 20% of all journal article titles (see Table 2.1) and are especially common in biology. It is worth noting that full-sentence titles are similar in form to newspaper headlines, virtually all of which are cast as truncated sentences (e.g., "Murder Suspect Apprehended in South City"). Although the percentages shown in Table 2.1 hardly come close to the high percentage of full-sentence headlines found in newspapers, the data for this 45-year period certainly show a trend in that direction.

Along with this increasing syntactic fullness, we find, as might be expected, a clear increase in semantic richness. As Table 2.2 shows, it is becoming more and more common to find the results of an investigation stated (or strongly implied) in the title of the article. If our sample of 350 articles is representative, we can make the following observation: In 1944 less than one third of all articles announced the main results at the outset (i.e., in the title), whereas in 1989 more than two thirds did. In short, more bottom-line information is being loaded into the most highly foregrounded part of any article, the title—the one part that is also listed in the table of contents. As one of Rymer's biologists stated, "I want to give it a title that's catchy, that's very informative. . . . Gotta sell the stuff. Doesn't mean that you gotta be dishonest. But it's gotta be something that really catches people's eyes, so they stand up and pay attention" (Rymer, 1988, p. 235).

TABLE 2.1
Title Syntax

| Year | No. of Titles | No. of Full Sentences | Percentage |
| --- | --- | --- | --- |
| 1944 | 50 | 0 | 0% |
| 1959 | 70 | 1 | 1% |
| 1974 | 110 | 3 | 3% |
| 1989 | 120 | 25 | 21% |

TABLE 2.2
Results in Title

| Year | No. of Titles | No. of Titles With Results | Percentage |
|------|---------------|----------------------------|------------|
| 1944 | 50  | 15 | 30% |
| 1959 | 70  | 24 | 34% |
| 1974 | 110 | 46 | 42% |
| 1989 | 120 | 82 | 68% |

*Abstracts*, which enable writers to foreground their most important claims, used to appear only in certain journals. Now, however, they are a standard feature of almost all scientific journal articles and even of quick reports and letters. Although *Physical Review* (founded in 1893) began using abstracts in 1920, the other journals in our corpus did so much later (see Table 2.3). Not only have abstracts become a standard feature of scientific journal articles, they also have been getting longer and more informative. Tables 2.4 and 2.5 reveal this trend by showing the average number of sentences and results statements per abstract for each of the 4 years in our study. As can be seen in these data, the average number of sentences per abstract has increased from 4.4 to 6.5 during this 1944–1989 period and the average number of results statements has increased from 2.6 to 5.0. If size and informational density are any indication, the Abstract has clearly been assuming more and more importance in the modern scientific journal article. This is not surprising, as the Abstract serves a number of valuable purposes for busy readers: (a) it foregrounds important information for easy access; (b) it serves as an early screening device, helping readers decide whether or not to read the rest of the article; (c) it frames the reading of the article as a whole; and (d) it provides a summary of the main points of the article for later reference. Our consultants clearly made use of the first two functions when reading as

TABLE 2.3
First Appearance of Abstracts

| Journal | Year Founded | Year Started Using Abstracts |
|---------|--------------|------------------------------|
| *Nature* | 1869 | 1970 |
| *Science* | 1883 | 1959 |
| *Physical Review* | 1893 | 1920 |
| *Journal of Biological Chemistry* | 1905 | 1966 |
| *Proceedings of the National Academy of Sciences* | 1915 | 1969 |
| *Physical Review Letters* | 1958 | 1967 |
| *Journal of Cell Biology* | 1958 | 1958 |
| *Journal of Molecular Biology* | 1959 | 1959 |
| *Biochemistry* | 1962 | 1962 |
| *Cell* | 1974 | 1974 |
| *Nucleic Acids Research* | 1974 | 1974 |
| *Molecular/Cellular Biology* | 1981 | 1981 |

TABLE 2.4
Length of Abstracts

| Year | No. of Articles | No. of Abstracts | No. of Sentences | Average No. of Sentences |
|------|-----------------|------------------|------------------|--------------------------|
| 1944 | 50 | 11 | 48 | 4.4 |
| 1959 | 70 | 36[a] | 201 | 5.6 |
| 1974 | 110 | 110 | 656 | 6.0 |
| 1989 | 120 | 120 | 785 | 6.5 |

[a]Includes one abstract 39 sentences long. The exceptionally long abstract appears in a paper submitted by French biologists and written in French, and may be attributable to cultural differences. If this abstract was excluded from the data, the average number of sentences for 1959 would be 4.6 instead of 5.6.

specialists, and they also commented on the value of the third function for times when they would be reading as nonspecialists.

The *Introduction* occupies the same physical location it always has, but it contains much more bottom-line results than it used to. Swales and Najjar (1987), in a survey of 66 *Physical Review* articles published between 1943 and 1983, found that statements of results appeared in the Introduction with increasing frequency, from 36% in 1943, to 44% in 1963, to 55% in 1983. In our own larger corpus, the data are shown in Table 2.6. Although these figures do not depict a uniform progression over time, the overall trend is in the same direction as that of the Swales and Najjar study. That is to say, authors of scientific journal articles are increasingly likely to include a statement of their main findings in the Introduction.

TABLE 2.5
Informativeness of Abstracts

| Year | No. of Articles | No. of Abstracts | No. Results Statements | Average No. of Results |
|------|-----------------|------------------|------------------------|------------------------|
| 1944 | 50 | 11 | 29 | 2.6 |
| 1959 | 70 | 36[a] | 169 | 4.7 |
| 1974 | 110 | 110 | 514 | 4.7 |
| 1989 | 120 | 120 | 602 | 5.0 |

[a]Includes one abstract with 38 statements of results (the same abstract referred to in Table 2.4). If this abstract was excluded from the data, the average number of results statements for 1959 would be 3.7 instead of 4.7.

TABLE 2.6
Results in Introduction

| Year | No. of Introductions | No. With Results | Percentage |
|------|----------------------|------------------|------------|
| 1944 | 50 | 28 | 56% |
| 1959 | 70 | 46 | 66% |
| 1974 | 110 | 67 | 61% |
| 1989 | 120 | 91 | 76% |

TABLE 2.7
Results in Subheadings

| Year | No. of Articles | No. of Subheadings | No. with Results | Percentage |
|------|-----------------|--------------------|------------------|------------|
| 1944 | 50              | 100                | 0                | 0%         |
| 1959 | 70              | 81                 | 2                | 2%         |
| 1974 | 110             | 293                | 22               | 8%         |
| 1989 | 120             | 446                | 156              | 35%        |

*Heading*  Also appearing with greater frequency are *informative subheadings*, used especially to announce specific results. Table 2.7 shows the percentage of subheadings containing results (from Results and Discussion sections only) in our 1944–1989 corpus. Two patterns can be seen in these data. First, there has been a steady increase in the *use* of subheadings: In 1944 there were about 1.3 subheadings per article, whereas in 1989 there were about 3. Second, there has been a dramatic increase since the 1970s in the use of *informative* subheadings, from *Informative (do as a subcategory)* 6% in 1974 to 38% in 1989. Within the traditional sections labeled "Methodology," "Results," and "Discussion," authors are using subheadings to foreground specific and important procedures and results. Not surprisingly, more and more of these informative subheadings are being cast as full sentences (e.g., "CR2 Binds Specifically to an N-Terminal gp350/220 Synthetic Peptide") rather than as ordinary noun phrases such as "Dowex 1-Chloride Separation." Table 2.8 shows the data for our corpus. Increasingly, these subheadings (whether informative or not) are being foregrounded typographically, that is to say, printed in bold type. Bold type is more eye-catching than italics (Benson, 1985) and yet, as recently as the mid-1970s, the journals in our corpus customarily set off subheadings only in italics: Only 32% of the articles that used subheadings in 1959 and 42% of the articles that used subheadings in 1974 put them in bold typeface. By 1989, however, the percentage had risen to 64%, a significant increase.

*Visual*  *Visual aids* have always been a prominent feature of the modern scientific journal article, but, as Bazerman (1988) noted, they have become more rhetorically and theoretically focused. Instead of tables of raw data, one more often today finds

TABLE 2.8
Subheading Syntax

| Year | No. of Subheadings | No. of Full Sentences | Percentage |
|------|--------------------|-----------------------|------------|
| 1944 | 100                | 0                     | 0%         |
| 1959 | 81                 | 0                     | 0%         |
| 1974 | 293                | 10                    | 3%         |
| 1989 | 446                | 83                    | 24%        |

graphs, line drawings, schematic diagrams, and photographs. These kinds of visual aids are all more directly representational than tables and hence more attention getting, just as they are in newspapers.[3] All of our consultants looked for visual aids as soon as they had finished reading the title and abstract, and all showed great facility in interpreting them. In talking about an article he had recently published in *Physical Review Letters*, one of our consultants pointed to a line drawing of a crystalline structure that constituted the primary claim of his paper, and proudly described how he had arranged to have it appear on the second page of his article.

To create more space for all this foregrounded information, most of these journals have shifted to a larger *page size*. Readers of *Cell, Nature, Physical Review Letters, Journal of Biological Chemistry, Nucleic Acids Research, Science*, and *Journal of Molecular Biology*, for example, can now take in almost all of a paper's major findings and claims, both in writing and in visual aids, without having to turn more than one page.

*Methodology* sections, once given much space and prominence, are now greatly de-emphasized. In some journals (e.g., *Journal of Biological Chemistry, PNAS*), the Methods section is the only one printed in small type. In others (e.g., *Cell*, one of the most prestigious molecular biology journals), the Methods section not only appears in small print but has been physically relocated to the end of the body of the article, just before the acknowledgments paragraph. At least one major journal (*Journal of Biological Chemistry*) occasionally prints the Methods section at the very end of the paper as a kind of supplement in miniprint. The editors note that "miniprint is easily read with the aid of a standard magnifying glass" (e.g., Vol. 264, No. 1, p. 318). In still others (e.g., *Nature*, one of the two most prestigious journals in the natural sciences), there is sometimes no Methods section at all. Instead, the experimental methods are described in small print as part of the captions to figures. Table 2.9 contains the full data from our corpus regarding how often the Methods section has been downplayed by either printing it in small type or moving it away from its traditional location after the Introduction. As can be seen, there has been a striking increase (from 0 to 45%) in the percentage of Methods sections that have been printed in smaller type or relocated to nontraditional places, such as at the end of the article or in captions beneath figures. None of this is to say that methodology is any less important to science today than before, only that interest in methodology by typical readers of journal articles may be somewhat less. Studies of the manuscript review process (by ourselves and by many other scholars, e.g., Chubin & Hackett, 1990, and the references cited therein) show that methodology continues to be a major factor in manuscript evaluation, with editors and reviewers insisting on relatively full methodological descriptions. Our guess, based on comments from our con-

---

[3]One of our biology consultants informed us that one reason for this improvement in visual aids is the advent of the personal computer, which has made it possible for many authors to draw their own graphics.

TABLE 2.9
Methods Sections Downplayed (Printed in Smaller Type or
Moved to Nontraditional Location)

| Year | No. of Methods Sections | No. Downplayed | Percentage |
|------|------------------------|----------------|------------|
| 1944 | 46 | 0 | 0% |
| 1959 | 68 | 11 | 16% |
| 1974 | 110 | 30 | 27% |
| 1989 | 120 | 54 | 45% |

sultants, is that journal subscribers rely on the gatekeepers (the editors and reviewers) to carefully inspect and validate the methodological details of a study, so that they (the subscribers) can concentrate on the actual findings. Our consultants said they would be interested in looking closely at the methodology only under special circumstances, for example, if they had serious doubts about it or if they planned to use it themselves.

Less important data, especially raw data, are also frequently relegated to a nonprominent position in the article, if they are there at all. *Journal of Biological Chemistry*, for example, sometimes puts all but the most important data and figures at the end of articles in miniprint.

Background information is less prominent in today's scientific journal articles than it used to be. Instead, background information is being published more and more in the form of review articles. *Cell*, for example, has recently created a new genre, the "mini-review," which has a much faster publication turnaround time than traditional review articles.

These changes bring the journal article as a genre closer to a related genre with which, in a sense, it competes, namely, the Quick Report or Letter (sometimes called a Communication). This latter genre, with its faster publication time, has generally become the primary mode by which major breakthroughs in physics and biology are officially announced in print. By taking on more importance in the competitive, fast-paced world of modern science, the Quick Report has also taken on more prestige. As such, it has increasingly been accorded the text features of regular articles. The prestigious journal *Physical Review Letters* (PRL) is the classic case in point. PRL originated (unofficially) in 1929 as an ordinary letters-to-the-editor column in the long-established *Physical Review* (PR). At first each letter *looked* like a letter, with the authors' names at the end. In 1941, however, PR changed the format so that the authors' names appeared at the top, under the title. In 1955, a larger type size was used. By 1958, this letters-to-the-editor column had become so important that the publishers decided to issue it as a separate publication, thus giving birth, officially, to PRL. In 1967, abstracts were added below the authors' names, in 1980, each "letter" started on a new page, and in 1985, a larger page size was adopted. In short, these "letters" have evolved over time to the point where they now more closely resemble conventional journal articles than they do ordinary letters.[4] But they have done so by adopting only some of the traditional features of regular articles, namely, those that help carry news value, such as an informative title, a results-oriented abstract, powerful visual aids, and prominent statements of findings and claims. Less newsworthy information relating to methods, materials, and raw data is downplayed and sometimes omitted entirely. It is as if the journal letter, as a genre, has evolutionarily leapfrogged over the journal article in terms of combining news value and respectability.[5]

All of the features discussed here serve to foreground important, newsworthy information by bringing it closer to the beginning of the article. In this respect, the scientific journal article is gradually taking on text features that are analogous to those of news reports, and in so doing is conforming more to the actual reading practices of working scientists. In an increasingly competitive world where they are deluged with information, scientists must read quickly and efficiently. A top-down layout of important information facilitates a selective reading process.

This evolution of genre features in the direction of a more reader-based schema has been occurring—and is likely to continue occurring—quite gradually, for there is strong countervailing pressure to retain at least a semblance of the traditional, writer-based schema. The primary role of the scientific journal article, after all, even more important than conveying new knowledge claims to the scientific community, is the *certification*, so to speak, of these claims. The initial dissemination of claims can be done in other ways, such as through meetings, phone calls, proposals, and preprints. It is only through journal article publication that scientists can provide complete scientific argumentation for these claims. Hence, there is obvious pressure on them, in this genre, to promote facticity and personal credibility. One way of doing this is by using the traditional narrative-of-science schema, which symbolizes adherence to what Gilbert and Mulkay (1984) called the "empiricist repertoire." This means, of course, that whatever rhetorical moves scientists can make to get the attention of their readership will have to be small ones, done discreetly within the conventional formats currently in use. According to our informants, only powerful journal editors are in a position to change the existing genre conventions in any major way.

## Rhetorical Moves in the Discussion Section

The tension between credibility and news value can be seen not only in the text features described earlier but also in the kinds of rhetorical *moves* that are made

---

[4]One of our physics informants, who publishes regularly in both *Physical Review* and *Physical Review Letters* and also serves as a referee for both journals, stated that the latter is "far more conventionalized" than the former. A second physics informant, however, felt that this sense of conventionality was due not to layout, but to the style of writing, which resulted, in his view, from the time pressure of shorter deadlines.

[5]Blakeslee (1994) described this process in more detail, showing how the increasing prestige of *Physical Review Letters* has caused it to acquire *archival features*.

*Swales — on Intro.* in specific sections of articles. Swales (1990) argued that Introductions to scientific journal articles are typically composed of three distinct moves: *Establishing a Territory*, *Establishing a Niche*, and *Occupying the Niche*. These moves are delineated as follows:

*Establishing a Territory*
  by:   • claiming centrality, and/or
        • making topic generalizations, and/or
        • reviewing items of previous research

*Establishing a Niche*
  by:   • counterclaiming, or
        • indicating a gap, or
        • question-raising, or
        • continuing a tradition

*Occupying the Niche*
  by:   • outlining purposes, or announcing present research,
        • announcing principal findings,
        • indicating the structure of the article

Swales saw these moves as performing a "public relations" role, in the sense that the writers try to show that their research is addressing an important problem in an interesting and useful way. In other words, the Introduction must show something of news value (either by offering some new and possibly unexpected solution to an established problem, or by raising a new problem) *and* it must establish the writer's credibility (by showing familiarity with past efforts to deal with this problem).

Little attention, however, has been paid to the Discussion section of journal articles. This is an unfortunate oversight because if we can generalize from our interviews with scientists who read these articles most closely, the Discussion section appears to be at least as important as the Introduction. All seven of our consultants read at least part of the Discussion, whereas only a few of them read the Introduction.

If we apply a Swales-type analysis to the Discussion sections of journal articles, we find basically the same three types of moves as in the Introduction, but in reverse order. First, there is typically a statement of principal findings. One of our biologist consultants, who serves on the editorial board of a major journal in the field, said that the first paragraph of the Discussion should always be reserved for the strongest claim in the study. Though he stated this as a prescription, our survey of articles in both biology and physics showed it to be a description of actual practice as well. Indeed, the first paragraph of the Discussion often reads like a paraphrased version of the Abstract, which always contains the main finding(s) of the study. In Swales' terms, the writer reasserts

*Introduction*
1. Establishing a territory
2. Establishing a niche
3. Occupying the niche

*Discussion*
1. Occupying the niche
2. (Re)establishing the niche
3. Establishing additional territory

FIG. 2.3.    Comparison of basic rhetorical moves in Introductions and Discussions, showing reversed ordering.

his or her claim to the "niche" created in the Introduction and occupied in the subsequent investigation. Second, there is a series of statements showing how these results respond to the larger issue stated in the Introduction. These statements usually include a comparison of the present results to related findings or claims made by other investigators, with the present results shown to be either superior or of a different nature. This section of the Discussion may be seen, in terms of rhetorical moves, as a re-establishing (and, in some cases, an expanding) of the niche. Finally, there is usually some commentary about the implications of the study, including in some cases a statement of plans for future work. This part of the discussion may contain some speculation, although some of our consultants insisted that the competitiveness of today's science and the emphasis on hard data have led to a major reduction in published speculation.

That these three moves are analogous to those of the Introduction, but in reverse order, can be seen by doing a pairwise comparison, as shown in Fig. 2.3. In their normal 1–2–3 ordering, the three moves of the Introduction can be seen as working "from outside in": first talking about the field as a whole, then progressively narrowing the scope so that only the current investigation is being addressed. In this way, writers situate their work within the interests of the discourse community. Having established their "credentials" through Moves 1 and 2, they are in a good position to offer newsworthy information in Move 3. Moves 2 and 3 can be seen as steps *away* from the consensual knowledge of the discipline. Conversely, the three moves of the Discussion can be seen as working "from inside out": The authors begin by referring only to the study at hand, but then progressively widen the scope to include related work by others. In doing so, they implicitly attempt to situate their novel findings within the body of knowledge previously accepted by their fellow specialists. As Hopkins and Dudley-Evans (1988) noted, "The discussion sections of articles and dissertations appear to be judged less on the actual results presented than on the way the writer relates them to previous work in the field" (p. 119).[6]

---

[6]Hopkins and Dudley-Evans (1988), drawing on a corpus of MSc dissertations in biology and conference proceedings in agricultural science, described a more detailed pattern for Discussion sections that resembles, in general, the "inside-out" pattern described here but applies in cycles. For example, a Discussion section might begin with a Statement of Result and then continue through these steps: (2) Reference to Previous Research, (3) Explanation, (4) Exemplification, (5) Deduction, (6) Reference to Previous Research, (7) Hypothesis, and (8) Recommendation. In our terms, Step 1 would represent "Occupying the Niche," Steps 2–6, "(Re)establishing the Niche," and Steps 7–8, "Establishing Additional Territory." If more than one important result is discussed, which was true

## CONCLUSION

The analysis of scientific journal articles put forth here suggests the following conclusions:

1. During the past half century, scientists have come under increasing pressure from the information explosion and, therefore, have been accessing and reading specialized journal articles in an increasingly selective manner, searching for the most newsworthy information; this reading behavior is not unlike that of ordinary people accessing and reading newspaper articles.
2. To accommodate this reading behavior, the genre conventions used in scientific journals have undergone gradual changes.
3. The dynamism that can be observed in this diachronic textual evidence of the past half century reflects changes in the way the scientific community goes about its work.

It appears that, in today's scientific world, front-line research scientists belong not to one but to two discourse communities, one embedded within the other. The traditional layout of the journal article, still in effect in many ways, symbolizes the scientist's membership in the larger scientific community. According to this layout, the background information and methodological details are accorded as much value as any other section of the article, which is consistent with their importance in the empiricist repertoire. But the gradual modifications of this layout that have taken place over time reflect the scientist's membership in a smaller community as well, the more personal, fast-paced one in which he or she plays a bigger role. Here there is little interest in background orientation and methodology, both of which are likely to be fairly common knowledge; instead, the scientist wants the "news." The changes in genre conventions that we have observed in this study seem designed to accommodate this interest.

These conclusions are supported by Rymer's (1988) study of the composing processes of eminent molecular biologists. Rymer found that in major research laboratories, where articles are usually written as a team effort with various apprentices involved, only the title, abstract, introduction, and discussion are written by the senior scientist or main author. The more routine parts of the article—the methods section and the presentation of raw results—are typically written by junior scientists or graduate students. In other words, it is only those elements of the article that promote news value that the laboratory head feels deserve his or her attention.

---

of most of these cases, the writer would repeat these same eight steps for each result. In contrast to the Hopkins and Dudley-Evans corpus, the articles we looked at typically focused on just one major finding and thus did not engage in this sort of cycling pattern.

*Compare with NIH, NSF proposals*

We are left to speculate, however, why it is that scientists today seem to place more emphasis on news value than they did in the past. After all, those things that have news value in science—discoveries, tentative claims, theoretical insights—have always been an essential part of the discipline, indeed a *sine qua non*. Does today's science simply have more of these things to offer? Whether it does or not is perhaps beside the point, for it is not so much the *amount* of news value that is remarkable in today's scientific journal articles as it is the *promoting* of it. Today's scientists seem to be promoting their work to a degree never seen before. We think there are two obvious and complementary explanations for this. First, the world of science is embedded within modern, postindustrial culture, which can be characterized as a "promotional" or "consumer" culture (Featherstone, 1991; Wernick, 1991). To the extent that scientists become accustomed to the promotionalism found in the modern world, it should not be surprising to see them incorporating some of it into their professional work. This would include, of course, discursive practices and their associated genres. As Fairclough (1993) noted, "[in today's promotional culture] there is an extensive restructuring of boundaries between orders of discourse and between discursive practices ... generating many new hybrid, partly promotional genres" (p. 141). The scientific journal article would appear to be evolving in this direction.

Second, on a more immediately pragmatic level, the need to promote one's work seems to be a response to the greatly increased competitiveness of modern science. More people are doing more scientific research today than ever before and are producing more data than ever before. Furthermore, their research is increasingly dependent on large amounts of external funding. Consequently, there is great pressure to publish, even if the work is not particularly exciting. And with citation indices often serving as the primary basis for professional advancement, there is great pressure to have one's work noticed and read. One way of doing this is by submitting manuscripts to prestigious journals that know how to showcase, in a sense, exciting results. As one of our consultants said, "If you want to publish, if you've got hot results, you can't afford to have it buried among pedestrian papers."

We agree with Bizzell (1992) that we need to "demystify" academic discourse for our students. One way of doing this is by helping them see the form–function correlations of discourse conventions. Forms by themselves have little meaning; it is only when they are seen as serving certain functions that they become meaningful. But often one cannot detect these functions without first noticing a pattern of forms, and often such a pattern cannot itself be detected without looking across genres and across time. In the present study, for example, we have seen how text features of a particular genre have been changing over time and have been coming to resemble those of a seemingly unrelated genre. By perceiving this dynamism as resulting from the situated cognition of individual scientists, we have gained some insight into the nature of the scientific community itself.

Bazerman (1988) argued that "scientific language needs to be studied as a historical phenomenon" (p. 313), and he postulated four levels of history: (a) the single living moment; (b) the transformation of private experiences into "community–wide, intersubjective, realities"; (c) "the genetic account of the community as a whole"; and (d) "the history of cultural forms" (pp. 314–315). The study we presented in this chapter belongs to this fourth level of history, for it has seized on identifiable regularities within a cultural form—in this case, a genre—and tried to make sense of them. We think the effort has been very much in the spirit of Bazerman's call for more studies of cultural forms using combined qualitative and quantitative methods:

> We need to understand why regularities emerge, evolve, and vanish; what the writers accomplish through the use of these features within the activity of the discipline; why these particular symbolic choices have seemed advisable to so many members of the community that they become regular practices; whether these habitual practices have become institutionalized; and what the effect is of regularities and institutions on science's ongoing work. (Bazerman, 1988, p. 315)[7]

---

[7]We wish to acknowledge the assistance of William McClure, Robert Kraemer, William Brown, John Woolford, Michael Widom, Robert Suter, Leonard Kisslinger, Charles Bazerman, and Jone Rymer in carrying out this work.

# 3

## YOU ARE WHAT YOU CITE: NOVELTY AND INTERTEXTUALITY IN A BIOLOGIST'S EXPERIMENTAL ARTICLE

*Intertextuality: Evidence, in a book, that the author has read some other book and remembers it.*

—Scanlan (1991, p. 3)

In this chapter we present a case study of a biologist's revisions of an experimental article that extends recent studies of news value or novelty in scientific writing. We raise the question, "What kinds of knowledge (of the genre, of research networks or the research front) must scientist–authors draw on to make the case for novelty?" Using case study data combined with linguistic and rhetorical analyses of the biologist's drafts of a research report, we document the process through which the author (in response to referees' comments) came to orchestrate for novelty when she had initially focused only on findings in the lab, that is to say, local knowledge.

To understand novelty from a rhetorical perspective, that is, in the context of the writer's textual and intertextual representations of laboratory activity, it will be helpful to provide the briefest of glimpses of that activity *in situ*. The following passage is a snapshot of the activity occurring in a university biologist's laboratory. The senior professor, June Davis, is a biologist at a technological university in an upper Midwestern state.

At one bench in Davis' laboratory, Beverly Cronin, a doctoral student, is busy cutting off the tips of mouse tails to draw blood for an assay. It is a delicate procedure: In order to get the mice to hold still, she must lure them into a test tube with food. Once there, they are secured and clipped at the end of the tail. At another bench in the long rectangular room, Davis does a cardiac puncture in order to draw blood directly from the hearts of the mice she is studying. She selects one anesthetized mouse at a time from a jar containing carbon dioxide and quickly makes an incision into its chest cavity. Pulling the ribs back, she exposes the heart of the animal to draw the blood with a small syringe. The samples taken from the tail clips and the heart are then placed into a centrifuge.

Two experiments are being conducted in Davis' lab this morning. Cronin is investigating the changes in blood serum for plasma fibrinogen, a clotting agent. She spreads a small amount of blood to which sterile saline has been added on the surface of an agar plate in order to determine whether the plate will grow colonies of *Candida albicans*, a common fungus that has been implicated in Toxic Shock Syndrome (TSS). She is performing an assay that involves coating and washing 96 tiny plastic wells and then filling them with mouse sera to be examined for the presence of a powerful monokine, Tumor Necrosis Factor (TNF), which the body produces in response to disease-producing agents.

Much of Davis' time is spent in the lab with her graduate students injecting mice with various infectious agents and toxins, drawing endless blood samples from an endless supply of mice, writing down different times and dosages in her lab notebook, performing assays and other procedures, doing statistical analyses of the data, looking for significant results, being disappointed, and trying again. Davis is one of many scientists engaged in what might best be described as "brickwork," the routine tasks that constitute much of what Kuhn (1970) called normal science. The tedium and monotony of this labor is considerable.

Such is life in the laboratory, a setting in which many scientists carry out the archetypical experiential activity (Bazerman, 1994) of conducting experiments. Scientists engage in this activity in order to play their role in carrying out what most believe to be a global, rational enterprise. Lewontin (1991) suggested:

> Most natural scientists are really positivists. They rely heavily both on confirmation and falsification, and they believe that the gathering of facts, followed by inference rather than the testing of theories, is the primary enterprise of science. *They are daily reinforced in their view of science by reading and writing the literature of science.* . . . Science consists, in this view, of the postulation of more or less general assertions about causation and the necessary interconnection between repeatable phenomena. These postulations demand the gathering of facts: observation from nature or from the deliberate perturbations of nature that are called experiments. When the facts are in, they can be compared with the postulated relations to confirm or falsify the hypothetical world. (p. 141; italics added)

Much of the literature of science is in the form of the four-part experimental article with its Introduction, Material and Methods, Results, and Discussion sections, each of which serves to codify scientific activity into a coherent narrative of inductive discovery (see Medawar, 1964). This is to say that the four sections function together to present a rational view of scientific activity as a cumulative enterprise, building on accepted wisdom, yet at the same time constantly seeking new knowledge.[1]

Our purpose in this chapter is to examine a particular narrative mechanism— the use of citation, or referencing—that is central to the generic function of the experimental article. Citation establishes the intertextual linkages that diachronically connect scientists' laboratory activity to significant activity in the field, and *source* thus serves to establish a narrative context for the study to be reported.[2] The use of citations is intrinsic to scientists' story making because it contextualizes local (laboratory) knowledge within an ongoing history of disciplinary knowledge making. Such contextualization is essential because it is only when scientists place their laboratory findings within a framework of accepted knowledge that a claim to have made a scientific discovery, and thereby to have contributed to the field's body of knowledge, can be made.

The concept of *novelty*, as it relates to scientific discovery, refers to the idea *novelty* that innovations (new postulations) are at the heart of the scientific enterprise as it is seen by its practitioners. If scientific activity is to be purposeful and cumulative, then a major criterion for publication is the novelty or news value of the researchers' knowledge claims, seen in the context of accumulated knowledge. As Amsterdamska and Leydesdorff (1989) suggested:

> In a scientific article "the new encounters the old" for the first time. This encounter has a double significance since articles not only justify the new by showing that the result is warranted by experiment or observation or previous theory, but also place and integrate innovations into the context of "old" and accepted knowledge. ... References which appear in the text are the most explicit manner in which the arguments presented in an article are portrayed as linked to other texts, and thus also to a particular body of knowledge. (p. 451)

From this perspective, experimental articles that are deemed by journal reviewers as novel or newsworthy have been positioned by their authors within an

---

[1]This textual representation serves to instantiate a view of science that has been questioned and analyzed by a number of sociologists of science interested in contrasting formal with informal scientific discourse (see especially Gilbert & Mulkay, 1980, 1984; Latour & Woolgar, 1986). These researchers argued that the rationalist view of scientific activity (as reproduced in the genre of the experimental article) brackets out the social and political variables affecting the laboratory decisions that scientists make.

[2]The textual mechanisms through which scientists establish the intertextual linkages between their own and others' experiments has been investigated rather extensively by sociologists of science (Gilbert, 1977; Gilbert & Mulkay, 1980; Latour, 1987; Latour & Woolgar, 1986); by rhetoricians (Bazerman, 1988; Myers, 1990); by scientometricians who study citation patterns within various specialties (e.g., Amsterdamska & Leydesdorff, 1989; Cozzens, 1985, 1989; Leydesdorff & Amsterdamska, 1990; Small, 1977, 1978); and by citation content analysts (e.g., Swales, 1986) who study researchers' citing behaviors.

intertextual web (Bazerman, 1988) or fabric (Amsterdamska & Leydesdorff, 1989).[3] The linguistic or rhetorical strategies for integrating innovation (new knowledge claims) into the existing knowledge structure of one's field must be, as Amsterdamska and Leydesdorff (1989) proposed, both implicit and explicit, diffuse and specific. This is to say that:

> In the most diffuse manner, but perhaps most importantly, [integration] takes place through the shared technical and "theory-laden" language and through shared patterns of argumentation. A more specific "integration" of the new claim occurs when the use of a particular concept or method is said to be warranted by reference to some precedent, a previous occasion or context in which it has been used. In the Introduction and Conclusion sections of an article, this "placement" of a claim takes the form of a specific requirement that the problem which is to be addressed, its significance, and sometimes also its implications, be specified and explicitly stated. In a somewhat more implicit manner, such integration also takes place in the other sections of the article. Thanks to this integration, the innovation—no matter how trivial, or how original—is not just another loose fact added to the heap but rather an extension of a thread, a new knot, a strengthened connection, or alternatively a bit of unraveling, an indication of a "hole," a bit of reweaving, etc. (p. 451)

The study described in this essay documents this process of integration of new claims into existing knowledge. Specifically, we focus on Davis and Cronin's efforts to get a manuscript accepted for publication by a major journal in Davis' field, *Infection and Immunity*. In our research we used a combination of sources for obtaining data, including field notes from lab observations, taped interviews with Davis (the senior researcher) and with Cronin (a doctoral student writing her dissertation) that took place between February 1988 and August 1990, the drafts of a single article written primarily by Davis, the comments on those drafts by the senior author (made in interviews), the reviewers' written comments, the editors' written comments, and the authors' written responses to the editor. To understand in greater detail the kinds of responses a reviewer might make when reading the drafts of their article, we also used three "penumbral readers," active researchers in fields close to but not identical to that of the author.[4] These researchers agreed

---

[3]However, it should be noted that an intertext representing the work of a research network (or that of overlapping networks) is organized by problems at the research front—which are in turn affected by a specialty's reputational structure: who is being cited, who is being funded, and, therefore, who is seen as working at the field's cutting edge. Moreover, the intertext is subject to continual revision as each newsworthy article appears in print, is read and, in turn, cited by interested colleagues. Thus, the textual matrix within which the activities of a particular community of scientists are communicated and acted upon cannot be regarded as a static entity, but rather a set of dynamic relationships that are more or less stable depending on the community's cohesiveness.

[4]One (B. A.) was a cellular immunologist specializing in the murine immune system, including TNF; another (K. B.) was a cellular immunologist specializing in the activation and regulation of T-cell responses; the third (J. W.) was a molecular immunologist/biologist specializing in mouse genetics.

*Research articles have two very different kinds of readers — the obvious ones in the text and the acquisition editor and referees of the journal. Books too, but often to a lesser degree*

*the most immediate target audience is the journal - peer review*

to read both the first draft and final draft of Davis and Cronin's article as reviewers, commenting on audiotape as they read. We call these readers penumbral because we see them not as part of the writers' immediate target audience (i.e., specialists in *Candida albicans*) but as typical of the larger readership for their article: grant proposal reviewers, journal reviewers, and colleagues in related fields.

We examine the way that Davis and Cronin, at the most abstract and diffuse level, use shared patterns of argument in the Introduction and Conclusion sections of their article; we examine their reference to a prior series of experiments reported in *Science* (1985 and 1986), whose methodology and conceptual structure they have replicated; finally, at the most explicit and specific level of argument, we examine their use of citations to demonstrate how they position their experiments in relation to other investigations of a related series of problems on which scientists at the research front of their specialty are working. This study of the peer review process uncovers the highly contingent and tentative epistemological status of the scientist's knowledge claim. Observing what goes on in the course of peer review clearly demonstrates the socially constituted, negotiational character of a genre of that has been most often analyzed only in the form of finished products (see Gross, 1990). Although something can be gained by studying published reports, certainly, we feel that tracking and analyzing the development of a report as it goes through various revisions yields unique insights about the epistemology of science.

## DAVIS' RESEARCH PROGRAM

For over a decade Davis has studied the role of *Candida albicans*, a common yeast in the mouth, intraperitoneal cavity, and vaginal tract. Although perceived by the medical community as a benign nuisance, *C. albicans* has been implicated in TSS, a life-threatening disease occurring primarily in women. In the early 1980s Davis' research suggested that *C. albicans* acted synergistically with *Staphylococcus aureus* bacteria, producing toxic effects in mice identified as having TSS. Since that early research she has moved on to study the effects of *C. albicans* on the immune system, having focused specifically on its relation to TNF. Immunologists have been interested in studying the mechanism of TNF production because it is one of the body's mediators when attacked by infectious agents. As an immune cell, TNF, it has been observed, produces potentially lethal effects. The majority of *in vivo* TNF studies have been on responses to invasion by endotoxin, a toxin that is released from certain bacteria as they disintegrate in the body (causing fever, shock, etc.), that can indirectly produce widespread tissue damage by generating an exaggerated and potentially lethal response from immune cells. A study published in *Science* in 1985 first established TNF's lethal overreaction to endotoxin invasion. The authors of this study noted that TNF functioned:

as a hormone to promote cellular responses which, in part, result in the mobilization of host energy reserves in response to invasion ... [thus] in the present study we reasoned that TNF might also play a role in the lethal metabolic effects of endotoxin mediated shock. Accordingly, we passively immunized mice with antibody to TNF and challenged them with lethal amounts of [endotoxin]. (Beutler, Milsark, & Cerami, 1985, p. 869)

Beutler et al. (1985) reported that when immune serum was administered to mice by "intraperitoneal injection 1.5 hours before the intraperitoneal injection of 400 μg of [endotoxin], a significant protective effect was demonstrable ... compared to the mortality rate observed among control mice treated with preimmune [nonreactive] serum or with serum from nonimmunized rabbits" (p. 870).

Though it established a cause-and-effect relationship between endotoxin and TNF, Beutler's study did not create such a relationship between external infectious agents and TNF. Hence, this was a natural direction for researchers to take using infectious agents like *C. albicans*. In 1988, a second group of researchers reported that "*C. albicans* induced TNF production *in vitro* by human monocytes and natural killer cells" (Djeu, Blanchard, Richards, & Friedman in Riipi & Carlson, 1990, p. 1). By the late 1980s Davis had become interested in determining the role *C. albicans* played in elevating the fibrinogen level in the blood, one of the effects of TNF. Davis and Cronin, at this time, were extending Beutler et al.'s *in vivo* study, by examining the *C. albicans*/TNF relationship. They sent a report of their initial findings to the journal, *Infection and Immunity*, noting that prior work on the *C. albicans*/TNF relationship had been done *in vitro*, and that theirs was the first *in vivo* study.

## CONSTRUCTING AN ARGUMENT FOR NOVELTY

The particular rhetorical problem that Davis and Cronin faced was creating sufficient surprise value or novelty for journal reviewers to concur that their experiments were indeed newsworthy. Because the stuff of their science is brickwork rather than the big ideas that challenge the status quo (see Myers, 1990), their argumentative strategies were necessarily quite different. For Davis and Cronin then, the rhetorical task was to justify the importance of their experiments by creating a research space in their discussion of recent work: They needed to show in the Introduction and Discussion sections of their article what had been accomplished in the recent research on TNF/endotoxin, and to propose in what ways their experiments extended this line of research on the production of TNF in mice by infectious agents. The importance of positioning their work in relation to a series of crucial experiments, that is, deploying the relevant line of research through citation, cannot be underestimated. As one of our penumbral readers observed:

In a good Introduction you can almost get the entire paper and background. A good Introduction, in a way, is like Kentucky Fried Chicken: The Colonel used to say if the gravy is good enough you can throw away the chicken. And you can almost throw away the paper, if the Introduction is set up well, because you can see the field, you can see where it all fits, you can see what they did.

## Draft 1: Getting the Basic Facts Down

Davis (who as senior researcher wrote the entire paper except for the Methods section) did not seem concerned about laying out the field and positioning her work within it, at least not initially. In Draft 1, the Introduction was local rather than intertextual, the author having cited only her own studies:

> We have previously found that a small dose of *Candida albicans* which had little adverse effect by itself, acted synergistically with *Staphylococcus aureus* to cause shock and death in mice (3 [self citation]). While attempting to identify the role of *C. albicans* in the *C. albicans/S. aureus* synergism, we had found that *C. albicans* alone at low doses which have no effect on a variety of blood parameters tested did elevate plasma fibrinogen levels (unpublished). In this study the ability of small doses of *C. albicans* to induce changes on blood chemistry and hematology and the role of tumor necrosis factor (TNF) in these changes were examined. (Davis, Draft 1)

The Introduction was curiously insular in this first draft. Davis did not situate her work within any body of experiments conducted by other specialists. Rather, she attempted only to link the current study to her own previous research on synergism between *Candida albicans* and *Staphylococcus aureus*, specifically to follow up on one result in a previous (unpublished) study, that *C. albicans* induction had produced elevated fibrinogen levels in the blood.[5] Although she mentioned TNF in this early Introduction, its significance in being induced by *C. albicans* was only alluded to in the last sentence. Reference to the experiments by Beutler, Milsark, and Cerami on the production of TNF by endotoxin was made only once, buried in the second paragraph of her Discussion section: "Endotoxin, cause of endotoxic shock, has been shown to induce TNF which is in turn responsible for shock in the mouse (2)."

## Draft 2: Building the TNF Connection

Although Davis was not unaware of the importance of positioning her work within a related literature, during the revising of the first and second drafts she was much more concerned with technical issues and questions that reviewers

---

[5]Fibrinogen is a globulin, or protein, which produces fibrin in the clotting of the blood. It is an important factor in heart disease. Because much of Davis' research has been supported by the National Heart Association, her interest in fibrinogen is understandable.

raised about the procedures used in the lab. For example, one reviewer wanted to know if precautions were taken to guard against endotoxin (LPS) contamination of *C. albicans* preparations and other reagents used. This information was thought to be important because even picagram amounts of LPS could act in synergy with *C. albicans*, thus contributing to the observed responses.

The polite and cautious tone of the scientist's language masked the somewhat hostile implication of the question that procedural sloppiness may have affected what was observed. The comment can thus be seen as an indirect request that Davis produce evidence showing that such was not the case. Responding to this and other questions of lab procedure occupied Davis' efforts through her first few revisions.

At the same time, it can be seen that the Introduction to Draft 2 possesses new intertextual features. For one thing, Davis substituted a reference to the work of Beutler et al. (1985), in place of the reference to her own unpublished study on *C. albicans* and fibrinogen (see sentence 3):

> We have previously found that a small dose of *Candida albicans*, which had little adverse effect by itself, acted synergistically with *Staphylococcus aureus* to cause shock and death in mice (3 [self citation]). This study was undertaken to determine how *C. albicans* contributes to this lethal shock synergism. It has been reported that induced TNF is responsible for endotoxic shock in the mouse (2 [reference to Beutler et al.]). Because *C. albicans* and endotoxin share a number of characteristics (for review see 12) the role of TNF in candidal-induced hematology and blood chemistry changes was examined. (Davis, Draft 2)

Not only did Davis link her study to the experiments of Beutler et al., but she also inserted another intertextual reference in sentence 4. In this sentence she also began to develop what one of our penumbral readers described as a "prospective rationale" in the form of a general warranting statement implied by her assertion. The warrant implied in sentence 4 can be seen to have the form of the following heuristic reasoning: If two chemical substances x and y share characteristics A through M, and if x is then found to possess the characteristic N, it is reasonable to suppose that y might also possess N.

This warrant was not made explicit, probably because everyone in Davis' discourse community already subscribed to it. Davis' claim that *C. albicans* shares characteristics with endotoxin was, in this sense, indexical, pointing as it does to a shared warrant within the field. This kind of logical appeal, we suggest, is based on tacit presuppositional knowledge within a discourse community. What is being warranted is Davis' assertion that a yeast and the cell wall of a bacterium have similar characteristics, one that our specialist readers questioned:

> J. W.:  When . . . they say something like "*albicans* and endotoxin share a number of characteristics," what are those characteristics? I don't know what they are. And it doesn't do me any good to tell me to go see a review because the last thing I'm

going to do is go look up a review to find out what the characteristics are, to understand the intellectual linkage that these things have.

B. A.:   I have no idea what they mean by *Candida albicans* and endotoxin sharing a number of characteristics. The response of an animal to *Candida albicans* and endotoxin may share a number of characteristics, but *Candida albicans* and endotoxin don't share anything. Very different stuff.

These two penumbral readers may have accepted the implied warrant but they rejected the specific grounds of the claim (i.e., that *C. albicans* and endotoxin share a number of characteristics). Davis' inclusion of a citation to a literature that purportedly demonstrates a connection between the two indicates her awareness of the need to provide such grounds for skeptical or uninformed readers.

Draft 2 was rejected by the editor of the *Journal of Medical and Veterinary Mycology*, although, as Davis pointed out in an interview, the reasons for rejection were most likely due to the lack of interesting data on the *C. albicans*/TNF relationship. What she meant by this observation is that the major newsworthy item was her *inference* that "TNF was induced in the mouse by *C. albicans* infection and that this TNF, in turn, was responsible for the observed increase in fibrinogen levels." This claim, however, was based on *indirect evidence* (the presence of elevated levels of fibrinogen in the mice *not* treated with TNF antibodies 18 hours prior to injection with TNF) rather than on direct observation. The reviewers found this inference alone to be insufficient to support Davis' claim regarding the *C. albicans*/TNF relationship. Thus, the editor rejected the paper on the grounds that it was incomplete, lacking data on TNF.

## Draft 3: Providing the Necessary Data on TNF Linking it to <u>Candida albicans</u>

Eight months and dozens of experiments later, using a new assay that enabled them to report the levels of TNF produced by injections in mice with *C. albicans*, Davis and Cronin produced quantitative data that directly supported their claims of *C. albicans* inducing TNF in mice and TNF being responsible for an increase in fibrinogen. Davis reported this information in a letter to the editor of *Infection and Immunity* to whom she sent her revision:

> We have included new data on candidal-induced TNF using a sandwich type ELISA [enzyme-linked immunosorbent assay]. . . . As you stated that you would be glad to look at this paper again should we provide this additional data, we are returning it to you with the hope of a better outcome. Specifically we have . . . determined with ELISA the levels of circulating TNF after selected doses of *C. albicans*.

To reflect their emphasis on the new data and especially to foreground the newsworthy finding that TNF could be induced by *C. albicans* (a yeast) as well as by endotoxin (cell walls of bacteria), the authors changed the title of their paper from "Elevation of Fibrinogen Levels Due to Injection of *Candida albicans* or Recombinant Tumor Necrosis Factor (TNF) in the Mouse: Protection with TNF Antibodies" to "Tumor Necrosis Factor (TNF) Is Induced in Mice by *Candida albicans*: Role of TNF in Fibrinogen Increase." Not only does the second title foreground the *Candida*/TNF relationship, it does so very emphatically by putting it in the form of a full predication, as is done in newspaper headlines (see chap. 2 for further discussion of this linguistic feature). Furthermore, Davis and Cronin changed the wording of sentence 4 in the Introduction somewhat to highlight their new central claim that *C. albicans* induces TNF production. Instead of saying "the role of TNF in candidal-induced hematology and blood chemistry changes was examined," they say, more directly, "*candidal*-infected mice were examined for induced TNF."

Both reviewers for *Infection and Immunity* approved of the direction the paper was taking, but they also had suggestions for further textual and rhetorical improvements, such as expanding the Introduction. One reviewer indicated that the new draft was on much firmer ground than the manuscript previously reviewed. This reviewer also submitted a checklist of several items that needed to be corrected, including expanding the Introduction to set the stage for the research that followed (the reviewer was bothered that the readers unfamiliar with TNF and fibrinogen relationships would not understand why fibrinogen was not selected for assay). The reviewer also wanted to see included in the Introduction the information buried in the second page of the Discussion. The second reviewer concurred, suggesting that further references to related studies (which had not appeared in the manuscript) should also be included in the Introduction, in particular the results of previous studies on the induction of TNF by *C. albicans* and the ability of TNF to potentiate the anticandidal activity of polymorphonuclear leukocytes, as reported in the *Journal of Immunology* (1986) and *Infection and Immunity* (1989). This reviewer suggested a further intertextual move by exhorting the investigators to be explicit with their finding that the monokine response of mice to *C. albicans* differs from that obtained with LPS (endotoxin). The reviewer added that these differences were important and should be addressed.

### Draft 4: Creating the "Phony Story"

Davis immediately saw the validity of this reviewer's comment about monokine response,[6] and set about doing "a thorough comparative study of the TNF responses to endotoxin and *C. albicans*," as she was to report to the editor of *Infection and Immunity* in the letter that accompanied her revision. On the rhetorical level, though, she was much less enthusiastic. Preparing to write the next

---

[6]See Gross (1990) for a discussion of scientists' rhetorical strategies in responding to peer reviewers.

draft of the manuscript, Davis alluded to the "phony story" that she would have to add to the Introduction. When pressed as to what she meant, she simply noted that "reviewers always expect you to say certain things." Davis' efforts to develop a "phony story," that is, to contextualize her experiments within a related literature, can be seen in Draft 4. First, in the Discussion section she added two paragraphs in which she compared her *C. albicans*/TNF data with that of Beutler et al., as well as the data from a second group of researchers (Zuckerman & Bendele, 1989) who had measured TNF levels in mice receiving lethal doses of endotoxin. Second, she expanded the citational base of the Introduction, incorporating references the reviewers had suggested and using accepted knowledge claims as scaffolding for the present study. An examination of the Introductions to Drafts 4 and 5 illustrates the ways in which Davis integrated the new with the old:

> We have previously found that a small dose of *Candida albicans* which had little adverse effect by itself, acted synergistically with *Staphylococcus aureus* to cause shock and death in mice (3). The present study was undertaken to determine how *C. albicans* contributes to this lethal shock synergism. It has been reported that induced tumor necrosis factor (TNF) is responsible for endotoxic shock in the mouse (2). Because *C. albicans* and endotoxin share a number of characteristics (for a review see 13) candidal-infected mice were examined for induced TNF. As exogenously administered TNF is known to induce acute phase proteins such as fibrinogen (9), plasma fibrinogen in infected mice was also measured and the role of TNF in the fibrinogen increase investigated.
>
> It has been reported recently that *C. albicans* induced TNF production by human monocytes and NK cells *in vitro* (8). Also *in vitro* TNF has been shown to potentiate the fungicidal activity of human neutrophils against *C. albicans* (9, 10). (Davis, Draft 4)

Davis made three major additions in this draft of the Introduction. The first of these, the last sentence in paragraph 1, was constructed in response to the comments of Reviewer 1 who had wanted to see information originally appearing in the Discussion foregrounded in the Introduction, and who was also concerned that "The reader who is not familiar with TNF and fibrinogen relationships does not have a clue as to why fibrinogen was not selected for the assay." To accommodate this reviewer, Davis combined two sentences from the previous draft. First she revised the sentence from the Introduction in Draft 3 ("In addition, the relationship between TNF and candidal-induced hematology and blood chemistry changes was examined.") and combined it with a sentence containing a citation that had appeared originally in the second paragraph of the Discussion section of Draft 3: "Also, exogenously administered TNF is known to induce acute phase proteins such as fibrinogen (9)." In the new sentence, one can see Davis building her study on an antecedent, and thus linking new to old, or given knowledge. This kind of linking continues to supply a prospective rationale, justifying the present study with what has previously been accomplished in the field. It creates the appearance of a chronology of scientific activity; one can therefore understand why Davis thought of herself as constructing a "phony story." She was, in fact, constructing a narrative. Davis also added two new sentences containing citations in a very brief second paragraph: "It has been reported recently that *C. albicans* induced TNF production by human monocytes and NK cells *in vitro* (8). Also *in vitro* TNF has been shown to potentiate the fungicidal activity of human neutrophils against *C. albicans* (9, 10)." These sentences were included to accommodate Reviewer 2, who had suggested that she add references to two in vitro studies in the Introduction and who had given her the citation for one of these, the other having been buried in the Discussion of Davis' previous draft.

## Draft 5: Strengthening the Argument

In the Introduction to Draft 5, these two sentences (sentences 5 and 6) are skillfully woven into the body of the first paragraph:

> We have previously found that a small dose of *Candida albicans* which had little adverse effect by itself, acted synergistically with *Staphylococcus aureus* to cause shock and death in mice (3). The present study was undertaken to determine how *C. albicans* contributes to this lethal shock synergism. It has been reported that induced tumor necrosis factor (TNF) is responsible for endotoxic shock in the mouse (2). Because *C. albicans* and endotoxin share a number of characteristics (for a review see 15) candidal-infected mice were examined for induced TNF. It is reasonable to suspect that *C. albicans* could induce TNF *in vivo* because it has been reported recently that *C. albicans* induced TNF production *in vitro* by human monocytes and natural killer cells (9). TNF has also been shown to potentiate the fungicidal activity of human neutrophils *in vitro* against *C. albicans* (10, 11). As exogenously administered TNF is known to induce acute phase proteins such as fibrinogen (12), plasma fibrinogen in infected mice was also measured and the role of TNF in the fibrinogen increase investigated. (Davis, Draft 5)

Embedded at the presuppositional level in these two sentences is a warrant in the form of a tacit methodological principle: If *a* produces *b in vitro*, then it is reasonable to suppose that *a* will produce *b in vivo* (other things being equal). This warrant underlies both the claim ("it is reasonable to suspect that *C. albicans* could induce TNF *in vivo*"—justification of the present study) and the grounds for that claim ("because it has been reported recently that *C. albicans* induced TNF production *in vitro* by human monocytes and natural killer cells (9)" and "TNF has also been shown to potentiate the fungicidal activity of human neutrophils *in vitro* against *C. albicans* (10, 11)"). The warrant itself is not explicit; however, once again, as in sentence 3, biologist readers are likely to infer it. The references further buttress the claim by providing evidence, and by being attached (by inference) to the underlying methodological principle. With its claim–grounds–warrant structure, sentence 5, like sentence 3, appears to fulfill the criteria for a Toulmin argument (1958). Sentences 4 through 6 appear to exemplify two kinds of intertextual integration that Amsterdamska and Leydesdorff (1989) described (although they did not use this term) when they referred to diffuse *shared patterns of argument* and the more specific integration of a new claim that occurs "when the use of a particular concept or method is said to be warranted by reference to some precedent, a previous occasion or context in which it has been used" (p. 451).

Looking at the Introduction as a microtext, we can trace a chronology or story that weaves together Davis' previous work with *C. albicans* and *S. aureus* synergism producing shock in mice, with related sets of experiments investigating the role of the immune system in response to infectious agents: *in vivo* studies that investigated the role of TNF production in endotoxic shock, *in vitro* studies of *C. albicans* induced TNF production, and experiments that induced the *in vitro* production of acute phase proteins by exogenously administering TNF. Bound together with citations and undergirded by presuppositional warrants, these sentences create a coherent narrative which functions to contextualize (and thus justify) the present study. The creation of this kind of narrative scaffolding is quite different from the *create a research space* rhetorical activity that Swales (1990) described.

## SPECIALIST READERS' PERCEPTIONS OF NOVELTY IN DAVIS' FIRST AND LAST DRAFTS

In this discussion of the revisions of Davis and Cronin's paper for the journal *Infection and Immunity*, we have focused on Davis' interactions with her editor and reviewers concerning the placing and integrating of her research into a related body of literature. One of our penumbral readers' responses to the first and final (published) versions of the manuscript illustrates how the scientist–reader looks for and responds to news. After reading the first draft of the manuscript, he reacted as follows:

> J. W.:   To me this is a rather mundane finding, but I have to spend more time reading it to see whether or not it's really unique in terms of science, or whether or not it's merely continuing what you'd expect. If you inject TNF into animals, I guess I'm not surprised that a lot of things happen, because it's nasty stuff. That's usually where the Introduction helps me a lot. They don't help me here.

Later, while reading the Discussion section of the final version in manuscript form, he commented on what caught his eye and interest:

> J. W.:   So now we get through everything and go to the Discussion. [Reads.] They're giving me their data and giving me their interpretation. [Reads.] They say this? I certainly didn't catch it [in the earlier draft]. [Reads.] Hm. I don't see it.

Starting this paragraph, [reading aloud] "Since endotoxin does not induce TNF in the C3 H/HeJ [endotoxin-resistant] strain, our finding that *C. albicans* did induce TNF in the endotoxin-resistant strain suggests that the induction of TNF by *C. albicans* is under a different mechanism of control and the induction of TNF by endotoxin." Now if they said that in here [Draft 1], I didn't even see it. But that's very interesting.

T. H.:   Why is that particularly interesting?

J. W.:   It gives me another pathway. They're now defining something which is novel to me. They're not saying that the induction of TNF by *Candida* is the same thing as the endotoxin-induction of TNF, they're saying that it's a different mechanism, because of the [prior] work on endotoxin-resistant strains. So, uh, that's telling me that this is new and novel. So if I'm reviewing it, they get a little click on the new and novel scale.

J. W.'s reaction as he read the first and last drafts of the manuscript (as well as our other readers' responses) provided important information regarding the ways that other biologists, and specifically immunologists, would have evaluated both the technical/scientific and the rhetorical dimensions of this experimental report. These responses make us somewhat cautious about framing our discussion of novelty strictly within a rhetorical context, something that researchers in our field are likely to do. On the other hand, it was also J. W. who provided the insight that, when written well, the Introduction enables the scientist–reader (with particular schema and purposes for reading [Bazerman, 1985]) to "see the field . . . see where it all fits . . . see what they did."

## CONCLUSION

The study reported in this chapter documents what happened in one case in one small arena of textual activity intimately connected to other domains of scientific activity: a scientist placing her work within an intertext. In many respects, Davis strikes us as a typical working scientist, one who sees laboratory research and rhetorical activity as distinctly *separate*. Her distaste for the disingenuous, her cynicism regarding the "phony story" she had to construct, suggests that she was very aware of the difference between recounting local history in her lab and contextualizing that history within a narrative framework, and that she considered only the former as constituting true science. She appears to be a very technical-minded scientist who devalues the rhetorical dimension, letting her reviewers tell her what is needed to create the necessary "phony story." Although she was a realist, her realism extended only as far as what she observed in her lab (unlike the more rhetorically savvy scientists described in Myers, 1990).

Davis' reviewers, on the other hand, made no such distinction between laboratory activity and rhetorical accommodation, insisting that to be science her

*You con't just prove, you have to argue*
*Not just the lab work, the article*

*[handwritten margin note: novelty (in science) is a central criterion for the argument.]*

report had to include an intertextual framework for her local knowledge. Rather than letting the laboratory research speak for itself, they helped inject surprise value into this article by insisting on background information and warrants and by asking the author to foreground her claims. In this sense it can be said that the reviewers aided Davis in the construction of knowledge, that is, in the claim to novelty.

Another framework for characterizing the reviewers' intellectual contribution is that of current narrative theory (Fisher, 1987), particularly with regard to narrative coherence or the sense of completeness that a good story has. Davis' initial accounts of her research depicted it as the story of her work in the lab: She obtained endotoxin-resistant mice, prepared *C. albicans* cultures, inoculated the mice, took blood samples, and so on. It was a distinctly "local" narrative. But Davis' reviewers had a much larger narrative in mind, the ongoing narrative of Tumor Necrosis Factor and its role in fibrinogen production. They knew that this larger narrative already commanded the attention of a certain segment of the scientific community, and they saw how Davis' local narrative fit within it. Far from being a phony story, as Davis put it, the larger narrative is, in a sense, the *real* story. At least, that is how the reviewers (and our penumbral readers) saw it.

*[handwritten margin note: How I did my research]*

A major question with which we are left is whether Davis' negative attitude toward writing phony stories and providing "the things that reviewers expect you to say," does not capture something more subtle about the ideological nature of the experimental article as a genre. This something more subtle has to do with the difference between Davis' perception of science and that of the reviewers. As we have said, Davis' view of science appears to be constituted largely by what goes on in the lab. In contrast, the perspective promoted by the reviewers, which sees laboratory activity in terms of its relevance to disciplinary intertextuality, functions to instantiate a rationalist view of the cumulative nature of scientific discovery that goes well beyond Davis' straightforward empiricism. This conception of science as an inductive, cumulative activity is what Lewontin (1991) seemed to be referring to (in the passage we quoted earlier) in his observation that scientists are "daily reinforced in their view of science by reading and writing the literature of science" (p. 141).

From an entirely different perspective, Amsterdamska and Leydesdorff (1989) hinted (although nonreflexively) at the ideological activity underlying scientists' conception of novelty: "Thanks to this integration [into a related literature], the innovation—no matter how trivial, or how original—is not just another loose fact added to the heap, but rather an extension of a thread, a new knot, a strengthened connection, or alternatively a bit of unraveling, an indication of a 'hole,' a bit of reweaving, etc." (p. 451).

The view here seems to reflect an assumption that is part of the methodological hard core (Lakotos, 1970) of scientists' beliefs concerning science as a knowledge-building, or cognitive, enterprise. However, we suggest that it is the unreflective use of the conventions themselves that reproduces this view of science.

That is to say, the conventions of the scientific journal article instantiate ideological assumptions that are regularly reinforced by scientists' routine, unreflexive use of the genre. As Bruner (1991) argued, "Genres . . . are ways of telling that predispose us to use our minds and sensibilities in particular ways. In a word, while they may be representations of social ontology, they are also invitations to a particular style of epistemology" (p. 15; see our discussion of principle 5 in chap. 1). In the case of the experimental journal article, scientists who wish to have their work published must adopt a slightly contradictory stance in which they (a) act as though scientific discovery is a purely inductive process (see Medawar, 1964, p. 41), but (b) explicitly acknowledge, via appropriate citations and warrants, that hypotheses are inspired by earlier research done by other scientists.

We think that this study opens an interesting line of inquiry in the rhetoric of science regarding the relationship between the conventions of the genre and the ideological assumptions embedded in those conventions. What do the narratives that scientists are socialized to produce and that reify scientific activity as perceived by the community reveal about the social dynamics of such texts? What does a study of the ideological character of the genre's conventions reveal about the deeply embedded epistemological assumptions that permeate scientists' discursive practices in general? More broadly speaking, what can researchers add to the provocative work in the rhetoric of science that draws on the rich interdisciplinary character of science studies to answer such questions? How do we draw on our own considerable expertise in analyzing the textual dynamics of discourse communities to begin to develop situationally located, grounded theories of genre? With hindsight we can claim that it was such questions as these that led to our developing the fifth principle that we enumerated in chapter 1: "Genre conventions signal a discourse community's norms, epistemology, ideology, and social ontology."[7]

---

[7]We wish to acknowledge, with appreciation, the constructive criticism that Charles Bazerman, Alan Gross, and Donald Rubin provided us during the writing of this chapter.

# 4

# Sites of Contention, Sites of Negotiation: Textual Dynamics of Peer Review in the Construction of Scientific Knowledge

*Speech Acts*

> *This is the paradox of journal peer review: The open sharing of knowledge through publication is preceded by secret deliberations among a few scientists acting with calculatedly restricted information, vague and unenforceable guidelines, and little accountability to authors. Scientists (as well as outsiders such as the public) are told that this system of evaluation and resource allocation is good for all concerned, that it allows the community to cohere, to sustain and reproduce itself. . . . It is important to ask how authors, editors, and reviewers together transform the raw material of manuscripts into the finished product of validated knowledge claims, that is, how they convert research resources into new knowledge.*
>
> —Chubin and Hackett (1990, p. 95)

> *Actions speak louder than words.*
>
> —Anonymous

Chubin and Hackett's interest in investigating the function of peer review interactions in converting the "raw material of manuscripts into the finished product of validated knowledge claims" has relevance for the material we report on in this chapter. Case study materials such as those that June Davis provided are rich in the sense that they continue to provide resources for inquiry as our research questions develop over time. In this chapter we shift our focus from Davis' revisions of her drafts to accommodate her reviewers, to the peer review correspondence between author and editor (and reviewers whose comments are part of the editorial correspondence). We examine the interactions between Davis and her reviewers, as mediated by the editor, and suggest that from a rhetorical perspective, journal peer review can be analyzed as a generically structured argumentative discussion. (A chronology of Davis' drafts and editorial correspondence can be found in Appendix A.)

Peer review, as it developed through the establishment of a referee system in the first scientific journal in 17th- and 18th-century Europe, has become, over time, a system for certifying new knowledge. The referee system has its historical roots in the efforts of Henry Oldenburg, the editor of the first scientific journal, the *Philosophical Transactions of the Royal Society*, and the council of the Royal Society to provide the institutional means through which scientists would be encouraged to report new experiments without fear of their work being stolen (see Zuckerman & Merton, 1973). The referee system has spread from the natural sciences to other knowledge-producing fields and can be seen as one indicator of disciplinary formation and professionalization. Although peer review is not infallible, it remains the primary means through which authority and authenticity are conferred upon scientific and scholarly papers by journal editors and the expert judges they have consulted. Figure 4.1 illustrates our conception of the discursive network of texts and actors that constitute the scientific publication system. The figure depicts the textual activities through which the research resources of the laboratory represented in the manuscripts are converted into the finished product of validated knowledge claims.

Peer review can therefore be seen as a social mechanism through which a discipline's "experts" maintain quality control over new knowledge entering the

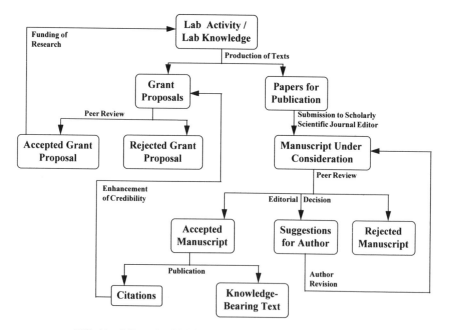

FIG. 4.1.   Life cycle of lab knowledge in scientific publication system.

*" status 'judges " - argue to get a positive result (accept)*

field. Quality control is, of course, a form of social control, and those who argue its utility share assumptions about the function of the referee system. Zuckerman and Merton (1973) put the matter this way:

> The referee system in science involves systematic use of judges to assess the acceptability of manuscripts submitted for publication. The referee is thus an example of status judges who are charged with evaluating the quality of role-performance in a social system. They are found in every institutional sphere. . . . Status judges are integral to any system of social control through their evaluation of role performance and their allocation of rewards for that performance. They influence the motivation to maintain or to raise standards of performance. . . . In the case of scientific and scholarly journals, the significant status judges are the editors and referees. ( p. 460)

According to this view, rational consensus is both goal and process of peer review (Gross, 1990). However, as numerous accounts have attested (see, e.g., Lloyd, 1985), there are many reasons for the process to go awry. Among scientists who may disagree with one another at the paradigmatic level, an author often encounters reviewers with competing research agendas. It is not too difficult for such referees to use their power as gatekeepers to prevent competitors from getting into print.

As a discourse, peer review correspondence generally has an agonistic character. The relationship between corresponding author and referees is generally asymmetrical. A reviewer's carefully worded questions can signal to an editor grounds to reject a manuscript. If the author's text is not flatly rejected, that author must convince the editor either that necessary repair of a manuscript has been made, or that a specific request of a reviewer is unwarranted. In the discussion that follows, we emphasize the highly indeterminate status of a scientist's textual representation at the peer review stage of knowledge production. Building on our research on June Davis' revisions (chap. 3), we analyze that data from a second analytical framework that has been developed from argumentation theory. Drawing on the work of argumentation theorists van Eemeren and Grootendorst (1983), we suggest that peer review correspondence can be viewed as an argumentative discussion consisting of illocutionary act complexes. This discussion consists of a set of negotiations among author, reviewers, and editor, all of whom draw on previously established generic conventions and argumentative moves.

Van Eemeren and Grootendorst (1983) extended the speech act theory of Austin (1975) and Searle (1969, 1979) to sequences of discourse longer than the *with the goal of reaching consensus* sentence to suggest that argumentative discussions can be analyzed as being constituted by various kinds of illocutionary act complexes. We have modified somewhat their analytical framework in analyzing the peer review correspondence that provides the context for Davis' revisions of her manuscript reporting Tumor Necrosis Factor (TNF) production of fibrinogen in mice injected with *Candida albicans*. Included in this sequence are the reviewers' comments appended to

*The reviews as a counter argument*

the editors' letters to Davis and her point-by-point replies to their comments and inquiries.

We wanted to determine what kinds of illocutionary acts participants in the correspondence used to negotiate the status of the author's knowledge claims. After a close reading of the peer review documents, we knew that there were sequences of comments that functioned as speech acts. Yet the Austin and Searle taxonomies of speech acts were designed to apply to single sentences (or utterances) in talk rather than longer stretches of discourse in a written mode. We then looked to the literature on discourse analysis and pragmatics to find if scholars had used speech act theory to investigate other kinds of discourse. Extending van Eemeran and Grootendorst's (1983) schema for analyzing sequences of sentences in oral argumentative discussions as illocutionary act complexes, we analyzed Davis' peer review correspondence to determine (a) what kinds of illocutionary act complexes could be identified in sequences of sentences that seemed to have a particular function, and (b) in what ways the institutional role of each interlocutor as either author, referee, or editor determined the illocutionary acts each could (or could not) deploy.

## ASSUMPTIONS AND THEORETICAL FRAMEWORK

According to both Austin (1975) and Searle (1969), a speaker's utterances manage to both *state* things and *do* things.[1] This is to say that utterances simultaneously convey a meaning, possess a force, and elicit an effect. For example, the sentence, "Shut the door," at the level of meaning, refers to accomplishing an action (shutting) in relation to an object (door). Depending on the intentions of the speaker, however, the sentence may be spoken with a particular force of an order, a request, or even a question. Force can thus be seen as "an element of utterances which is dissociated from their meaning, although it is often indicated by the speaker's use of a certain verb [such as] promise, order, state and so on" (Potter & Wetherell, 1987, p. 17). This aspect of a speech act is referred to as its *illocutionary force*. A second feature of utterances is the effect or consequence of its meaning and force on the hearer, or hearers. Thus, "Shut the door" may be uttered with the force of an order, but it may have more than one effect, for example, making the hearer annoyed and resolved to ignore the order, or making the hearer comply. This characteristic of a speech act is referred to as its *perlocutionary effect*. The importance of Austin's theory of speech acts, as Potter and

---

[1]Potter and Wetherell (1987) made this point in their succinct and lucid discussion of speech act theory as one of the foundations of discourse analysis. See *Discourse and Social Psychology: Beyond Attitudes and Behavior*, pp. 14–18. We have drawn on their commentary for this section of our discussion.

Wetherell (1987) noted, is that it "draws our attention to the role played by the web of social conventions in the achievement of actions through talk, and thus sensitizes the researcher to features of the social context surrounding language use" (p. 18).

Because speech act theory is not empirically grounded in studies of language-in-use, it has been criticized for being decontextualized and removed from the actual situated practices of language users. Nevertheless, the theory has, we believe, heuristic power when used as a deductive analytical framework for describing the moves that actors make in the texts intended to persuade, as is the case with peer review correspondence. If we consider peer review correspondence to be a generically structured interaction in which actors know what moves are appropriate, given the *range of actions* that is available to them through their use of various speech acts, we can become attuned to the rhetorical character of this activity. In journal peer review correspondence, it is possible to see predictable kinds of rhetorical moves and strategies in the same way that one sees predictable moves and strategies in a chess game. This is because experienced scientists, like competent chess players, have highly developed genre schema (as well as domain knowledge) and thus a considerable repertoire of argumentative strategies.

## PEER REVIEW CORRESPONDENCE AS ARGUMENTATIVE DISCUSSION

June Davis, the biologist–subject of chapter 3, submitted a number of drafts of a research report to the editors of two journals in her field, *Infection and Immunity* (*IAI*) and the *Journal of Medical and Veterinary Mycology* (*JMVM*), before finally receiving word from the editor of the former that the manuscript had been accepted for publication. The correspondence, including the exchange of letters between Davis and both editors and the appended reviewers' comments to which she responded in her correspondence, provides evidence that author, editor, and reviewers were engaged in well-rehearsed argumentative moves, and that an analysis of the constituent speech acts would provide valuable information about this kind of frequent interaction among scientists.

Analyzing journal peer review correspondence as an argumentative discussion requires that we move away from Austin's (1975) and Searle's (1969) view of speech acts as grammatical sentences isolated from larger units of discourse to a perspective that regards *sequences of utterances* as the unit of analysis. This rather novel approach to analyzing argumentative discourse from the framework of speech act theory was developed by van Eemeren and Grootendorst (1983), who constructed a hierarchical model for analyzing what they called "complexes" of speech acts. They suggested that:

This (partly) shows the relevance of Speech Acts and von E & G to longer texts. Like Toulmin it works best at the paragraph level

66

4. TEXTUAL DYNAMICS OF PEER REVIEW

> Argumentation can be treated as an illocutionary act complex. This act complex is composed of elementary illocutions ... which at the sentence level maintain a one-to-one ratio with (grammatical) sentences. The total constellation of the elementary illocutions constitutes the illocutionary act complex of argumentation, which at *a higher textual level* maintains, as a single whole, a one-to-one ratio with a (grammatical) sentence sequence. The compound illocutionary act of argumentation does not, therefore, stand in a one-to-one ratio to individual sentences, but to a *combination of sentences ordered into a sequence.* (p. 34, italics added)

Van Eemeren and Grootendorst's model includes sentences and elementary illocutions at the sentence level and a *higher textual level* that consists of compound illocutions or illocutionary act complexes. Their conception of illocutionary complexes is important for the following analysis of Davis' peer review correspondence because it conceives of larger units of discourse than the single sentence as illocutionary acts, and because in doing so, it introduces a macrolevel focus for interpreting these larger sequences of text.

Two additional points need to be made. First, as suggested previously, peer review correspondence is conducted within an institutionalized textual sequence, that is, "an institutional unit more or less determined by tradition, [which is] linked to a specific *sociocultural context*" (Van Eemeren & Grootendorst, 1983, p. 38).[2] Second, text sequences should not be regarded as deterministic structures, but rather are subject to change precisely because of alterations in pragmatic rules arising from language users' intentions. This is to say that the genres through which scientific communication is conducted are constituted through language users' illocutionary acts as they participate in the discursive activities of their communities; yet, reciprocally, language users invoke and reproduce disciplinary norms in drawing on rules-for-use in performing illocutionary acts. This, of course, is the view we arrive at when we apply structuration theory (Giddens, 1984) to scientists' textual practices and discursive activities. (See the discussion of Giddens' conception of "duality of structure" as underlying principle 4 in chap. 1.)

In the following analysis of Davis' peer review correspondence, we identify examples of assertives, directives, declaratives, commissives, and expressives. These categories constitute the *taxonomy of illocutionary acts* that Searle (1979) enumerated in his essay of the same name. What follows is a brief description of each of these classes:

---

[2]Although van Eemeren and Grootendorst (1983) argued here that, in contrast, illocutions are *functional* units determined by pragmatic rules that are primarily linked to the *specific intentions of language users* (p. 68), this distinction is, we believe, spurious. Text genres, as they have been analyzed in our work and the work of others (Bazerman, 1988; Miller, 1984), cannot be separated from individual language users' intents. Indeed there is a *reciprocity* between intent and genre, between social typification and situated artful action of the language user.

intent and genre - reciprocity

- *Assertives:* According to Searle (1979), the "point and purpose of members of the assertive class is to commit the speaker (in varying degrees) to something's being the case, to the truth of the expressed proposition. All the members of the assertive class are assessable on the dimension of assessment which includes *true* and *false*" (p. 12).

- *Directives:* This illocutionary act has as its purpose the attempt by the speaker to get the hearer to do something. Searle (1979) pointed out that these may "be very modest attempts as when I *invite* you to do it or *suggest* that you do it, or they may be very fierce attempts as when I *insist* that you do it" (p. 13, italics added). Verbs that belong to this class include *ask, order, command, request, beg, plead, pray, entreat, invite, permit*, and *advise*. Verbs that are part of the fiercer illocutionary group include *dare, defy*, and *challenge*.

- *Commissives:* The point of this type of illocutionary act is to commit the speaker (in varying degrees) to some future course of action. The editor of the *Journal of Medical and Veterinary Mycology*, who rejected an early version of June Davis' paper, nevertheless qualified that rejection by telling her that if she thought she could satisfactorily deal with all of the points raised by the referees and could send him a substantially revised paper, then he would be happy to reconsider it. Such a comment is an example of a commissive, "I would be happy to consider it," embedded in a directive, "If you feel that you can satisfactorily deal."

- *Expressives:* This class of acts has as its illocutionary purpose the expression of the psychological state of the speaker that is specified in the sentence's propositional content. Hence, the speaker can variously "thank," "congratulate," "apologize," "condole," "deplore," and "welcome," but not have as one's purpose when apologizing for stepping on someone's toe, either to claim that the toe was stepped on (assertive) or to get it stepped on (directive).

- *Declarations:* This class of illocutionary acts might best be described as "saying makes it so." Searle (1979) noted that the successful performance of a member of this class "brings about the correspondence between the propositional content and reality," ergo, "If I successfully perform the act of appointing you chairman, then you are chairman; if I successfully perform the act of nominating you as candidate, then you are a candidate; if I successfully perform the act of declaring a state of war, then war is on" (p. 17). Declarations are the prerogatives of presidents and popes, that is, they involve an extralinguistic institution, a system of constitutive rules in order that the declaration be successfully performed. Searle (1979) argued, "It is only given such institutions as the church, the law, private property, the state and a special position of the speaker and hearer within these institutions that one can communicate, appoint, give and bequeath one's positions, or declare war" (p. 18).

## ANALYSIS OF PEER REVIEW CORRESPONDENCE BETWEEN JUNE DAVIS AND THE EDITORS OF INFECTION AND IMMUNITY AND THE JOURNAL OF MEDICAL AND VETERINARY MYCOLOGY

The peer review correspondence between the scientist of this study, the journal editor, and the peer reviewers can be seen as taking place in three stages that we describe—modifying van Eemeren and Grootendorst's (1983) schema—as the Opening Stage, the Argumentation Stage, and the concluding Negotiating Stage.

### Assertives and Directives in the Opening Stage ~ Not arguments?

Stage 1, or the Opening Stage, consists of two rounds of letters between Davis and the two editors, who included the reviewers' comments with their letters of rejection.[3] Davis' letter like other such letters can be seen as a directive in the form of a request. The letter from the editor of *JMVM* is a declaration (rejection), with an embedded directive ("resubmit when you have substantially revised the paper") that softens the negative effect of the declaration.

> Dear Editor:
>     We wish to submit our manuscript, Elevation of Fibrinogen Levels Due to Injection of *Candida albicans* or Recombinant Tumor Necrosis Factor (TNF) in the Mouse: Protection with TNF Antibodies, for publication in *Infection and Immunity*. (**1**) We suggest it be included in the Fungal and Parasitic Infections and Immunity section. (**2**) I also request it be sent to [Editor in Chief] or [Editor]. (**3**)
>     Although I realize the Editor will select reviewers, I recommend _____ (University of _____) and _____ as highly knowledgeable and interested in this area of research. (**4**) (letter from June Davis to editor of *Infection and Immunity*)

Davis' letter is simple and straightforward, although it contains more directives than we would expect to see in a letter of this kind, especially the bold requests in sentences 3 and 4.[4] The *JMVM* editor's letter contains the generic illocutionary

---

[3]The correspondence of Stage 1 described on pp. 68–70 includes Davis' letter to the editor of *Infection and Immunity* (*IAI*) and the letter of rejection that she received from the *Journal of Medical and Veterinary Mycology* (*JMVM*) editor, who included the reviewers' comments with his letter. Reviews on the first draft of Davis' manuscript from the *IAI* reviewers were unavailable, as was the *IAI* editor's initial letter of rejection to Davis.

[4]In an interview, Davis revealed that she had made this move to circumvent getting for a reviewer a colleague who was in competition with her and who was in a larger and more prestigious lab. This colleague had previously written negative reviews of her grant proposals and papers. Because the price of receiving a positive review from this colleague had been to "cut him in" on important projects in her research, she hoped that, by this rather aggressive strategy, she could avoid getting him as a referee.

acts that we would expect in a rejection letter to a senior professor, well established in the field. The message, although a rejection, is mixed with a directive in the form of an invitation to resubmit.

Ref: MS 89/211
Dear Professor Davis:
I have now received the referees' comments on your paper entitled "Elevation of fibrinogen levels due to injection of *Candida albicans* or recombinant tumor necrosis factor (TNF) in the mouse: Protection with TNF antibodies." (1) I am sorry to say that neither referee felt that they could recommend publication of this article, at least in its present form. (2)

However, if you feel that you can satisfactorily deal with all the points raised by the referees and can let me have a substantially revised paper, then I would be happy to reconsider it. (3) One of the referees has penciled in some suggested changes to the manuscript and I am letting you see these so you can consider them should you decide to undertake the revision. (4)

I am sorry that the outcome is not better at this point in time. (5) (letter from editor of *Journal of Medical and Veterinary Mycology* to June Davis)

Note that the declaration (sentence 2) is stated as an expressive and an assertive that has as its subject the reviewers' advice. This is an example of an indirect speech act (Searle, 1979) that functions rhetorically as a hedge, taking the heat off the editor. The second paragraph of this letter is interesting in that at the macrolevel it functions as a directive and at the sentence level it contains a combination of directives, assertives, and a commissive ("I would be happy to reconsider it"). Sentence 5 is a generic expressive, that is to say, the kind of statement we would expect to find at the end of a letter of rejection. In the reviews that accompanied the letter, one of the reviewers made only perfunctory comments on the first draft, suggesting that she believed the manuscript did not merit a response in any great detail. In contrast, the second reviewer, whose letter follows, by strategically deploying assertives coupled with directives, severely damaged the credibility of Davis' claims.

MS 89/211
Elevation of Fibrinogen
The authors have presented a study in which they demonstrate that *C. albicans* caused an increase in plasma fibrinogen levels which was partially abrogated by pretreatment with anti-TNF-α. (1) In general, this is a simple, straight-forward study. (2) In addition to several grammatical considerations penciled onto the manuscript there are several addition[al] concerns. (3)

1. It is not clear why the authors have chosen to present the actual mg/dl data in the figures and percentage increases in the tables and in some of the text (e.g., p. 6, lines 3–4). (4) Why not present mg/dl uniformly, perhaps along with percentage increases. (5)

2. In Table 2, why are data from two of the control groups presented as footnotes.

(6) It gives one the impression that they were data acquired during the course of a separate experiment. (7) If that is true they should be summarized in the text as data gathered from additional experiments and not included in Table 2. (8)

3. I have a problem with one of the conclusions drawn by the authors and presented on page 7, lines 1 and 2. (9) The data for anti-TNF are limited, and the truncated experimental design does not allow the authors to conclude that "additional mechanisms are operative at later times". (10) The authors do not know the half-life of their exogenously-administered antibodies, for example, which could explain the lack of effect after 24 hours. (11) Perhaps the antibody titer was relatively low and clearance of a heterologous antibody was relatively fast, limiting the available antibodies to neutralize the TNF produced. (12) (included in letter from editor of *JMVM* to June Davis)

Reviewer 2 's comment in sentence 3 ("In addition to numerous grammatical considerations penciled onto the manuscript, there are several addition[al] concerns") appears innocuous enough, until one sees item 3 of the list that follows. This tactic suggests that underlying the assertive of sentence 3 is an implicit directive that might be translated as "Editor, be cautious." Of the three concerns that follow, items 1 and 2 would not by themselves merit rejection. They address problems concerning the representation of data on which referees frequently comment. However "concern" 3 is damning, the referee arguing that:

> The data for anti-TNF are limited, and the truncated experimental design does not allow the authors to conclude that additional mechanisms are operative at later times. (10) The authors do not know the half-life of their exogenously-administered antibodies, for example, which could explain the lack of an effect after 24 hours. (11) Perhaps the antibody titer was relatively low. . . . (12)

The assertives in sentences 10 and 11 function to make the case that the paper is incomplete, that is, lacking sufficient data to support one of Davis' major claims. Note that sentence 12 contains a rival hypothesis that also argues against Davis' claim. To summarize this opening set of exchanges, we have seen the interlocutors—Davis, her editor, and the referees—using both macrolevel and microlevel illocutionary acts aimed at producing *uptake* (Austin, 1975) on the part of the addressee.

## Uptake and Intertextuality in the Argumentation Stage

In the next round of correspondence between Davis and reviewers (Stage 2 or the argumentation stage), the previous activity is even more pronounced as the correspondence takes on a <u>dialogical character</u>. In this exchange, a round of five letters, it is not difficult to discern the moves of an argumentative discussion between interlocutors. The macrolevel illocutionary point or purpose of this exchange at this second stage is to bring the manuscript (and the science that the manuscript depicts) to the point where it will pass muster before a readership of scientists. This process is what Zuckerman and Merton (1973) have described as quality control. The status of the manuscript has changed, from one that is incomplete to one that is capable of repair, although still problematic (see Gross, 1990).

The exchange is initiated by Davis' directive in the form of a request that indexes the consensus of the first exchange.[5]

Dear Dr. _____:

Thank you for your June 16 review of our manuscript IAI 485–89, which described a possible relationship between *Candida albicans* induced TNF a and an increase in fibrinogen in the mouse. (1) Please recall that your main concern was that our original paper was incomplete, lacking data on TNF. (2)

We now feel that we have addressed all comments of the two reviewers. (3) Besides clarifying specific questions, we have included new data on candidal-in-duced TNF using a sandwich type ELISA employing rabbit polyclonal and hamster monoclonal antibodies to mouse TNF-α. (4) As you stated you would be glad to look at this paper again should we provide this additional data, we are returning it to you with the hope of a better outcome. (5)

Specifically we have. . . . (6) [Here Davis indicates in the form of a list the new experimental procedures she and her assistant used, and she notes as well the changes that she made in the manuscript in response to the reviewers' comments and queries.]

We thank you again for your initial suggestions. (7) We agree with you that the data on TNF greatly strengthens such studies and we are happy we are now able to include this study. (8) We believe our changes and additional work has greatly improved our manuscript. (9) We look forward to hearing your response. (10) (letter from June Davis to editor of *Infection and Immunity*)

We might paraphrase Davis' macrolevel directive as "accept this manuscript with the changes we have made." The perlocutionary effect of this illocutionary act is based on an assertive that communicates a major claim, a response to the reviewer who had previously seen the data as being incomplete: "We now feel that we have addressed all comments of the two reviewers. (3) Besides clarifying specific questions, we have included new data on candidal-induced TNF using a sandwich type ELISA [assay] employing rabbit polyclonal and hamster mono-clonal antibodies to mouse TNF-α" (4).

Although sentence 3 begins with an expressive, it functions rhetorically as an assertive. We observed Davis using expressives fairly frequently, perhaps to tone down the force of her assertives or perhaps because she feels the need to use politeness markers. At any rate, the letter contains a number of these expressives: "Thank you for your June 16 review of . . ."; "We thank you again for your initial suggestions"; and "We look forward to your response." Many of these

---

[5]In this sense the illocutionary acts have more of an interactional character than Austin or Searle conceived of in their taxonomies.

expressives are formulaic, stock phrases of the genre. However, the expressive in sentence 9—"We believe our changes and additional work has greatly improved the manuscript"—can also be read as an assertive, and represents Davis' second major argumentative claim. This macrolevel claim is supported by the assertives that appear in sentences 3 through 6. Sentence 5 calls the editor's attention to the commissive that had appeared in his letter of rejection.

As the initial move of the second or Argumentation Stage, Davis' letter functions in a manner similar to an opening serve in a tennis match (see Freadman, 1987). Its assertives are strong enough to have considerable perlocutionary effect, although certainly the accompanying manuscript plays a major role in determining the reviewers' uptake (Searle, 1969, 1979). Within 2 weeks there were two new sets of reviewers' comments for Davis to address. (These were the same reviewers who had read the previous draft for *IAI*.) Both referees' initial macrolevel comments are assertives that indicate the positive response of each to the extensively revised manuscript. Reviewer 1 opined, "The results provide *new information on in vivo* host response to *C. albicans*," and Reviewer 2 observed, "Scientifically, this paper is on much firmer ground than when previously reviewed." Reviewer 2's assertive, however, is followed by a second qualifying assertive (which may be also be interpreted as an indirect directive): "In terms of its presentation, however, there are several items that remain to be corrected." What follows in each review is a laundry list of tasks that remain to be accomplished for the paper to merit publication.

Thus, at the microlevel, the illocutionary acts in the reviewers' comments are a mixture of assertions and directives. Unlike the first round of comments, these are not truncated; indeed, to the contrary, they are exhaustive. Many of the comments in this round of peer review correspondence have been discussed in chapter 3. Suffice it to say that the force of the illocutionary act complex in each review is argumentative, specifically the directives to Davis to (a) clear up the questions concerning various procedural problems that relate to the thoroughness of her work in the lab, and (b) present a complete literature review so as to position the present study in the context of related scientific work.

It took 2 months for Davis to revise her manuscript and to write a cover letter to the editor of *IAI* in which she responded point by point to each of her reviewer's concerns. This letter is heavily intertextual, the numbered comments of her letter consisting of rejoinders to her reviewers' criticisms. Davis' comments each contain a blend of assertives and commissives[6] in which she either accepts the reviewer's directive or presents counterarguments. For example, in response to Reviewer 1's assertive/directive:

---

[6]We are calling the illocutionary force of these sentences commissive, although strictly speaking, they refer to completed actions rather than promising such actions. The illocutionary point in either case is the same, the speaker having committed herself to the act specified.

Were precautions taken to guard against endotoxin (LPS) contamination of *C. albicans* preparations and other reagents used? This is important since even pica-gram amounts of LPS could act in synergy with *C. albicans*, thus contributing to the observed response.

Davis countered with an assertive/commissive:

We took precautions to guard against endotoxin contamination using nonpyrogenic saline and heat treated glassware (p. 4, paragraph 2). In addition there was no reason to suspect endotoxin contamination because *Candida*-induced TNF differed in a number of important ways from what has been found in the case of endo-toxin-induced TNF.

However, in response to Reviewer 1's directive:

The investigators need to discuss their finding that the monokine response of mice to *C. albicans* differs from those obtained with LPS [endotoxin]. . . . These differ-ences are important and should be addressed. Comparative experiments with LPS would be most appropriate and should be considered by the authors.

Davis responded affirmatively with the commissives:

We have now discussed our finding where TNF response to *C. albicans* differed from that reported for endotoxin (p. 9, paragraph 4; p. 10, paragraph 1). We agree with Reviewer #1 that this difference is important and we are currently doing a thorough comparative study of the TNF responses to endotoxin and *C. albicans*.

This exchange demonstrates the intertextual/dialogical character of the dis-cussion that appears in Davis' peer review correspondence. Over and over again the reviewers call the author's attention to procedures in the laboratory, making sure she leaves no stone unturned, no rival hypothesis unexamined. In order to do this they call on considerable background knowledge of this research area. In her response or *uptake*, as we are calling it, Davis can either accommodate them or offer a rebuttal, which we see her doing in the previous example. What we see occurring here is a negotiation of expertise among interlocutors in an argumentative discussion that will be adjudicated by the editor. As the adjudicator who represents, in speech act terminology, an extralinguistic institution (in this case the scientific journal), the editor is the one actor among the interlocutors who is empowered to make a declarative illocutionary act. Thus, the editorial judgments voiced in the following letter conclude the second Argumentative Stage of this discussion and initiate the third, concluding stage (what we are describing as the Negotiation Stage):

I am writing to you about your manuscript, IAI #____ (formerly IAI #____. (1) Both reviewers agree your modification is an improved version. (2) I believe you *register of politeness*

have responded to Reviewer #2 properly and adequately. **(3)** Reviewer #1 had a few additional minor suggestions that I knew you would like to respond to. **(4)** I enclose those suggestions. **(5)** Moreover, that reviewer opined to me that the data in Table 1 and 2 were better represented in tabular form. **(6)** What do you think? **(7)** Would you rather present Table 1 and 2 as originally intended? **(8)** I will accept your decision. **(9)** The Production Editor's opinion is not binding and I would rather present your results the way you would like to see them presented. . . . **(10)** I look forward to your response: we seem close to acceptance now. **(11)** (letter from editor of *Infection and Immunity* to June Davis)

## Directives and Commissives in the Negotiation Stage

There are several linguistic and rhetorical features in the editor's letter worth noting. At the macro (whole text) level, the letter can be seen to be a declaration. Within this declaration, at the micro (sentence sequence) level, there are a number of directives that are communicated as indirect speech acts, for example, sentence 4: "Reviewer 1 had sent a few additional minor suggestions that I knew you would like to respond to." This was somewhat of an understatement because Reviewer 1 had sent a page's worth of directives. Nevertheless, it is important to understand the illocutionary force of sentence 4 as an indirect speech act—a directive in the form of a polite invitation. The *negotiational* character of this communication is reflected in this sentence and in such other directives as (in sentences 7–9) "What do you think? Would you rather present Table 1 and 2 as originally intended? I will accept your decision." Note that sentence 9 is a commissive. When we consider the complex illocutionary act that this sequence of utterances communicates, it seems apparent that the editor's letter "declares" to the author a new status for her manuscript. This change in status is also communicated by the editor's altered register, denoting the altered relationship between editor and author. As represented both by the illocutionary acts and register, this letter rhetorically signifies acceptance, despite the editor's cautiously worded declaration in the last sentence: "We seem close to acceptance now." This sentence may in fact be a stock phrase for the editor to use on this occasion, combined as it is with, "I look forward to your response."

The two other texts that constitute this round of correspondence include a page of brief directives by Reviewer 1 and a set of rejoinders from Davis that follow the pattern of the previous argumentative stage, but which this time are much more truncated. (We have all had a Reviewer 1 who remains zealous to the very end. This tenacity is an important element in peer review, as we shall see.) This reviewer's "brief suggestions" are prefaced by the formulaic assertive/directive: "The revised manuscript by Drs. _____ and _____ is much improved over the earlier submission. Some minor comments/suggestions are listed below:" These two stock phrases are followed by a brief list of directives, some of which refer to lab procedures, others of which merely offer suggestions for editing for clarity. As in the previous round of correspondence, Davis submits a numbered list of rejoinders, most of which are commissives, save a single rebuttal to a suggestion by the reviewer that a *new* ELISA assay be conducted to distinguish between the cytotoxicity induced by TNF-α or TNF-β. In the response to the reviewer's directive, Davis argues that the ELISA is not necessary, "since the commercially available ELISA kit highly similar to ours reacts with both TNF-α and TNF-β, our ELISA probably reacts with . . . TNF-β as well as TNF-α. We have added this information (p. 6, paragraph 1)." The illocutionary force of this rejoinder is that of an assertive (which counters Reviewer 1's assertive), combined with the commissive, "We have added this information." Once again, this kind of exchange puts the editor in the position of determining whether or not Davis' response will suffice; however, her commissive suggests that she is negotiating with the reviewer.

One can see in Davis' final statement that she intends that this round of correspondence be the last: "We wish to thank you and your reviewers for the great deal of time and effort that you have given to our work." Although the statement appears to be an expressive, it could be an indirect speech act. Davis' closing comment also signals the commissive, "We're signing off." This letter was in fact to be her last. A month after writing it, she received a set of page proofs to be corrected for publication.

## CONCLUSION

As a set of activities exemplifying rational consensus among interlocutors (see Gross, 1990), the preceding discussion of peer review suggests that argumentation in the form of illocutionary act complexes serves a major function in this process. Knowledge claims are vigorously disputed and the laboratory procedures from which such claims are adduced are rigorously scrutinized, their instrumentality debated as the scientist–author struggles to defend the thoroughness and rigor of her method. Over and over we can see that *what happens in the lab*, as it is perceived by reviewers, forms the ground upon which knowledge claims are disputed and ultimately adjudicated by the editor.

The roles of the players can also be clearly delineated in this study: scientist–author as protagonist, referees as antagonists, and editor as adjudicator. Each of the actors, if sophisticated and knowledgeable of the script, has a repertoire of rhetorical actions. The reviewers seem almost like pit bulls guarding the queen's jewels; their tenacity is their best asset, as we saw in the case of Reviewer 1. The editor also has well-defined functions. It is the editor who determines at what stage the reviewer is evaluator, and at what stage the reviewer is collaborator and repairer. It is the editor who plays a critical role in adjudicating the argumentative discussion between author and reviewers, as when Davis' editor wrote "I believe that you have responded to Reviewer 2 properly and adequately. Reviewer 1 had a few additional suggestions that I know you would like to respond to." By using indirect speech acts, the editor may also mitigate the harshness of the reviewer's judgments and sometimes hostile comments.[7] But perhaps the editor's most important function is declarative power in certifying new knowledge. This editorial power has its roots in the efforts of the Royal Society to provide the institutional means through which "men of science" would be encouraged to report new work and through which that work be deemed authoritative. As Zuckerman and Merton (1973) noted, "Through the emergence of the role of editor and the incipient arrangements for having manuscripts assessed by others in addition to the editor the journal gave a more institutionalized form of the applications of standards of scientific work" (p. 469).

Certification of new knowledge thus depends on a collaborative effort of author, reviewers, and editor. The ways in which the uneven distribution of power can nullify this collaborative process have been more than amply documented (see Chubin & Hackett, 1990, for a review of this literature). As can be seen in this study, Davis herself made a rather unorthodox move in her initial letter to keep her manuscript out of the hands of a colleague whom she felt would not hesitate to exploit his gatekeeping power to his advantage. Despite this and other difficulties in the peer review process that have been discussed in the literature, this study suggests that when the players in the peer review process are being conscientious about their responsibilities, the process works well. Certainly Davis' referees made every effort to insure that the textual representation of her lab work (including both written text and graphic material) be accountable. The editor depended on their rigorous scrutiny of every aspect of the reported experiments and the claims based on those experiments.

On the other hand, it is equally the case that the individual who is the most savvy about the kinds of generic moves possible in editorial correspondence has an edge. As an old experienced hand in such communications, Davis was well aware of the moves available to her: She knew, for example, how to cast her resubmitted manuscript in the best light possible by making a strong case in the cover letter that accompanied her revision. She also knew when to bring on board a tough reviewer by deferring to his judgment, and when to make a counterargument, criticizing that judgment.

But perhaps what is most striking in the foregoing analysis of the illocutionary acts of the peer review interlocutors is that it provides empirical evidence that illocutionary acts *do* get things done in the world, either through direct or indirect means. Using the illocutionary acts (and power contained therein) of declaratives and commissives, an editor can reject a manuscript while simultaneously inviting an author to resubmit. This mixed message is delivered through the editor's combining assertives with directives and commissives. Similarly, a reviewer's

---

[7]Gross (1990) pointed out in an insightful discussion of peer review as an example of Jurgen Habermas's *ideal speech situation*, that one function of editors in conveying the results of peer review is to "shield authors from the worst of referees' excesses" (p. 134).

*Interesting empirical test of speech act theory*

politely worded questions can serve to damn a study through a combination of assertives and directives. An editor's assertive, "I think we are close to acceptance," can function also as a declaration of acceptance, given an editor's institutional authority. In all of these cases, *speech not only means things but does things as well.* Speech acts *are* louder than words, are more than the sum of the meaning of the words.

The rhetorical functions of the many texts, oral and written, that constitute scientific activity are still only dimly understood; it is a difficult concept to grasp that texts have action in human projects and that genres have activity in our most basic and everyday enterprises. Because the typifications that constitute genres are so deeply embedded in our daily actions, in our professional and disciplinary activities, we are hardly aware of their presence, much less their function. Nevertheless, given the recent resurgence of interest in the rhetorical functions of genre, we may begin to understand the role that genre and the constituents of genre, speech acts, play in scientific and other knowledge-producing enterprises.[8]

---

[8]Van Eemeren and Grootendorst's (1983) stage model of argumentative discussion is useful in this respect for examining from the perspective of the *higher textual level* of compound illocutions, the kind of rhetorical action that we find operating within this sequence of linked texts.

CHAPTER

# 5

# EVOLUTION OF A SCHOLARLY FORUM: READER, 1977–1988

*There is nothing that fully predicts my production of a sign. Nor is the textual instantiation of any one generic type ever like any previous instantiation, even in conditions of great external constraint. Even in a situation of great constraint and awareness of convention, I can act unpredictably, assessing in a particular instance the consequences of my action differently to what would normally be predicted. I can speak formally to my partner over the dinner table when there seems no clear, contextually plausible reason for doing so; and I can speak informally to my superior in a formal situation, prepared to accept the consequences in both cases. But even my decision to act in conformity with an understood convention is the result of an act of choice, and as such is my new production of the meaning of conformity.*

—Kress (1993a, p. 176)

Kress' assertion of individual choice—even to act in accordance with understood conventions—brings us once again to the concept of *duality of structure* (Giddens, 1979, 1984) described in chapter 1: As actors draw on genre rules to engage in professional activities, they constitute social structure (in professional, institutional, and organizational contexts) and simultaneously reproduce those structures. It is important to understand that structure is not "out there." Rather its existence is virtual, instantiated through symbolic interaction among individuals as they draw on stocks of knowledge in the course of communal enterprises. The following case study of the evolution of a scholarly forum describes this process as it occurred over time for a group of scholars who were members of an emergent discourse community. As in previous chapters, we focus on writers' situated artful actions.

79

Because the communities that we discuss in this chapter and the next are so nascent, we have had the opportunity to examine the process of disciplinary formation (at an early stage) in relation to the appearance (and disappearance) of various genre features in writers' texts.

Chapter 5 tracks the changing discursive practices of members of a fledgling discourse community of reader-response critics and practitioners (part of the larger community of literary scholars) through an examination of its members' contributions to a scholarly forum. It is a historical, text-based study of the evolution of a scholarly journal from newsletter to full-fledged academic forum. The changing genre features that we examine in this chapter provide evidence of the textual character of institutionalization of the forum and, by implication, of the discourse community.

## BIRTH OF A COMMUNAL FORUM

At the Modern Language Association (MLA) meeting in New York City, December 26–29, 1976, several hundred English professors attended a series of sessions on "The Reader of Literature." As Robert Crosman and James Slevin, the organizers of the program, had anticipated, the subject aroused considerable interest. A plenary session attracted 1,000 people, and the six scheduled workshops drew audiences ranging in size from 50 to 150. At a final impromptu workshop, about 20 people discussed what had been accomplished and planned seminars for the 1977 Convention under the general prefix, "The Reader of Literature." Members of that workshop also decided to publish a newsletter.[1]

In the first newsletter issue, published in January 1977, the editor, Robert Crosman (1977a), explained his conception of the purpose of such a forum:

> The need for such a publication seems clear. At present it is hard to know exactly what "reader-oriented criticism" is, or where it is headed. Wayne Booth, Jonathan Culler, Stanley Fish, Norman Holland, Gerald Prince, David Bleich, Walter Ong, Michael Riffaterre and others all use the concept of the "reader" in their criticism, but they often mean different things by the word. Is reader-oriented criticism a system, a method, or is it rather a tendency, a direction in which many critical minds are moving at present? *It is to help answer these questions, to put those minds in contact with each other, and thus to learn more about the nature and direction of their collective critical enterprise, that this newsletter is conceived and begun.* (p. 1, italics added)

It is also quite clear from his remarks that Crosman conceived of the newsletter as serving an alternative function to mainstream journals of literary criticism:

---

[1]The details of this account of the meetings that took place at the Modern Language Association Conference are drawn from Robert Crosman's (1977a) description of the event appearing in Issue 1.

> It won't of course be able to fill the major function of a professional journal—the large scale publication of formal articles—yet in this limitation there is also a kind of freedom. [The newsletter] can explore new ways of communicating with a readership, can be responsive to the desires of those readers, can change tack, can even criticize itself, in ways that established journals cannot. It can even come close to being what other publications only pretend to be—a forum for discussion among members of an intellectual community. (p. 1)

Crosman's description of the new forum suggested that he understood the powerful role that the scholarly forum plays in the formation of a new disciplinary subspecialty. Studies on the functions of forums within scholarly communities are still relatively rare (Bazerman, 1988; Herrington, 1989); however, they are a rich source of information about emergent genre features and conventions in a dynamic social context.

Historically, the forum was a physical site (usually the marketplace or public square of a Roman city) where business and judicial affairs were conducted, and where orators debated questions of public interest before crowds. By evoking the term's origin, we might characterize *forums* as places or locations where discourse is conducted among the members of a scientific or academic community. The forum provides an enduring connection between rhetors and their audiences. It institutionalizes community norms through its conventions, thus both constraining writers and providing them with resources for argument. This chapter documents one such forum's function in the development of an academic community's discourse. Using case study techniques combined with textual and linguistic analyses of the various issues, we traced the evolution of a scholarly forum, *Reader*, from its inception as a newsletter in the late 1970s to its present status as a journal included in the *Arts and Humanities Citation Index* and *Current Contents/Arts and Humanities*. *Reader*'s title, format, and objects of study have changed over the last 17 years, as have the conventions that its contributors employ.

Some of these changes occurred as the journal changed in format from a newsletter to a refereed journal. Other changes in *Reader* reflect historically evolving issues and themes as defined by contributors to the journal. To what extent did *Reader*'s contributors determine the priorities of a newly emerging field? And to what extent did the development of the forum from an informal newsletter to a full-fledged academic journal affect the production and dissemination of knowledge within the reader-response community? Finally, what can studies of forums, such as *Reader*, reveal about the role that texts play as "dynamic causal entities in the social environment"? (Bazerman & Paradis, 1991, p. 3)

Perelman and Olbrechts-Tyteca (1969) suggested that "every social circle or milieu is distinguishable in terms of its dominant opinions and unquestioned beliefs, of the premises that it takes for granted without hesitation: these views form an integral part of its culture, and an orator willing to persuade a particular audience must of necessity adapt himself to it" (pp. 20–21). Perelman and Ol-

*[handwritten marginal notes: "writer as an insider", "write within a discourse community of to an audience"]*

brechts-Tyteca appear to have anticipated the interest in discourse communities;[2] and indeed, the idea of a writer being a member of such a community requires that we reconceptualize our notions of audience in important ways. Writing within academic communities requires more than understanding the beliefs and interests of a particular audience. Academic writers who publish must also understand what is accepted knowledge within the community in order to position their claims in relation to that knowledge.

Bazerman and Paradis (1991) used the phrase "textual dynamics" to refer to the idea that:

> Written discourse is produced by a complex of social, cognitive and rhetorical activities that precipitates the various contexts and actions that constitute the professions. . . . Out of provisional clusterings of people, activities and language emerge highly organized professions of great social consequence. Once established, professions maintain their organization, power and activity in large part through networks of texts. (p. 4)

Studying the evolution of a disciplinary forum is one way to make the construct of textual dynamics operational, that is, to see how a professional forum carries out the work necessary for building a new field and launching scholars whose object is to promote activities relevant to field development, as well as enrolling novices into a burgeoning scholarly area.

It is important to keep in mind that such texts do not spring out of a meeting of the minds alone, but also out of the material conditions of academic culture. These conditions, as most of us know, involve a system of rewards that hinge on publication and national recognition. Academics accumulate "cultural capital" (Bourdieu, 1977) or credibility in various ways, including winning grant monies, publishing, being cited, and serving on editorial boards of journals. Part of the novice academician's socialization into the culture of the university involves learning the best means through which to promote one's work, or become "visible." The struggle for visibility engages the time and efforts of many assistant professors. This is not to suggest that literary scholars or scientists are solely extrinsically motivated to do research and write, but that the cognitive and material conditions of academic scholarship and research exist in a dynamic tension. The following discussion of the role that *Reader* played in the constituting of the reader-response community needs to be seen in light of both sets of conditions.

We have divided the following discussion of *Reader*'s history into three distinct periods, each period distinguishable in two ways: by changes appearing in the external features of the forum (e.g., length of contributions, appearance of citations, table of contents), and by the policies and agendas of *Reader*'s three

---

[2]For a discussion of recent scholarship on discourse communities, see Rafoth's (1990) essay, "The concept of discourse community: Descriptive and exploratory adequacy." For an examination of the relationship of the concept of discourse community to the concept of genre, see Swales (1990).

*[handwritten note at bottom: "Could try annual messages by MLA president"]*

*[handwritten margin note: A seems late to be a reaction to New Criticism]*

editors, Robert Crosman, Wendy Deutelbaum, and Elizabeth Flynn. The first of these periods may be seen as a time during which contributors attempted to respond to and elaborate on the issues raised by Crosman's (1977a) question in the first newsletter: "Is reader-oriented criticism a system, a method, or is it rather a tendency, a direction in which many critical minds are moving at once?" (p. 1). The contributions that appear in Issues 1–3 (1977–1979) reflect a free-flowing exchange of ideas by a number of writers deeply immersed in the reader-response movement. The second period, Issues 4–8 (1979–1980), during which Crosman and then Deutelbaum assumed editing responsibilities (Crosman re-signed the editorship after Issue 5), can be characterized by the editors' attempt to bring about some sort of integration between theory and pedagogy. The third and longest period (1983–1989), during which Issues 9–21 were published under the administrative editorship of Flynn, can best be described as a period of professionalization, that is to say, a period during which the routines of academic production that constitute normal science or scholarship become stabilized.

The appearance of the newsletter was a timely response to a shifting of the ground within the MLA constituency. This kind of movement is also common in the social and natural sciences: A period of rebellion against one body of theory or school of criticism (in this case the New Criticism whose proponents argued that bona fide literary inquiry is limited to the investigation of textual phenomena) is heralded by the appearance of an "invisible college" (Crane, 1972) of theorists whose writings challenge the methodological and epistemological status quo. This group becomes the vanguard of a new movement that attracts many younger scholars who debate and discuss the issues that the major figures have raised in their writings. In this sense, *Reader* met a need within the profession. The writings of Fish (1971, 1973a, 1973b, 1976), Bleich (1975a, 1975b, 1976a, 1976b), and Holland (1973, 1975a, 1975b, 1975c) on this side of the Atlantic and those of Iser (1971, 1974, 1975) in Europe had attracted a critical mass of followers disenchanted with the narrowness and scientism of the New Criticism, which limited the object of study to the literary text and ignored the reader and social context of the reading act. Thus, the time was ripe for a forum that would be responsive to the needs of this new constituency.

## 1977: GETTING A CONVERSATION INTO PRINT, ISSUES 1–3

### Issue 1

*[handwritten margin note: argue]* In the first issue of the newsletter, Crosman described what the new forum could provide for its readers: a dialogue between committed participants. Crosman suggested that future issues be devoted to identifying and discussing issues and questions relating to reader-oriented criticism and classroom practice. Thus, he defined the focus of the newsletter, which was emphasized by its title, *Reader:*

*a newsletter of reader-oriented criticism and teaching.* The bulk of the first issue was devoted to Crosman's summarizing the 1976 MLA Forum on "The Reader of Literature," which consisted of a very large general meeting with a panel of well-known theorists and critics (Riffaterre, Ong, Bleich, Fish, Holland), each describing his conception of the reader, and a series of smaller workshops organized around issues broadly related to reader-oriented theory. Important figures in the MLA establishment such as Bleich, Fish, and Prince served as panelists, and up-and-coming young (and not-so-young) scholars delivered papers, often on their mentors' theories. Crosman summarized the general meeting as well as the various workshops and described the plans for another sequence of meetings planned for the MLA the following December. Noting that "bibliography should be a regular concern of this letter" (p. 1), Crosman included three pages listing articles and books that he and a colleague, Susan Elliott, considered relevant to reader-oriented criticism.

## Issue 2

Crosman's invitation elicited a number of responses from readers interested in raising issues and themes that they thought were important. Rabinowitz (1977) asked to see "some intense discussion of the last word in the newsletter's title, since all of these theories do have serious implications for what goes on in the classroom" (p. 2). Tompkins (1977) enumerated issues and questions that she thought reader-response enthusiasts needed to address:

> If readers really do make meaning, then what are our responsibilities as teachers to the critical traditions that have preceded us? Do we insist on talking about "the romance," when we teach Hawthorne simply because everybody else has, or should we urge students to become articulate about what happens inside their heads and to their feelings as they read? Why bother to choose "definitive" editions if we can never recover the author's intention anyway? What constitutes knowledge about a literary text—knowledge of interpretive strategies? of our own insides? of the interpretive strategies that lie behind our feelings? (p. 3)

Like Crosman, Tompkins (1977) saw *Reader* as a nontraditional forum "where people can try out writing that would be rejected automatically by traditional journals in the field." In Issue 2, as well as elsewhere in the early issues, Crosman (1977b) went to great pains to elicit writing from readers that would be simple and straightforward, thus avoiding what he perceived to be "the tedious formalities of the journal style":

> The idea is not to write a formal essay or to make your arguments unassailable, but to "think out loud on paper," so to speak, to contribute feelings and ideas to a general discussion. . . . Don't censor yourself, you're among friends. I think that you'll have fun writing something not too elaborate on these topics, and in reading

what others have written on the same topic. You can even list it as a publication on your vita. (p. 5)

Pleased at the response that he got to the first issue, Crosman proposed topics for the following two issues. For Issue 3 he asked readers to write their reactions to the essays appearing in *New Literary History* (*NLH*; 1976) on "Readers and Spectators," which contained articles by "famous critics on both sides of the Atlantic." Responding to suggestions by a number of readers, Crosman proposed that Issue 4 be devoted to letters describing how readers applied reader-centered criticism in their classrooms.

## Issue 3

In contrast to the informal style of the letters published in Issue 2, in Issue 3 we see the appearance of *microessays*, generic mixtures of 1,000–1,500 words or less in which readers responded to one or more essays that had appeared in the *NLH* issue on "Readers and Spectators." Because these microessays referred to ideas and arguments appearing in another forum, readers not familiar with the essays appearing in *NLH* would not be able to make much sense of the statements in *Reader*. This kind of discourse depends on writers and readers sharing knowledge in the same sense that, in conversation, speakers depend on mutual knowledge with their listeners (Nystrand, 1986; cf. our discussion in chap. 3 of June Davis' use of biologists' presuppositional knowledge in creating warrants for her claims).

The essays ranged from a brief note to more fully developed essays containing many of the features of formal belletristic prose. Crosman arranged them according to their degree of formality. The note appeared first, then two very brief statements (one page) with titles suggesting an informal response: "A Reply to Christian Metz" and a review by a journal referee, "Tsvetan Todorov, 'The Origin of Genres,' *NLH* (Autumn, 1976), 159–170." The author of the first of these, Rabinowitz (1977), used the first person pronoun, and opted for less formal syntax: for example, "I personally would be more interested in a live broadcast of the opening night of the Met than in a replay shown two weeks into the season" (p. 2). In contrast, Hedrick (1977), who wrote the second of the two pieces, employed a register characteristic of formal writing (Chafe, 1982), as indicated by his complex syntax: for example, "He [Todorov] relieves us of some current temporal parochiality by arguing that literature has in fact never existed without genres, and that rejections of old genres become new genres in a process of continual 'transformation' (a term that seems loosely adopted to give the idea more status)" (Hedrick, 1977, p. 3). In essays following those of Rabinowitz and Hedrick, Rubin and Elliott used formal titles, wrote introductions and summations, and used direct quotations and citations. The last two writers, Miller and Crosman, presented an overview of essays in the "Readers and Spectators" issue.

*sharing knowledge — can only be inferred from what is written and what is not, written, or is only alluded to without elaboration*

Like Rubin and Elliott, these writers used direct quotations and citations in their *source* *x* *ref* statements, although none of the four authors included a bibliography. Although Miller and Crosman did not title their contributions, these last four essays can be seen as incorporating more of the features that we would be likely to associate with formal written composition—unlike the shorter pieces that preceded them.

A closer look at some of the differences between the essays that appeared in Issue 3 illustrates not only differences in the formal features that the various writers used, but also in the varying degree of *intertextuality* that the essays exhibited. The concept of intertextuality figured importantly in chapter 3. Here again it enables us to see the social constructionist nature of a genre convention. Through the explicit use of references and citations, quotations, paraphrases, *source* summaries, and syntheses, writers evoke for their readers a prior literature, which enables them, as members of a discourse community, to communicate in concise fashion with one another. Similar to the conventions that speakers use that depend on shared knowledge with their listeners, the intertextual devices that writers employ depend on their awareness of shared knowledge with their audiences. Among reader-response enthusiasts, we can assume that a body of shared knowledge existed regarding various approaches to the literary canon. This knowledge would have been acquired in graduate school, through reading the discipline's various journals, and through participating in various MLA forums, especially in the areas of literary criticism and theory.

Perhaps the most interesting difference among the essays that appeared in Issue 3 is that the authors who wrote the more formal statements tended also to use intertextual conventions to refer their readers to both the essays appearing in *NLH* and to other essays in the canon of literary criticism that they considered relevant. In order to illustrate these differences, it will be helpful to compare the first paragraphs of three of the responses. (We have italicized intertextual features for clarity.)

### Writer 1 (Daniel Laferriere)

Dear Rob:
Sorry to be so slow in responding to your invitation. (**1**) I did indeed read the issue of *NLH* on "Readers and Spectators." (**2**) I did it because you asked me to, and, having done it, I can't believe I read the whole thing because it was a bad meal and now I have heartburn. (**3**)

### Writer 2 (Peter Rabinowitz)

A Reply to Christian Metz

Many of us turned to reader-oriented criticism partly because other critics so often ignored readers; but some of us are also concerned that exclusive attention to readers may make the *texts* disappear completely. (**1**) *Christian Metz's "The Fiction Film and Its Spectator" (NLH, No. 1, pp. 75–105)* illustrates the problem in

*[handwritten margin note: relation of sources to 1st narrator? and register / ad hoc – not fixed]*

nightmare form. (2) In its thirty dense, jargon-filled pages of psychological analysis, not a single film is mentioned—except in two footnotes, one of which is by the translator. (3) This lack of specificity dilutes the argument; Metz fails to recognize that different films act on us in different ways. (4)

## Writer 3 *(Stan Rubin)*

*The "Valuing Relation" in Naumann's "Literary Production and Reception":*
Some Theoretical and Practical Conclusions

*Barthes, in his famous 1966 "Introduction to the Structural Analysis of Narrative," acknowledged the way in which narration "opens out into the world where narrative is consumed" (NLH, Winter, 1975).* (1) Naumann's Marxist perspective takes us into this broader terrain, which Barthes (at that time) had deemed beyond the realm of literary analysis. (2) *From a consideration of the social relations of production and consumption, Naumann leads us back to the reading act itself, not as a "causal relationship" in which the work figures as cause, and the processes in the reader as effect, or, conversely, in which the effect of the work has its cause in the reader, but as a "special form of relationship whose two constituents mutually permeate each other."* (3)

No intertextual features appeared in Writer 1's brief note, the most informal of all the essays in Issue 3. He used the first person pronoun as the topical, as well as the grammatical, subject of his sentences (Faigley & Witte, 1983) and employed an informal register characteristic of conversation. Writer 2's first paragraph contained a single citation, but no summary, no direct quotation, no paraphrase, or any other convention associated with intertextuality. His piece was a response to the essay to which he referred—as indicated by his title: "A Reply to Christian Metz"—and by his use of a more formal register than Writer 1. In contrast, Writer 3 deployed a variety of intertextual devices. His title contained a reference to a concept in the source text; he cited and summarized the gist of an essay by Barthes in sentence 1; he also used paraphrase, summary, and direct quotation in sentence 3, all of which refer to prior texts with which his readers were presumably familiar. In addition, Writer 3 used a number of "literate strategies" (Tannen, 1982) characteristic of scholarly journal writing in literary studies. For example, his title, an indicator of genre, forecasts that a formal belletristic essay is to follow. The average sentence length of his first paragraph is 40 words, as compared with Writer 1's 17 words and Writer 2's 16 words. The register is more formal, more characteristic of a literary critic or scholar, than that of Writers 1 and 2. Finally, sentence 3, which is 69 words long, contains 10 embedded clauses. Writer 3's register and convoluted syntax remind one of the "tedious formalities of the journal style" that Crosman had exhorted his readers to avoid. However, in this and subsequent issues, we see the appearance of the traditional literature scholar's journal style, as well as the intertextual conventions one would expect to see in a disciplinary forum.

## 1978–1980: IDENTIFYING MAJOR ISSUES AND
## CONCERNS WITHIN THE COMMUNITY

Between 1978 and 1980, a growing number of books and articles in mainstream forums were published that were to join the canonical texts published by Bleich, Holland, Fish, Iser, and others.[3] Among the influential new works were Bleich's (1978) *Subjective Criticism*, Iser's (1978) *The Act of Reading*, and Fish's (1980) *Is There a Text in This Class?*, as well as the collections *Reader-Response Criticism: From Formalism to Post-Structuralism* (Tompkins, 1980), and *The Reader in the Text* (Suleiman & Crosman, 1980). Many academics in the early stages of their careers sought an opportunity to discuss the issues raised by these works and others being discussed through the forums provided by the MLA and elsewhere. Other *Reader* contributors were interested in discussing or presenting classroom applications of those reader-centered theories (Bleich, Fish, Holland) that centered on the responses of "real" readers. Because mainstream journals in literary studies were not interested in discussions of classroom practices, *Reader* provided a forum where it was possible to publish such accounts. Two issues of *Reader* published between 1978 and 1980 were devoted to essays by teachers who had introduced reader- response techniques to students in their literature classes.

During this period, Bob Crosman and Wendy Deutelbaum shared editorial responsibilities with the help of Susan Elliott. Crosman, Deutelbaum, and Elliott also contributed essays to the issues they edited, a somewhat unorthodox maneuver suggesting that they saw themselves in the dual role of editor and contributor. The published issues during these years reveal constellations of younger academics who wrote about concerns raised by the first generation of theorists. Issue 6 (1979), for example, was devoted to readers' responses to Bleich's *Subjective Criticism*. A number of these readers were colleagues (and in one case, Elliott, a student) of Bleich. Steven Mailloux, a contributor between 1977 and 1980, had been the student of Fish. Mailloux's name was often seen in the "Announcements" section as organizer of MLA sessions developed around the theories of Fish, Bleich, and Holland. Because of the informal exchange of ideas that appeared in these early issues, a number of these students and young colleagues were able to establish a voice, at least among a limited number of the journal's subscribers.[4]

Issues of *Reader* published between 1978 and 1980 reflected a broad spectrum of scholarly and pedagogical interests. At one end of this spectrum were contributors who argued that reader-oriented critics should not narrow their focus to real readers in actual classrooms, but should seek to make connections among

---

[3]Interestingly, Rosenblatt's (1978) *The Reader, the Text, the Poem: The Transactional Theory of the Literary Work* did not receive attention in *Reader* during this time.

[4]Beth Flynn recalls that Deutelbaum sent her a list of 200 subscribers when Flynn assumed the editorship in 1982.

those theories that nodded toward the reader in one fashion or another. Suleiman argued for this position in 1978, at which time she was editing the essays that would appear in *The Reader in the Text*, many of which were by major figures in the MLA establishment:

> What we need is to recognize reader-oriented criticism for what it is: not a move-ment, not a school, not even, strictly speaking, a category, but rather an attitude, a frame of thought—or, if one may be permitted, a tired (but in this case apt) metaphor, a theoretical horizon. A horizon is what is always there, something we cannot choose not to see the moment we lift our heads enough to look at a whole landscape. . . . Reader-oriented criticism then becomes the kind of criticism that, whatever else it looks at in the foreground, never loses sight of the text's horizon. (pp. 4–5)

Another contributor, Mistacco, also appears to have been primarily concerned with making connections between various poststructuralist theories that dealt with the implied reader. In describing a course that she taught at Wellesley, Mistacco (1977) noted that although the course dealt with different theorists' representations of the reader, it was not designed as a "pedagogical experiment of the type 'real' reader proponents such as Jane Tompkins or David Bleich might undertake" (p. 7).

At the other end of the spectrum were contributors who were concerned with the teaching of so-called real readers and who wished to address issues related to the radical epistemology of Bleich, Holland, and Fish. Issue 6, which featured responses to Bleich's (1978) *Subjective Criticism*, dealt with many of the issues and concerns that his approach to the literature classroom raised. Briefly, Bleich had argued for a social constructionist approach to literary reading based on the assumption that knowledge begins as an individual emotional response to a literary work "which is [then] negotiated into communal knowledge, to which all members of a community freely assent" (Crosman, 1979, p. 6). In foreground-ing student readers' perceptions (as seen through their writing) as the object of study in the literature classroom, Bleich had (as had Holland) rocked the epis-temological, as well as the institutional, boat. At the center of Bleich's pedagogy was a challenge to conventional sources of authority—in the classroom, in the library, and in the professional journal. In a brief essay in which he responded to the statements that appeared in Issue 6, Bleich (1979) wrote:

> Scholarly publication is a means of creating authority; if the subjective source of that authority is not given, the claim to authority is, I believe, unethical. In order to continue to present ethical claims of authoritative knowledge, scholarly publi-cation ought to become more like the present publication, READER, whose purpose of intracommunity contact outweighs, so far, its prestige on university tenure com-mittees. (p. 26)

Bleich's comments here are quite perceptive regarding the unique character of *Reader* as a forum, the primary purpose of which was to facilitate intracom-munity contact. At the same time, however, writing for a small newsletter may

*How were early issues distributed and paid for?*

*Seems like a listserv in print*

have been too time consuming for many young assistant professors who may have been reluctant to list publication in *Reader* on their vitas. It may have also been the case that editing the newsletter became more and more time consuming (and thus more of a career liability) for the two editors. By mid-1979, Crosman had left the editorship in the hands of Deutelbaum. In late 1980, Deutelbaum, under pressure from a contributor who had not granted permission to publish her essay, recalled Issue 8, which consisted of reprints of papers delivered at a 1979 MLA session on gender and reading. No new issues appeared between 1980 and 1983, at which time Issue 9 was published under the editorship of Elizabeth Flynn, whose university had underwritten the costs of production.

With the exception of the essays in Issue 8, which were reprints of papers delivered at the 1979 MLA, submissions in Issues 4–8 were informally written and generally around 1,000 words, as the editors had requested. One sees few intertextual features in these essays, which also did not include bibliographies, although lists of new bibliographical entries were published at the end of each issue. "Announcements" and "Calls for Papers" also appeared in the first eight issues. Thus the forum enabled subscribers to keep in touch with what was going on in the field and where they might find the opportunity to be on panels within the various divisions and special interest groups of the MLA. A number of the newsletter's early issues can be seen to reflect the concerns of a group of young scholars who were seeking to understand the implications of the theories of Bleich, Fish, and Holland for their literature classrooms, many of which were filled with nonmajor, introductory-level students. Other issues reflected the musings of contributors seeking to compare various currently popular theories that acknowledged the existence of readers, whether ideal, implied, or real. How long *Reader* could have maintained its identity as an informal forum reflecting the immediacy of intracommunity contact seems a moot question given the fact that after the publication of eight issues, two editors had resigned and a system of guest editors, which had been proposed to make editing and distributing a communal responsibility, had not materialized.

## 1980–1988: FROM NEWSLETTER TO SCHOLARLY JOURNAL

When Elizabeth Flynn became editor in 1983, she made a number a major changes in the format of *Reader*. First, she changed the title from *Reader: a newsletter of reader-oriented criticism and teaching* to the more formal *Reader: Essays in Reader-Oriented Theory, Criticism, and Pedagogy*. This decision, as well as others, Flynn described in "A Note from the Editor," a preface that was to become a regular feature in subsequent issues:

> I conceive of *Reader* then, as continuing to provide an "alternative" to other journals: it is relatively inexpensive ... and it still provides a forum for discussion of reader-oriented issues. But it will do so in a somewhat different way. Essays will

be longer (12–15 double-spaced pages) and more formal; issues will have an interdisciplinary emphasis; and there will be a deliberate attempt to include the perspectives of "outsiders," i.e., those who would not consider themselves to be part of the reader-response community. (Flynn, 1983, p. ii)

The issues published between 1983 and the first half of 1986 constituted a series of symposia on diverse topics selected by colleagues of Flynn who served as guest editors of the journal. These included *reading/writing relationships, deconstruction, gender and reading,* and *teaching noncanonical literature.* Flynn described her use of guest editors as "a system of collaboration and quality control" (personal interview, June 1989). Typically, she invited a colleague to edit an issue; in turn, that colleague solicited manuscripts from other colleagues. Some guest editors developed an issue from papers that had been delivered at a Midwest Modern Language Association (MMLA) session or, in one instance, at a small prestigious conference held to bring together literary theorists, rhetoricians, and writing researchers.[5] In other cases, a guest editor asked colleagues working in a common area to contribute essays. This kind of informal networking provided the social scaffolding upon which many issues of *Reader* were constructed during the first 3 years that Flynn was editor. By Autumn 1986, however, Flynn was able to report that she had received enough high-quality material to publish an issue that was composed of unsolicited manuscripts. This issue, on "Pedagogy," was followed by two more during 1987–1988 that were edited by Flynn (rather than a guest editor). By this time, Flynn had enlisted the support of a number of colleagues in her department to serve as reviewers to handle the steady flow of submissions from "individuals with national visibility, or untenured assistant professors who have not yet established themselves but have promising careers" (personal communication, March 1987). She was thus able to report in her prefatory note:

The number of fine submissions we have been receiving recently is certainly an indication of *Reader*'s development over the past few years and of the development of the response community whose conversation it records. *Reader* is no longer the small newsletter we took over in 1982. We have subscribers from five continents, institutional subscriptions from major universities in this country and abroad, exchanges with a number of other journals, and the support of leading researchers and theorists in several fields. We've gone from a newsletter that employed an informal format and that was published occasionally to a journal that has a professional appearance and that is issued regularly. (Flynn, 1986, pp. i–ii)

## Protean Possibilities in a Newly Emerging Field

Flynn's editorial policies can be seen at work in the first several issues, which were essentially conference proceedings. For example, Issue 10 (edited by Flynn) consisted of papers that had been delivered at an MLA session titled "Relationships

---

[5]"The New Rhetoric and the New Literary Theory," Carnegie Mellon University, April 1985.

Between Response Theories and Reading Research." Issue 11, edited by Flynn's fellow teacher and colleague, the late Bruce Petersen, was developed from an MMLA session, "Relationships Between Reading and Writing: Cognitive, Social, and Interpretive." The editors of Issues 13 and 14 continued this trend of exploring relationships between diverse areas. Issue 13 dealt with connections between feminist criticism and reader-oriented criticism, a subject that Flynn and Patrocinio Schweickart (the editor of the issue) had pursued in their edited collection of essays, *Gender and Reading* (1986). Issue 14, which was conceived by Kathleen McCormick, was a collection of edited papers from a conference designed to bring together empirical researchers and scholars of literary theory.

Given the guest editors' efforts to make connections among different fields with their own methodologies and literatures, the citations appearing in the essays published between 1983 and 1988 suggest that the field of reader-oriented criticism was fairly nebulous. Writers made reference to a variety of literatures including psycholinguistics and cognitive psychology, empirical reading and writing research, and composition and rhetoric. Also frequently cited were the theorists whose work first drew attention to reader-oriented criticism: Bleich, Iser, Fish, and Holland. Rosenblatt's work, which had not been cited during the early years of *Reader*, was mentioned with increasing frequency. This broad pattern of citation is, as Bazerman (1988) noted, constitutive of, "a newly emerging field with a small and loosely structured literature [which] draws on the literary capital of other specialties out of which it emerged; however, the protean possibilities of a newly emerging field offer opportunities for direction-setting innovations" (p. 324).

Flynn's decision to publish a forum with an interdisciplinary emphasis was responsible, in part, for the ecumenical nature of the scholarship that appeared in *Reader* between 1983 and 1988. Constructs from other fields, such as schema theory from cognitive psychology, were described in articles by well-known reading and composition researchers, such as Carey, Beach, and Purves. Reports of interdisciplinary collaborations, such as Hunt and Vipond's (1985) transactional model of literary reading, which integrated context, text, and reader, suggested that creative young academics could synthesize from fields as disparate as literary scholarship and criticism on the one side and cognitive psychology and empirical reading research on the other. Despite the range of the scholarship appearing in *Reader* during Flynn's tenure, however, it is also quite clear that a body of canonical reader-oriented theory had emerged to which writers referred with regularity. References to the theories of Bleich, Holland, Iser, and Fish outstrip references to any other single critic or theorist, especially in the period between 1983 and 1986. References to Rosenblatt's work, however, increased dramatically between 1983 and 1988, suggesting that her work had also become part of the established critical canon, as Fig. 5.1 illustrates.

Looking at the distribution of citations over 2-year periods (1983–1984, 1985–1986, and 1987–1988) to the work of Bleich, Holland, Fish, and Iser, we see that references to their work remained fairly constant over the 6-year period.

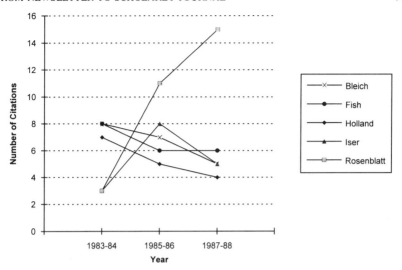

FIG. 5.1. Theorists most frequently cited in *Reader*, 1983–1988.

Bleich was cited 8, 7, and 5 times, respectively; Holland 7, 5, and 4; Fish 8, 6, and 6; and Iser 3, 8, and 5, suggesting a very slight drop in citations during this period. In contrast, Rosenblatt was cited 3 times during 1983–1984, 11 times during 1985–1986, and 15 times during 1987–1988. A large part of this dramatic increase was due to the publication of a 1988 issue on Rosenblatt's work. Fifteen citations to her books and articles appeared in the essays in that year's issue. Were we to subtract them from the total citations appearing in 1987–1988, Rosenblatt's citations over the 6-year period would be 3, 11, and 4, a pattern resembling that of Iser. One could argue, then, that Rosenblatt's increase in citations was due to chance; had one of the other canonical figures been the subject of Issue 20, we would expect to see a similar dramatic increase. It is also conceivable that the increase in citations to Rosenblatt's work appearing during 1985–1986 (from 3 to 11), as compared with the stable number of citations to the work of other theorists, indicates a swelling of interest in Rosenblatt's transactional theory of reading. Whatever the case, it seems clear that the increase in references to Rosenblatt's work signals the acceptance of her scholarly works into the canon of reader-response theory and criticism.[6]

---

[6]John Clifford (1988), the guest editor of the special issue on Rosenblatt's work, argued that "Rosenblatt's ideas about the dialectical simultaneity of the reading process, about the contextual complexity of language in its social and private dimensions, were simply a generation ahead of their time" (p. 1). Clifford's view that Rosenblatt's ideas anticipated the current interest among literary theorists in readers and the act of reading may have parallels in the sciences. One account of prematurity has been made recently by Carolyn Miller (1992) who argued that *kairos*, or appropriate timing, has much to do with the acceptance of new knowledge among the members of disciplinary communities.

## ROLE OF THE FORUM IN DISCIPLINARY FORMATION

Earlier in this chapter we raised three questions: To what extent did *Reader*'s contributors determine the priorities of a newly emerging field? To what extent did the development of *Reader* from an informal forum to an academic journal affect the growth and dissemination of knowledge within the reader-response community? And what does this study of an evolving forum tell us about its function as a dynamic causal entity in constructing a community of scholars and teachers interested in reader-oriented criticism? The present study of *Reader*'s alteration over the last 11 years from newsletter to journal provides only a partial picture of the growth of knowledge within the constituency of reader-oriented critics and teachers. Other texts, meetings, and events, obscured from our view, will also have played a role in constituting the new subspecialty.

With this qualification in mind, looking back over the three editorships, it is first of all apparent that the field of reader-oriented criticism and pedagogy is still very young and in a state of flux. Although the forum underwent a period of professionalization under its most recent editor, which led to the emergence of a prior literature (through citation and other forms of overt intertextuality) against which writers could position their claims, this prior literature is still evolving. And although the field was initially established around a core of theoretical texts appearing in the middle and late 1970s and early 1980s, there appears to be little consensus regarding the theoretical ground on which rival notions of the reader are based. As one of *Reader*'s most recent contributors noted:

> Contemporary reader-response critics are still divided according to whether they study real readers, as Norman Holland and David Bleich do (though their "subjective" criticism is clearly at odds with Rosenblatt's more socially-oriented approach) or whether they postulate ideal constructs such as Wolfgang Iser's "implied reader," Michael Riffaterre's "superreader," Stanley Fish's "informed reader," and Jonathan Culler's "competent reader." (McCormick, 1988, p. 48)

Furthermore, the infusion of theory and research from such fields as psycholinguistics and cognitive psychology, rhetoric and composition, and empirical research on reading and writing make it difficult to point to a body of shared assumptions around which a community ordinarily constitutes itself. Thus, at this point in *Reader*'s evolution, one can only point to general trends that have appeared since its inception.

During Crosman's and, later, Deutelbaum's tenure as editors, a good deal of enthusiasm was generated by the early contributors, who expressed a desire to use the forum as a place to raise questions concerning the new theories and to exchange information. The newsletter format seemed appropriate, especially because Crosman's goal was to provide readers with an alternative to other MLA scholarly publications. In its first incarnation, *Reader* was, therefore, a place in which readers identified issues and concerns growing out of the scholarship of the first generation of reader-oriented theorists. Many of these issues and concerns revolved around the epistemological question that Tompkins posed in Issue 2: "What constitutes knowledge about a literary text?" (1977, p. 3). The early issues of *Reader*, in which contributors identified issues and concerns central to the new movement, can be seen to constitute an epistemic core around which a loosely formed constituency could organize itself. The essays appearing in the newsletter were generally informal pieces, without footnotes, citations, bibliographies, or other intertextual devices (with the exception of Writer 3's contribution in Issue 3) that characterize the (MLA) journal style that Crosman sought to avoid. Until 1983, when Elizabeth Flynn took over the editorship, the essays appearing in the forum did not deploy the intertextual mechanisms that allow for reference to a prior literature, necessary for warranting knowledge claims. Flynn's alterations in format led to the appearance of essays that exhibited the features of formally structured literary arguments utilizing all of the available means of persuasion acceptable within a community of scholars trained in literary studies. *Reader* was then positioned within the larger constituency of the MLA (and related constituencies such as National Council of Teachers of English) to become a recognized source of scholarly information, as indicated by its inclusion in various bibliographies and citation indices. Without the forum's contributors having utilized the intertextual mechanisms necessary for the production of formal academic discourse, it is unlikely that *Reader* would have had any lasting influence within the profession of English studies.

At the same time, as a scholarly journal, *Reader* lost much of the immediacy of intracommunity contact that its first editors strove to maintain. However, as early as Issue 8, an issue based on papers delivered at an MLA session on "Woman as Reader" and edited by Deutelbaum, the forum had begun to evolve into a more conventionally structured scholarly journal. Issues 9–11 followed this trend, all having been compiled from papers delivered at MLA or MMLA panels. This subtle but significant alteration reflects an early sign of institutionalization within the new field, that is, a shift toward the routines of academic production that characterize *normal scholarship*. As a newsletter, *Reader* had served the function of building community among adherents of a new critical movement identified by a small number of texts written by a vanguard of critics, who, by the middle to late 1970s, were well established figures. By 1979–1980, however, many enthusiasts had become a second generation of theorists and critics who were in their own right publishing scholarly books and collections. A number of this younger generation of reader-oriented critics had, therefore, entered the mainstream of literary criticism, as can be seen by the proliferation of books and collections published by Johns Hopkins and other university presses. By the early 1980s, a number of graduate students and young assistant professors exposed to reader-oriented criticism in graduate school, were entering the field, which, as we have seen, was inclusive enough to admit scholars combining

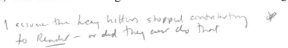

I assume the heavy hitters stopped contributing to *Reader* — or did they ever do that?

interests in reader-oriented theory and feminist theory, composition studies, psy-cholinguistics, and reading research. A small journal, yet a bona fide source for scholarly output, *Reader* offered an opportunity to publish for this latter group whom Flynn (1986) identified as young assistant professors who [had] not yet established themselves but [had] promising careers, and who would have experienced considerably greater difficulty breaking into major academic forums.

Thus, as a small, newly established journal with a system of guest editors who built its early issues out of an informal networking system rather than the conventional system of academic gatekeeping, *Reader* created an opening, or professional space (see Miller, 1992), for unestablished scholars to get their ideas "into the pipeline," an opportunity that could lead to citation and further publication. At the same time, *Reader* was also establishing its own professional credentials as a forum for reader-oriented scholarship. Unfortunately, it is beyond the scope of this study to determine the impact that *Reader* essays may have had on the scholarship appearing within other forums. Long-term citation analyses of clusters of researchers, or *social circles* (Crane, 1972), although common among sociologists of scientific knowledge, are new to studies of the diffusion of knowledge in fields of the humanities. Such studies would enhance our understanding of the role that the scholarly forum plays in disciplinary formation and, conversely, of how the growth of such forums is affected by the social, historical, and material conditions of academic culture. We have just begun to appreciate the dynamic nature of these processes.

# 6

# GATEKEEPING AT AN ACADEMIC CONVENTION

*Institutional gatekeeping is ubiquitous in modern societies.*
—Erickson and Schultz (1982, p. xi)

The Conference on College Composition and Communication (CCCC) is the primary professional organization of postsecondary writing instructors in the United States. Started in 1949, its membership and influence have grown steadily over the years, to the point where it now represents more than 10,000 college and university writing teachers nationwide. Every year it organizes a 4-day convention that is attended by about one third of the membership.

The main activity at a CCCC convention is the presentation of scholarly papers. Ten months before the convention takes place, members (and nonmembers) are invited to submit proposals to give a paper. These are reviewed by the program chair, assisted by a panel of about 150 to 200 external reviewers representing different areas of interest within the field. For the most recent convention (1993), approximately 4,000 proposals were submitted, about 1,000 of which were accepted for presentation.

The heart of a CCCC proposal is a one-page abstract. Each abstract undergoes blind review, usually by two or more external reviewers and the program chair (Blind reviewing was initiated in 1992). Reviewers are asked to rate abstracts on a 4-point scale, including *Excellent* (4), *Good* (3), *Adequate* (2), and *Weak* (1). A high score makes it likely that the paper will be included in the program, but does not guarantee it: Other factors, such as a balance of topics, broad geographical representation, and the program chair's particular interests, can intervene.

Submitters are given relatively little guidance in how to write an effective abstract. Instructions to submitters typically include this statement: "Insofar as possible, the chair will try to include sessions that focus on current topics of interest and on critical issues in the profession. Proposals submitted will be chosen on the basis of their clarity, organization, and potential interest to people attending the convention." But unlike some academic conferences, the winning abstracts are never published and thus are never made available as models for the larger membership; only the program chairs, their local helpers, and the external reviewers get to see them. Hence, the typical submitter can only guess as to what makes for an appealing abstract. Indeed, in talking with many members of CCCC who regularly submit abstracts to the annual convention, we found widespread uncertainty about what constitutes a good CCCC abstract.

## PILOT STUDY

We were intrigued by this question as well and decided to do an empirical study to try to answer it. Accordingly, during the summer of 1987, one of us visited the program chair for the 1988 convention and interviewed her about the selection process, then underway. With her assistance, we also compiled a stratified, randomly selected subset of 96 abstracts. To maximize the representativeness of the sample, we selected four abstracts (one for each rating level) from each of the 24 designated areas on the submission form (*Basic Writing, Rhetorical Theory, Composing Processes*, etc.). We thus had 24 Excellents, 24 Goods, 24 Adequates, and 24 Weaks, representing a cross section of the field. (Note: We deliberately selected only abstracts that had been submitted as individual presentations, not as a part of panels. Panel proposals are a somewhat different genre in terms of textual features and elements.)

Our first step in analyzing this corpus was to examine it holistically, looking for general patterns that could be converted into hypotheses for more detailed study. We based our analysis on an assumption that the genre called "CCCC abstracts" should be defined not by the full range of abstracts submitted but only by those deemed successful according to the community and its gatekeepers. This meant that there were basically two levels of patterning to be observed: (a) those features found in all the successful abstracts but also in most or all of the unsuccessful ones, and (b) those features found only in the successful abstracts, that is to say, those rated Good or Excellent. We might call the former *general* features and the latter *distinguishing* features. As to general features, almost all of the 96 abstracts we examined addressed a topic clearly relevant to the field of rhetoric and composition, raised some issue and proposed to develop it in some way, and were reasonably well organized and well written. Almost all were typewritten or computer printed and confined to one page.

It was the distinguishing features, of course, that were more interesting, and here three distinct patterns stood out. First, the high-rated abstracts seemed to be more "abstract" (i.e., more theoretical or scholarly, less "practical") than the low-rated ones. Instead of discussing course design or teaching techniques, for example, they emphasized research, theory, or history, often citing references to the scholarly literature. Second, the high-rated abstracts seemed to address social issues more often than the low-rated ones. They used language associated with the emerging "social view" of writing, including words like *social, community*, and *the self*. Third, the high-rated abstracts seemed to be longer, more complex, and more problematized.

To test these impressions, we did a count of text features that seemed to be plausible indicators of these patterns. For example, we counted the number of scholarly references in each abstract; the number of times words like *social, community*, and *the self* appeared; and the total number of words per abstract. Not surprisingly, the results confirmed our impressions: Abstracts rated Excellent or Good had significantly more scholarly references than Adequate or Weak ones (2.16 vs. 0.49), used more social view key words (2.1 vs. 0.8 of the three words listed previously), and were longer (289 vs. 246 words).[1] To further explore the *abstractness* dimension, we had three raters independently sort the abstracts into four general categories—practice, research, theory, or history—with the first category referring to more concrete, localized descriptions of teaching techniques, curriculum design, and so forth and the latter three categories referring to more conceptual, scholarly investigations.[2] We then compared the resulting classifications with the scores given to these abstracts and found that only 32.5% of the practice-oriented abstracts were rated Good or Excellent, compared to 62.5% of the more scholarly ones,[3] a statistically significant ($p < .003$) difference.

A good example of a successful 1988 CCCC abstract is shown in Fig. 6.1. This abstract was submitted to the Writing Center area and was rated Excellent. In contrast to many other Writing Center abstracts, which tended to be very local and practice oriented (e.g., "Here's what we do at our writing center"), this one is quite theorized. The writer started on a practical level, describing a problem familiar to anyone who has ever worked at a writing center, but he quickly broadened the scope of the problem, citing Freire, Brannon, and Knoblauch and promising to discuss "some philosophical and pedagogical dimensions of this dilemma." Other concept-names were drawn into the discussion: Bakhtin, Harris, Bartholomae, Bowles, and Gintis, all of whom are associated with the social view of writing. The writer deepened and problematized the issue not only by invoking an extensive body of scholarly literature on it, but also by stating that he would "discuss the advantages and problems of both positions"; in saying this, he implies that it is a complex issue with no simple answers. Furthermore, by putting quotation marks around the terms *right words* and *error*, he indicated

---

[1]All of these results were statistically significant at $p < .05$.

[2]In 61% of the cases, there was unanimous agreement on categorization, and in the remaining cases there was two thirds agreement.

[3]A more detailed account of this study can be found in Huckin (1992).

---

**"If the Words Are 'Right,' Is the Tutor Wrong?"**
Joseph Janangelo

How many times have students come to writing conferences seeking "the right words" for their papers? They badger the instructor in the hope that he or she will provide them with the precise alchemical combination of language that will ensure them a better grade. When this happens, instructors are faced with a dilemma: do we perform the "service" (Freire) the students have been socialized to expect, or do we deny their requests (Brannon and Knoblauch), remaining secure in our refusal to become their ghost-writers?

In an oral presentation, I will discuss some philosophical and pedagogical dimensions of this dilemma. I will use my original research, conducted at - - - - - - University's Writing Center, to dramatize the above-mentioned theoretical positions. If, on the one hand, we fulfill the students' expectations, are we little more than word suppliers—language "dealers" who dispense "fixes" to desperate writers? Do we also impose our own "authoritative discourse" (Bakhtin) on students? (It is naive to imagine that our "right words" could ever be their "right words.") If we deliberately withhold words and meanings from students (particularly ESL students), are we not letting "error" become an opportunity for intellectual growth (Harris, Bartholomae)? What is worse, are we being socratic rather than honest, not sharing what we know about language? Are we, in effect, further "disenfranchising" (Bowles and Gintis) students from the academic community?

I will discuss the advantages and problems of both positions. I will conclude by suggesting ways of helping students find the "right words" without ghost-writing their texts; ways of sharing language which encourage them to abandon isolated word searches and to concentrate on conceptual revision.

---

FIG. 6.1. A high-rated abstract from the 1988 convention, submitted in the "Writing Centers" area.

his awareness of the contested nature of such terms in the rhetoric and composition community. All of these things mark this writer as not just a dues-paying member of CCCC but as an insider familiar with the literature, terminology, and ideology of the scholarly community.

In general, our pilot study suggests that successful 1988 CCCC abstracts tended to be scholarly and tended to embrace a social view of writing. In this respect, one can say that the genre was shaped significantly by the interests of the program chair. In her 500-word theme statement included with the *Call for Program Proposals*, she gave major emphasis to the social view of writing, repeatedly using key words like *social, society, community, the self,* and *context,* and, as a well-known scholar in the field, she might be expected to favor scholarly topics over purely practical ones. In evaluating individual abstracts, she did not seem to hesitate to impose her own judgment over that of external reviewers whenever there was a difference of opinion,[4] and she stated matter-of-factly in conversations with one of us that she was trying to find the "most interesting"

---

[4]In the 52 cases (out of a larger corpus of some 250 abstracts) where we were able to compare the program chair's rating to that of another referee, there were 35 cases of disagreement. In all these cases the program chair's rating prevailed.

abstracts she could. Such influence by the program chair is not at all unusual at CCCC conventions; indeed, we have heard many veteran attendees say they *expect* program chairs to "put their mark on" the convention. At the same time, however, it must be kept in mind that this program chair, like all others, was chosen partly because she was highly respected within the CCCC community and was viewed as an outstanding *representative* of that community. One could argue, therefore, that it was not her "personal" interests that she was exercising here so much as those of the community, especially if one takes a constructionist or poststructuralist view on autonomy and subjectivity.

These observations bring to mind those of Lynn Quitman Troyka, who was program chair for the 1980 convention. Reflecting on the abstracts submitted to that convention, Troyka wrote that they "were most compelling when characterized by clarity of ideas coupled with a sense of where those ideas fit, or do not fit, in relation to *the mainstream of current thinking on the subject*. The weakest proposals unavoidably elicited the thought, 'Where have you been these past few years?'" (Troyka, 1980, p. 229, italics added). The annual program guidelines mentioned earlier contain similar language ("Insofar as possible, the chair will try to include sessions that focus on current topics of interest and on critical issues in the profession. Proposals submitted will be chosen on the basis of their clarity, organization, and potential interest to people attending the convention"), but the results of our pilot study suggested that this language did not really capture the degree to which "interestingness" plays a role.

## EXTENDED STUDY

We came away from this exploratory study with some initial notions of what constituted a good CCCC abstract for 1988. But this was only a single convention, and we were curious to see what our findings would be if we looked at abstracts from several conventions. More importantly, we felt we had not really done justice to the genre even for that one year, for there were many exceptional cases for which we had not accounted. For example, although scholarly abstracts had been far more successful, in general, than practice-oriented ones, there was still a substantial number of the latter that had received scores of Good or Excellent. Likewise, not all successful abstracts (of either type) had taken a social view. In short, we were missing something.

Our guess was that although we were correct in taking "interestingness" as the key criterion in the evaluation of CCCC abstracts, we had not developed an adequate characterization of it. Thinking that a more longitudinal study might help out, over the next few years we compiled a similar set of randomly selected abstracts for each of the years 1989, 1990, and 1992 (1991 was inadvertently excluded). This yielded a full corpus of 441 abstracts (see Table 6.1). In analyzing this enlarged corpus, we departed from the methodology we had used in the pilot study: Instead

TABLE 6.1
The Full Study Corpus

| Year | Chair | No. of Areas | No. of Abstracts |
|------|-------|--------------|------------------|
| 1988 | Lunsford | 24 | 96 |
| 1989 | Peterson | 26 | 104 |
| 1990 | McQuade | 32 | 112 |
| 1992 | Gere (blind) | 40 | 129 |

*Note.* In some areas, there were no individual abstracts for a certain rating level, thus accounting for the fact that in 1992, for example, we have only 129 abstracts instead of 160.

of trying to isolate and quantify specific text features, we decided to take a more holistic approach in hopes of getting a more comprehensive picture of the genre. Accordingly, one of us went through the entire 1989–1992 corpus, reading each abstract carefully (often several times) and noting patterns that seemed to distinguish high-rated abstracts from low-rated ones; a doctoral student in rhetoric and composition, Brenton Faber, working independently, did likewise. Both analysts then sat down together and compared notes. In some cases, they had observed the same patterns; in most other cases, one of them observed a pattern that the other had not, but the other quickly acknowledged it when it was pointed out.

What emerged from this extended study were the following findings:

1. The high-rated abstracts all addressed topics of current interest to active, experienced members of the rhetoric and composition community; the low-rated abstracts often did not.

2. Almost all of the high-rated abstracts clearly defined a problem; the low-rated abstracts often did not.

 3. The high-rated abstracts all discussed this problem in a way that would be seen by experienced insiders as novel and therefore interesting, whereas virtually none of the low-rated abstracts did.

4. The high-rated abstracts usually projected more of an insider ethos through the use of terminology, special topoi, and/or explicit or implicit references to the scholarly literature of the field than did the low-rated abstracts.

Some of these features bear a striking resemblance to those identified by Raymond (1993) in his description of how he evaluated personal reflection essays as editor of *College English* during the years 1985–1992. Noting that "few [personal reflection essays] seemed to escape the inertia of particularity and local interest," Raymond went on to describe several exceptions. Each of these exceptional cases was distinguished by three qualities: "topical relevance," "the energy of novelty and dissent," and "authoritative voice" (p. 479). Judging from Raymond's discussion of these qualities, we would argue that they are similar to Points 1, 3, and 4 just delineated.

## Topic

To see the role of topic in differentiating high-rated abstracts from low-rated ones, we have listed the topics of all Excellents and all Weaks from our 1990 sample in Figs. 6.2 and 6.3. For experienced members of the rhetoric and composition community in 1990, the topics listed in Fig. 6.2 would be seen as addressing, in the words of the program guidelines, "current topics of interest."

| Area | Topic |
| --- | --- |
| Advanced composition | Montaigne and the writing of nonconfessional first-person prose |
| Assessment | Analysis of a "community" of graders |
| Basic writing | What does "remedial" mean? An ethnographic study |
| Business comm. | Comparative study of two real-world writing teams |
| Collaboration/schools & colleges | [none] |
| Collaborative writing | Desirable disorderliness in peer-group discussions |
| Composition & literature | Composition for Asian-American students via Asian-American literature |
| Computers | Computers, disabled student writers, and new accessibility requirements |
| Critical thinking | A consensus conception of what "critical thinking" means |
| Curriculum design | Co-teaching as theorizing |
| Discourse analysis | Major genres of written medical discourse |
| ESL | Contrastive rhetoric: Chinese vs. American |
| Freshman composition | [none] |
| Gender issues | Gender & language in the 1637 trial of Anne Hutchinson |
| History of rhetoric/instruction | Rev. C. L. Franklin and the black folk pulpit |
| Ideology | *Voice* as ideological metaphor: cognitive vs. critical theory |
| Innovative teaching | Integrating composition and the study of local literature |
| Literacy | Experiencing "illiteracy" by spending a year in Japan |
| Race & class issues | [none] |
| Research on composing | How do writers respond to readers' difficulties with a text? |
| Research methods | Ethnography in anthropology vs. ethnography in composition |
| Research on reading | [none] |
| Social contexts | The social origins and meanings of genre |
| Teacher training | [none] |
| Technical communications | How novices learn the communicative practices of discourse communities |
| Terms & conditions | [none] |
| Theories of composition | Social constructionism vs. social interactionism |
| Theories of knowledge | Problematizing the idea of "shared beliefs" in argumentation |
| Theories of rhetoric | Using classical rhetoric to explicate Native American rhetoric |
| Two-year colleges | Using a reading notebook to respond to literature |
| WAC | Teaching composition in foreign language courses |
| Writing centers | The writing center as a *subversive activity* |

FIG. 6.2.   Topics of high-rated abstracts in the 1990 sample.

| Area | Topic |
|------|-------|
| Advanced composition | Using problem–cause–solution papers in Intermediate Composition |
| Assessment | Using a personal profile chart for each student in class |
| Basic writing | Using newspaper headlines to teach language structure |
| Business comm. | Incorporating P. A. L. (purpose, audience, and lists in Business Writing |
| Collaboration/schools & colleges | Articulation procedures between a Florida high school and a Florida university |
| Collaborative writing | Using collaborative writing in first-year composition to build a sense of community |
| Composition & literature | The growing fragmentation and dissolution of Composition Studies |
| Computers | How to get students through the first 3 weeks of computer writing labs |
| Critical thinking | Dialectic is more useful than rhetoric for invention |
| Curriculum design | Fostering community and individuality through Vedic Science |
| Discourse analysis | [none] |
| ESL | ESL students have trouble with English essay conventions |
| Freshman composition | What "Composition" means to me |
| Gender issues | [none] |
| History of rhetoric/instruction | Memory and delivery are regaining importance in age of secondary orality |
| Ideology | [none] |
| Innovative teaching | Enabling students to express an opinion through the process approach |
| Literacy | Punctuation can affect how readers perceive texts |
| Race & class issues | [none] |
| Research on composing | Creating a voice through collaborative learning |
| Research methods | How to recognize a student's *voice* |
| Research on reading | Writing an ethnographic narrative from improvisational theater |
| Social contexts | The *Canterbury Tales* as paradigm for the composition class |
| Teacher training | A program of language instruction/grammar for education majors |
| Technical communications | Designing instructional materials instead of using a textbook |
| Terms & conditions | [none] |
| Theories of composition | [none] |
| Theories of knowledge | Children's books show that "all communication is narration" |
| Theories of rhetoric | Kinneavy's *Theory of Discourse* fails to consider historical context |
| Two-year colleges | We need to improve attitudes in two-year colleges |
| WAC | [none] |
| Writing centers | [none] |

FIG. 6.3.   Topics of low-rated abstracts in the 1990 sample.

The program chair's theme statement is a helpful guide in this respect (see Fig. 6.4). Clearly, the major theme of this statement is *diversity*. The term is fore-grounded in the title and then repeated eight times in the body of the text. The concept is also evoked through a variety of near synonyms (in this context) such as *pluralism, multiculturalism,* and *breadth (of interests),* and through the various examples given. *Community,* which was highlighted in the 1988 convention, also continues to be emphasized here.

Not surprisingly, the topics of those abstracts given high ratings (see Fig. 6.2) were much more in line with the theme statement than the topics of those abstracts given low ratings (Fig. 6.3). Among the high-rated abstracts, we found many topics related to diversity: Asian-American students, Native-American rhetoric, disabled student writers, gender differences, the Black folk pulpit, and so on; among the low-rated ones, we found virtually none. Likewise, many of the high-rated abstracts addressed the topic of community (a "community" of graders, real-world writing teams, social constructionism vs. social interactionism, dis-course communities, etc.), whereas only two of the low-rated abstracts did.

The correlation of topicality (current interest) and rating illustrates to some extent one of the principles discussed in chapter 1, namely, that genre knowledge embraces both form and content, including a sense of what content is appropriate to a particular purpose in a particular situation at a particular point in time. This sense of appropriateness and timeliness, also known as *kairos,* has been widely discussed in both classical and modern rhetoric (e.g., Carter, 1988; Miller, 1992).

## Problem Definition

Another prominent feature of the high-rated abstracts was the clear definition of a problem or need. Usually, the problem was explicitly laid out and was identified with a concessive conjunct like *but, however, while,* or *although* (e.g., "There is a massive body of research on how White students learn and master language skills, but few studies focus on specific minority populations"). In most other cases, the problem was not explicit but could readily be inferred. In a few cases, there was not a problem per se, but rather a gap in our knowledge; these abstracts tended to be in one of the History categories. In any case, the problem-description in these high-rated abstracts was almost always quite lengthy, usually constituting anywhere from one third to two thirds of the entire abstract.[5] In general, this seemed to be necessitated by the complexity of the problem and by the need to situate it, via various forms of intertextual reference (citations, terminology, etc.), within the ongoing discourse of the community. A good example of such extended problematization can be seen in Fig. 6.1, the 1988 abstract we discussed earlier, where the problem description is so elaborated that it takes up four fifths of the entire text; only the last paragraph goes beyond it.

---

[5]In 1992, for example, 70% of the abstracts had problem descriptions of this length.

## Strengthening Community through Diversity
### Donald McQuade

Through its conventions, workshops, and publications, CCCC maintains a supportive and spirited community of inquiry within which its members have established an admirable record of accomplishment in composition theory, research, and classroom practice. As we lead our discipline into the final decade of the twentieth century, we can look to the 1990 CCCC Annual Convention in Chicago as an opportunity collectively to consolidate the remarkable achievements of the past few decades.

Our discipline has made these advances because it has welcomed diversity and encouraged risks. And at a time when reclaiming a restricted educational legacy is prescribed as the cultural antidote to nightmarish visions of "a nation at risk," we ought to remind ourselves—and others—that arguments about reading the "right" materials are long-standing in the United States. Yet, there is an equally strong cultural tradition in this nation that makes more than a grammatical distinction between passively being at risk and actively taking risks—a tradition that suggests that taking risks is the right way to live, that taking risks creates special opportunities.

The CCCC convention program reaffirms each year the benefits of taking risks and demonstrates that "access," "excellence," and "diversity" are fully compatible terms—in theory and in practice. The 1990 CCCC Convention provides the occasion to celebrate—and to focus sustained attention on—the specific ways in which diversity infuses excellence and strengthens our community. In this spirit, the 1990 Convention can also increase the diversity of our community and its interests by providing access to—and working imaginatively with—new texts for reflection that to date have remained publicly unsung or unheard—from the literature that students write in freshman courses to the autobiographies of twentieth-century working men and women as well as the narratives of nineteenth-century slaves.

Many of the problems and issues that challenge our discipline have an immediacy to them, and all of them surface within the context of late twentieth-century American ethnic, social, economic, and political diversity and, more generally, of America's cultural pluralism. Consider, for example, such issues as responding imaginatively and responsibly to changing demographics, to recruiting and retaining minority students as well as female and minority faculty, to creating equitable terms and conditions for employment, or to mapping the intersections of literacy, literature, rhetoric, critical theory, and classroom ideology. Few, if any, of these issues are what John Dewey called "transient excitations." Despite their immediacy, both experientially and in their formulation, these strikingly different kinds of issues have strengthened the resolve of our community—to learn what we should know and to learn what we can and should do. Our organization's diversity makes it strong, and our shared purposes dignify the work each of us does.

In principle and design, the 1990 CCCC meeting will present as expansive a view of the field of composition studies as the membership proposes. And as scholars and teachers, we should continue to move unhesitatingly across the intellectual demarcations and institutional enclosures implicit in the "field" metaphor and resist strenuously the limitations of the professional identity embedded in what William Carlos Williams called "specialists in a certain pen." If the courses we teach serve as the dynamic locus where the processes of intellectual development and change infuse every aspect of our work with a broad range of students and texts, then our national organization, open to all, must continue to encourage diverse, interdisciplinary, and multicultural views of that work and to help accelerate its progress most productively and collegially. By identifying, understanding, and highlighting the breadth of our professional interests, we can discover the specific ways in which that diversity can strengthen our sense of community and shared purpose—our collective commitment to the principle and practice of a fully literate democracy.

FIG. 6.4.  Theme statement for the 1990 CCCC convention.

The conventional text schema, or rhetorical structure, of CCCC abstracts is that of problem—method—findings/conclusions. Thus, following a lengthy description of the problem, the reader might expect to find equally lengthy descriptions of the method employed and the findings/conclusions reached. But, although this may be the norm for many other disciplines, in CCCC it seems not to be. Instead, highest priority is given to the problem description with sometimes relatively little attention accorded the other two parts; indeed, we found many high-rated abstracts that barely even mentioned method and findings/conclusions. This can be explained in part by the fact that CCCC abstracts must be submitted in more than 10 months prior to the convention. Participants are likely, therefore, to submit "promissory" abstracts based on a "good idea" they would like to pursue rather than a more traditional abstract reporting on research already completed or well underway. Emphasis on problem descriptions may also be explained, in part, by the thematic nature of the convention. If each convention is oriented toward a certain theme, and if that theme is announced only 1 or 2 months before the submission deadline for abstracts, then submitters have only that short time to develop an idea that accords with the theme.

We would like to suggest, however, that there are two other factors involved here that have nothing to do with time constraints or other practical matters, but rather with epistemology. First, the field that CCCC represents, rhetoric and composition, is a highly interdisciplinary one and is still in a fairly early stage of development. Unlike older fields that have a narrower disciplinary focus, a well-established set of methodologies, and a large body of knowledge, rhetoric and composition is a heteroglossic field open to new directions and new intellectual currents. These new ideas need to be framed in a way that fits into the ongoing "conversation" of the field, an effort that often requires considerable space.

At the same time—and this is the second factor—the field seems, in recent years, to be moving increasingly toward a more hermeneutical mode of inquiry by adopting from literary studies the activity of problematization. A good example can be seen in the abstract from the 1989 convention shown in Fig. 6.5. This abstract, which was rated Excellent by both an external reviewer and the program chair (who called it "a must"), devotes well over 200 words to the problem description alone. The hermeneutic nature of the approach taken would seem to require such elaboration.

## Novelty

A third characteristic feature of the high-rated abstracts is that they all discuss the topic and problem in a way that would likely be seen by experienced insiders as original and therefore interesting. Consider the example from the 1992 convention presented in Fig. 6.6. This abstract contains originality on two levels. First, the author claims that neither of the two prevailing attitudes on portfolio evaluation are well founded. Drawing on extensive personal experience, he opens the way for an alternative approach. But instead of simply offering such an

---

### Composition, Rhetoric, and the Place of Writing
Rex Olson

Since the shift in focus from arrangement to invention in Composition study, our increased knowledge of the composing process and how to teach it has enabled Composition to present itself as a "discipline" in itself, independent of literary study and other disciplines. At the same time the preoccupation with process at virtually every level has displaced the more central, theoretical question: What is composition? What is its relation to "rhetoric" and "writing"? Despite what may appear as a resurgent interest in composition study, at least insofar as the academy recognizes literacy as one of its more pressing priorities, its place will never be secure unless it can demonstrate knowledge of its object, knowledge being the act of disciplining, of assigning an object its name and proper place.

The problem for composition is that it still does not know itself. We find evidence throughout the literature that terms such as "rhetoric," "writing," and "composition" are randomly substituted for one another as if interchangeable names for the same object/activity. Working in a (post)modern age, which has forced every discipline to re-think the origin and object of its knowledge, these terms can no longer be treated as sharing the same essential "place." Writing simply is not the "same" as composition or rhetoric, and until these differences are acknowledged as "real," as having "places" of their own, "writing" programs will always remain at risk of being displaced in another time.

In an oral presentation this paper will examine the source of confusion between these terms on the question of place, returning to Aristotle's *Rhetoric* and *Metaphysics* where Rhetoric and Composition are first named and placed as philosophic terms to control the displacing power of writing. This will allow us to see the "place" of misreading and the differences between Composition, Rhetoric, and writing, each of which comes by its name in locating the "same" object in different places. This means that if we claim our central object as the writing of texts, then Composition in its concern for achieving *transparency* (meaning) will be shown as inherently theoretical, despite longstanding criticism to the contrary; Rhetoric, in looking at *modalities* of persuasion on any given subject whatever, will have its place determined as texts "of such a kind," expository, persuasive, expressive, critical, etc.; and writing, naturally and necessarily (self) transgressive, will be concerned with its own *specificity*, the play of text in and against meaning. Unlike Rhetoric and Composition the place of writing cannot be contained by its name and definition, because we find it everywhere (Derrida, *Of Grammatology*). Whereas modernism may define writing as either "Composition" or "Rhetoric," postmodernism lets writing *be* writing—a place open in being defined, a place (of a place) which displaces.

In recognizing that such terms mean differently in a postmodern era, there is much more at stake in thinking about how we are to teach writing. This paper concludes by discussing the implication for teaching writing as something "other" than Composition or Rhetoric but which cannot exist without Composition or Rhetoric.

FIG. 6.5. A high-rated abstract from the 1989 convention, submitted in the "Theories of Composing" area.

alternative, he surprises us by complicating things. There *is* another approach, he says, but it is not a perfect one. Indeed, he suggests that there *cannot* be a perfect approach to portfolio evaluation, because of built-in limitations and an inherent trade-off (or "paradox," in his words) among the criteria involved.

Novelty is a highly valued feature of many forms of academic discourse, as we have pointed out in several chapters of the book up to this point (see chaps.

---

**Two Cheers for Portfolio Evaluation**
Jack Blum

While some experts in assessment and evaluation have suggested that portfolio grading is pedagogically neutral—nothing more than another method of gathering data about student writing—the majority of administrators and instructors seem to have adopted an attitude toward portfolio grading that is not only more enthusiastic but also less critical, seeing in portfolio evaluation the vessel of their hopes for liberating students from the insensitivities of impromptu instruments of assessment and for finally establishing an evaluatory system that is philosophically and pedagogically consonant with process theories of instruction.

My presentation will critique each of these attitudes in light of the experience of implementing a system of portfolio evaluation in a large composition program (2,000 students; 115 instructors). I will argue that portfolio evaluation is not pedagogically neutral: that it entails consequences in curriculum and pedagogy as well as in assessment, and that these pedagogical effects are not in all cases unalloyed benefits, even in terms of the process theories most often cited by advocates of portfolio grading. The paper will have three sections. I will begin by establishing a context for my analysis, briefly reviewing some of the criticisms leveled against prepared-impromptu holistic assessment. I will then discuss the three criteria used in our program to help design our portfolio evaluation system: low intrusiveness upon instructional diversity, low time-demand upon instructors, and low susceptibility to plagiarism or illegitimate collaboration. In doing so, I will illustrate what I consider a major difficulty with portfolio evaluation: that to optimize the evaluation system in terms of any one of these criteria is to undermine the other two. I will conclude by suggesting that to realize the genuine potential of portfolio grading we need to remain alert to its inherent limitations and paradoxes.

---

FIG. 6.6. A high-rated abstract from the 1992 convention, submitted in the "Portfolio Evaluation" area.

2 and 3 especially). Here too, in CCCC abstracts, it emerges as a key ingredient of the genre. But it is not the same kind of novelty that one encounters in science or in other positivistic disciplines. In those fields, novelty is generally seen as the contributing of a new bit of knowledge to a well-defined and gradually increasing body of knowledge; our informants in the "News Value" study used expressions like "another piece of the puzzle" and "adding to our knowledge." It almost always refers to the *results* of investigations, the *findings*, which are what readers of scientific journals, for example, almost always seek (see chap. 2).

In the case of CCCC, however, novelty is different. It is generally not seen as a piece of knowledge or the result of an investigation. Rather, novelty in CCCC appears to be associated primarily with the *framing* of a study, that is, how a topic is selected and problematized. Given the fact that most CCCC members received their academic training in English departments, we might expect a heavy reliance on the kind of problematization commonly found in literary criticism (as described earlier). Fahnestock and Secor (1991), in identifying five special topoi frequently employed by literary critics to construct arguments (appearance vs. reality, ubiquity, the paradox, *contemptus mundi*, and the paradigm), state that:

Ultimately all the topoi we have discussed reduce to one fundamental assumption behind critical inquiry: that literature is complex and that to understand it requires patient unraveling, translating, decoding, interpreting, and analyzing. Meaning is never obvious or simple for, if it were, the texts under scrutiny would not be literature and therefore would not be worthy of unraveling, interpreting, decoding, etc. (pp. 89–90)

A good example of the complexity prized in literary criticism can be seen in an abstract from the 1990 convention shown in Fig. 6.7.

The author of this abstract addresses a timeworn topic familiar to all compositionists: voice. Over the years, this topic has been so worked over that the author's chances of giving it a novel spin seem pretty remote. But she does, mainly by problematizing it on several levels. By the end of the first paragraph, one might expect her to simply rise up and defend the term against the attacks by Hashimoto and Axelrod. But she does not, at least not in any straightforward way. Instead, she shifts the ground slightly and talks about "the territory with which that term has become associated." We soon discover, however, that this "territory" itself is not without problems of its own. At this point, we might expect her to shift the ground again, but the author again surprises us: Instead

---

**The Ideology of Voice, the Fearsome Metaphor**
Kate Gardner

In a CCC article of February 1987, I. Hashimoto attacked the term 'voice' as "evangelical" and "anti-intellectual"; Rise Axelrod, in an MLA presentation of 1987, attacked it as part of the myth of presence, deconstructed by Derrida. Both Hashimoto and Axelrod held its metaphorical nature against it; both attacks are part of a larger debate about the nature of writing—a debate between what I will call the cognitive and the inspirational camps. This debate links critical and composition theory and has direct implications for writing pedagogy.

I want to use Hashimoto's and Axelrod's papers, not precisely to defend the term 'voice,' but to explore and defend some of the territory with which that term has become associated: territory defined by words like life, force, spirit, breath, honesty, originality, authenticity, truth. These are, of course, problematic terms, overused and sometimes misused, and our new wariness in using them—a wariness for which we are largely indebted to critical theory—has distinct benefits. But to excise them from our critical and teaching vocabularies seems to me at least as dangerous as to espouse them unthinkingly or simplistically. In particular, nervousness in the face of metaphor—the fear of vagueness or imprecision—indicates a paradoxical allegiance to knowability, to singleness of intention and effect, which current critical theory has posited as unattainable.

Voice and its attendant territory, then, define a nexus at which concerns and concepts drawn from critical theory, composition theory, and pedagogy come together; my aim will be to examine some of the ways in which the ideas and experiences from these three areas bear on each other.

---

FIG. 6.7.  A high-rated abstract from the 1990 convention, submitted in the "Ideology in Writing Instruction" area.

of abandoning this problematic territory, she deconstructs it. We should be "wary" about this, she advises, but not "nervous": Nervousness "indicates a paradoxical allegiance to knowability." Everything seems to hinge on the distinction between "wariness" and "nervousness," a distinction that may seem overly subtle to naive readers but which is presented as being highly significant in critical theory and perhaps a key to understanding the concept of voice.

Many of the high-rated abstracts in our corpus are based on such problematization, particularly those taking a more hermeneutical approach. But there are many others that embrace more of an empirical approach, and although these abstracts do engage in some problematization, it is not as extensive and intricate as the hermeneutical ones, nor does it typically constitute the main activity of the abstract. MacDonald (1987) described problem definition in academic writing in terms of a continuum, with literary interpretation near one end and scientific writing near the other. Scientific problems are usually clearly defined, because the scientific disciplines have communally agreed-upon goals and a system of central principles; the goals usually involve finding the broadest generalizations possible for a given set of data. Literary interpretation, by contrast, is relatively unconventional and unregulated; there are no agreed-upon goals or set of principles, except perhaps the principle that literature is too complex to be reduced to broad generalizations.

Let us summarize briefly at this point by suggesting that the three features of CCCC abstracts we have discussed—topic selection, problem definition, and novelty—together consititute the vague notion of "interestingness." They do not always carry equal weight; in a particular case, one dimension may sometimes override the other two. In the 1990 ("Voice") and 1992 ("Portfolio Evaluation") abstracts, for example, the topics by themselves are not particularly arresting. What makes these abstracts interesting is the way the authors define the issues and develop them. In some other cases (not presented here), the topic itself is so timely and so interesting that the abstract received a high rating even with a less than exciting discussion of the problem. In any case, whatever interestingness is to be found in a CCCC abstract will almost always be located in one or more of these features.

## Ethos

In addition to interestingness, the high-rated abstracts also typically project more of an *insider* persona do than low-rated abstracts. This factor may serve to reassure reviewers that the author is capable of following through on promises and will deliver a high-quality paper at the convention. After examining these hundreds of abstracts many times, our impression is that authors establish their ethos partly through their general knowledge of the genre (as represented by the three features just mentioned), and also by their use of terminology, special topoi, and explicit or implicit references to the scholarly literature of the field. As in any field, rhetoric and composition has its own technical argot. Each of the four sample abstracts we have looked at illustrates this. The 1988 abstract (Fig. 6.1) uses terms like *socialized, disenfranchising*, and *conceptual revision*, all of which would mark the author as conversant with current idiom. As we noted earlier, he also shows his awareness of community usage by putting quotation marks around the terms *right words* and *error*, both of which are associated with unfashionable prescriptivism. The 1989 abstract (Fig. 6.5) features deconstructionist terms like *place, displacement, specificity*, and *(self) transgressive*; and the author gives special meaning to ordinary terms by putting quotes around them, for example, "*other*," "*writing*," "*discipline*," and "*real*." The 1992 abstract (Fig. 6.6) uses terms from the language of assessment like *low intrusiveness, instructional diversity, time-demand*, and *prepared-impromptu holistic assessment*. The 1990 abstract (Fig. 6.7) features words associated with critical theory like *knowability, the myth of presence*, and *problematic terms*.

All four abstracts also illustrate the use of implicit or explicit references to the scholarly literature. The 1988 ("Tutoring") abstract explicitly cites Freire, Brannon and Knoblauch, Bakhtin, Harris, Bartholomae, and Bowles and Gintis. The 1989 ("Place of Writing") abstract cites Aristotle and Derrida. The 1990 ("Voice") abstract cites Hashimoto, Axelrod, and Derrida explicitly, and refers implicitly to Flower and Hayes, Scardamalia and Bereiter, Elbow, Macrorie, and other figures associated with the "cognitive and inspirational camps." And the 1992 ("Portfolio Evaluations") abstract, though not citing any scholars by name, refers to "some experts in assessment and evaluation" and "process theories of instruction," both of which would evoke, for knowledgeable insiders, specific names.

A third and equally important way of establishing ethos is through the use of recognizable special topoi. As Fahnestock and Secor (1991) put it in their analysis of the rhetoric of literary criticism:

> From a rhetorical point of view the locus of all the topoi is the interaction between arguer and audience, between logos and ethos. In other words, to invoke the topoi of paradox, appearance/reality, ubiquity, paradigm, *contemptus mundi*, and complexity serves to announce one's membership in the community of literary scholars who in turn will listen most attentively to the speaker with such credentials. Thus the special topoi inform the logos and constitute one manifestation of the ethos projected in a literary argument. (p. 91)

Almost all of the high-rated abstracts in our corpus draw on clearly identifiable special topoi, what Kinneavy (1983) called *ethnologics*, to develop their arguments. The most common special topos used for hermeneutical arguments is the complexity topos, supported by the appearance versus reality topos and the paradox topos. The abstract previously discussed in Fig. 6.7 is a good example. The most common special topos used for empirical arguments is what we might call the *extension of knowledge*, which might be paraphrased as follows: "We thought

---

**Placing Assessment in a Social Context: Grading in an
Interpretive Community**
Christopher Gould

Current theories place literacy in a social context. Since reading, responding to, and evaluating texts have thus become rhetorical acts with political consequences, they are appropriately addressed through collaboration. Although a variety of classroom practices have been devised to accommodate collaborative learning through the stages of planning, drafting, and revising, little headway has been made in the area of assessment.

This presentation will describe a collaborative project involving three instructors of first-year composition. Modeling the negotiations of a collaborative reading and written analysis of a published essay, the instructors were able to portray themselves as a distinct interpretive community. Subsequently cross-grading student analyses of a similar published essay, the instructors were able to enrich and complicate the notion of audience. The presentation will begin by setting forth the theoretical framework of the project, pointing out the inadequacies of conventional alternatives to the authoritative teacher as the sole reader and evaluator of student writing. These alternatives, despite the aims that impel them, lead to the formulation of an ideal text. The presentation will then describe the design and execution of the project and analyze results using data collected from student journals, participant observation, and the scoring of essays from experimental and control groups.

---

FIG. 6.8.   A high-rated abstract from the 1992 convention, submitted in the "Collaborative Writing/Learning" area.

we had a pretty good handle on this subject, but here is something we did not consider." This special topos is usually supported by a *multiple perspective* topos (similar to the ethnographer's *triangulation*, but not as systematic). In 1992, 19 of the 32 abstracts rated Excellent in our corpus were constructed around these two topoi. A good example is given in Fig. 6.8. The writer begins by establishing *a research space* (to borrow a term from Swales, 1990): He notes that collaborative learning has been given substantial attention as it relates to planning, drafting, and revising but that it has been relatively neglected when it comes to assessment. He thus deploys the *extension of knowledge* topos: We need to extend our knowledge and fill this gap. He proposed to do so through the *multiple perspectives* topos, specifically by "using data from student journals, participant observation, and the scoring of essays from experimental and control groups."

In both of the cases just discussed (Fig. 6.7 and 6.8), the writers establish a strong "insider" ethos by using special topoi that are not only recognizable but apparently highly valued within the CCCC community, at least for the year in question.

## CONCLUSION

Writing in 1990, we described composition studies as being engaged in a "turf war" between the empirically and hermeneutically oriented, and suggested that the pendulum seemed to be swinging toward the latter: "Interests reflected in the

[1990] CCCC program may be moving closer to those represented in the forums of the MLA" (Berkenkotter, 1991, p. 157). The present study lends some confirmation to that statement. Of the 25 abstracts rated Excellent in our 1990 corpus, 10 clearly follow a hermeneutic methodology and several others are partly hermeneutic (see Table 6.2). But it appears to have been a 1-year phenomenon. In 1991 the program chair's theme statement did not foreground literary hermeneutics, and in our 1992 corpus the number of empirical studies among the high-rated abstracts greatly exceeds (19 to 6) those taking a hermeneutic approach.

Looking at these figures, one is tempted to conclude that there was simply a reversal of the pendulum between 1990 and 1992, favoring empirical research at the expense of hermeneutic interpretation. On the surface, this might be true. But the real story, we think, is a bit more complicated. What we find, when we do a close textual analysis of each abstract, is what appears to be the development of *generic blends* in which the writer combines features from two, or even all three, of the subgenres indicated in Table 6.2. For example, an abstract might describe an empirical case study of some kind but draw on hermeneutics to first either problematize the issue or help interpret the findings. Or, it might propose some practical course of action but frame it in layers of interrogation. A good illustration of the former can be seen in Fig. 6.8, which is basically a report on an empirical study but with the discussion cast in hermeneutic terms (cf. the reference to an "interpretive community" [evoking Fish] in which the instructors were able "to enrich and complicate the notion of audience"). A good illustration of the latter can be seen in Fig. 6.6, where the writer offers his personal opinion about portfolio evaluation based on his years of experience as a writing program director. This falls into the category of *practice*, but it is not a simple here's-what-I-do type of abstract. Instead, the writer enriches it by problematizing the issue on several levels, to the point where he ends up describing an "inherent paradox" in portfolio evaluation. It is this problematization, as much as anything, that makes his abstract so interesting.

This blending of discourses seems most appropriate, in our view, for a field that is still searching for an identity. Rhetoric and composition is a highly interdisciplinary field, not yet a true discipline unto itself, and the theme statements from recent CCCC conventions, including some we have not covered in this study, all reflect this fact. It is a field made up of diverse elements and interests, held together in an ever-changing constellation. (See Appendix B, "Theme Statement for the 1992 CCCC Convention.") But there seem to be at least three constants in the field: training in literary/humanistic studies, a commitment to

TABLE 6.2
Basic Categorization of High-rated Abstracts

| Year | "Empirical" | "Practice" | "Hermeneutic" |
|------|-------------|------------|---------------|
| 1990 | 10 | 5 | 10 |
| 1992 | 19 | 7 | 6 |

> pedagogy, and an interest in grounded (situated) research. These three features are routinely interwoven in rhetoric and composition, and the hybridization of the CCCC abstract reflects this fact. Indeed, the "perfect" abstract for 1992, based on our sample, would be an empirical case study of some kind framed in hermeneutical problematization and having a clear pedagogical application. (We did not find any such perfect exemplars in our sample, but there were many that came close.) Ethnographies, case studies, and other kinds of contextualized empirical investigations featuring multiple methods of inquiry would seem to be particularly amenable both to hermeneutic framing and interpretation and to practical application.

On the other hand, our study has been limited to only 4 years' worth of conventions, and there have been clear differences from one convention to the next. One must be cautious about making any generalizations beyond any particular year. As noted earlier, the role of the program chair as gatekeeper is considerable. Program chairs are authorized to shape the program in whatever way they deem fit, and they generally do exercise that power. To see this, consider that there are at least two levels of gatekeeping: (a) the external reviewers and (b) the program chair. We have observed many cases where the reviewers rated an abstract Excellent and yet it was not included on the program. Presumably, the chair disagreed with the reviewers' judgments (although there are sometimes other considerations involved, such as putting papers together to form a cohesive panel).[6] In short, each convention bears the stamp of its principal gatekeeper, and it would be a mistake to project any trends from our data.[7]

In this chapter we have illustrated at least two of the principles laid out in
> chapter 1, namely those of form and content and of community ownership. The former states that "Genre knowledge embraces both form and content, including a sense of what content is appropriate to a particular purpose in a particular situation at a particular point in time" (p. 13). It is clear from our study, we think, that the ability to write a successful CCCC abstract depends on a knowledge of what constitutes "interestingness" to an insider audience, which in turn depends on timeliness, or *kairos*. The principle of community ownership states that "Genre conventions signal a discourse community's norms, epistemology, ideology, and social ontology" (p. 21). Here, too, we think our study provides some insight into the intellectual constitution of the rhetoric and composition community. It

---

[6]In one particularly unfortunate case, a very interesting abstract was submitted to the Technical Communication area one year, where it received an Excellent rating from a reviewer and the program chair but was not included in the program (presumably because of a bad "fit"). It was revised slightly and resubmitted the following year to the Discourse Analysis area. Again it received an Excellent rating, but again it was not included in the program. The author of this abstract probably never knew that she had written such an outstanding abstract. All she would have been told was that her paper had been rejected for the program.

[7]Unfortunately, we would not be able to test any such projections anyway (using post-1992 data), because the CCCC Executive Council decided in 1993, in the face of several logistical and ethical isssues, to no longer allow CCCC abstracts to be used for research purposes.

is a community so diverse that the 1992 program chair is probably right in describing it as a site where "multiple and overlapping communities" intersect (see Appendix B) rather than as a single, monolithic one. At the same time, though, if the abstracts from that 1992 convention are any guide, these overlapping communities may be going through a process of what we might call, after Bakhtin, *centripetalization*. Only time will tell.

# 7

# CONVENTIONS, CONVERSATIONS, AND THE WRITER: AN APPRENTICESHIP TALE OF A DOCTORAL STUDENT

[with John Ackerman]

> *A community of practice is an intrinsic condition for the existence of knowledge, not least because it provides the interpretive support necessary for making sense of its heritage. Thus participation in the cultural practice in which any knowledge exists is an epistemological principle of learning.*
> —Lave and Wegner (1991, p. 98)

This chapter presents a tale (Van Maanen, 1988) of a doctoral student learning the conventions and conversations of one community of practice. In it we develop the view that "the significance of generic categories . . . resides in their cognitive and cultural value, and the purpose of genre theory is to lay out the implicit knowledge of the users of genre" (Ryan, 1981, p. 112). We return to the notion of situated cognition, the principle of *situatedness* that we discussed in chapter 1:

> Our knowledge of genres is derived from and embedded in our participation in the communicative activities of daily and professional life. As such, genre knowledge is a form of situated cognition (Brown, Collins, & Duguid, 1989) that continues to develop as we participate in the activities of the [ambient] culture. (p. 7)

We contend that genre knowledge develops out of what Lave and Wegner (1991) called *legitimate peripheral participation* in a community of practice. Legitimate peripheral participation, they suggest:

> Provides a way to speak about the relations between newcomers and old-timers, and the activities, identities, artifacts, and communities of knowledge and practice. A person's intentions to learn are engaged and the meaning of learning is configured

through the process of becoming a full participant in sociocultural practice. This social process includes, indeed it subsumes, the learning of knowledgeable skills. (p. 29)

The study of the graduate student that we describe in the following chapter is one of cognitive apprenticeship. This student's growing understanding of the registers and other conventions of the academic discourse of his new community was both cognitive and the result of sociocultural processes. Thus, the acquisition of genre knowledge like other kinds of apprenticeship learning occurs, as Lave and Wegner (1991) suggested "through centripetal participation in the learning curriculum of the ambient community" (p. 100). Students begin as novices, or newcomers to the community and begin their enculturation through peripheral forms of participation that change over time as apprentices change their status from newcomers to members.

We believe this process of legitimate peripheral participation in professional and disciplinary communities is a unique feature of graduate or professional school life. It has been noted more than once that lack of access to a community's discourse is a major problem for undergraduate students. For example, Bizzell (1982a, 1982b) and Bartholomae (1985) argued that students entering academic disciplines must learn the genres and conventions that members of the disciplinary community employ. Without this knowledge, they contend, students remain locked outside of the community's discourse. Yet understanding the appropriate linguistic and rhetorical conventions is only a part of the difficulty that students entering an academic discipline confront. They must also become aware of the *conversations of the discipline* (Bazerman, 1994). Bazerman's metaphor refers to the issues and problems that are currently under discussion within the community. These issues and problems reflect the research programs or methodology that members of the community acknowledge within a scientific or scholarly field's prevailing paradigm. As June Davis' case illustrates (chap. 3 and 4), publishing work in professional journals or having grant proposals accepted for funding requires writers to negotiate their claims within the context of their subspecialities' accepted knowledge and methodology. This accepted knowledge and methodology is most often transmitted through course work and through working on research projects with established researchers or scholars who have achieved credibility within the field.

Understanding both the conventions and the conversations of an academic discourse community appears, therefore, to constitute a special kind of practitioner knowledge or what Bartholomae (1985) has called *advanced* literacy. We have illustrated in chapters 2–6 how writers draw on practitioner knowledge when they write for professional forums. How are the literate behaviors that accompany practitioner knowledge acquired? What is the process through which novices gain community membership? And what factors either aid or hinder students learning the requisite linguistic behaviors?

We examine these questions by documenting the struggles of one skilled novice writer, "Nate," during his first year in a PhD Rhetoric Program at a major university. Our focus is on the writer's texts, including both formal writing assignments submitted to professors, and self-reports given to one of the authors once or twice a week. Nate's texts are of particular interest as research data because they constitute the visible index of his initiation into an academic discourse community. The linguistic changes that these texts exhibit show a skilled novice learning the conventions and the conversations of the Rhetoric Program community and, by implication, those of larger research and scholarly subspecialities. These subspecialties include classical and contemporary rhetoricians, and cognitive psychologists interested in studying writing and reading processes.

## AN OVERVIEW OF THE STUDY

Our purpose was to examine the effects of the educational context on one graduate student's production of texts as he wrote in different courses and for different faculty members over the academic year 1984–1985. We used participant–observer and case study data collecting techniques, then analyzed the data using a combination of qualitative and quantitative measures. (See Appendix C for a discussion of methods.) Although the focus of this report is on the student's texts, much of the data on the educational environment was in the form of one of the investigator's field notes, audiotaped interviews of faculty and students in the rhetoric program, and the student's written self-reports.

### The Setting

The project site was Carnegie Mellon University (CMU), a private technical university known for its strength as a research institution. Several departments, including cognitive psychology and computer science, are ranked among the best in the United States. The research reported here was conducted in the university's English Department, specifically in the Rhetoric Program, which has been in existence as a doctoral program since 1980. The Rhetoric Program is interdisciplinary; the faculty teaching in it include cognitive psychologists, classical and contemporary rhetoricians, a linguist, a speech communication specialist, and a computer scientist. The program has strong ties with the Psychology Department, and it is quite common for English Department students to engage in directed research with psychology faculty. As students proceed through their graduate course work, they take a number of courses in historical rhetoric and contemporary rhetorical theory, but the spine of the program is the training that graduates receive in empirical research methodology.

This training is quite rigorous. Students take an introductory course, "The Process of Research" (team taught in 1984–1985 by a rhetorician and a cognitive psychologist), in which they are introduced to the principles of what faculty members call *rhetorical research*. In this course, first-year students read an introductory textbook on research in the social sciences, learn how to formulate research questions, learn the principles of experimental research design, and receive basic instruction in statistics. After taking this introductory course, students often choose to take advanced quantitative research courses in which they learn more about experimental research design and statistical procedures. Students also learn the technique of protocol analysis (gathering and analyzing data from subjects who "think aloud" while performing writing and reading tasks). Second-year students are encouraged to take courses on information processing theory in order to learn the intellectual model and theoretical assumptions that underlie protocol analysis methodology.

The Rhetoric Program's interdisciplinary curriculum appears to be aimed at producing an intellectual hybrid: a scholar familiar with historical and contemporary rhetorical theory, who can communicate through such journals as *College English* and *College Composition and Communication*, yet also a competent researcher who can write social science expository prose for educational research publications such as *Research in the Teaching of English* and *Written Communication*. Students therefore need to become knowledgeable about invention theory as well as ANOVA tables, Aristotle and Ong (1982) as well as Campbell and Stanley (1966), and experimental design confounds and the Pearson product-moment $r$ as well as contemporary writing pedagogy. Course work often includes carrying out research projects, giving oral presentations, and writing publishable or national conference quality papers. With these assignments, many faculty members in the Rhetoric Program attempt to introduce graduate students to the major communicative forums for research and scholarship.

## What Nate Brought to the Rhetoric Program

We were able to construct a picture of Nate as a writer before entering the Rhetoric Program through the following means: We read the writing Nate produced during the Summer 1984 as a Fellow in the National Endowment for the Humanities (NEH) Summer Seminar for College Teachers, used material from a personal history he authored describing his writing background, and reviewed his self-reports and taped interviews. Like any student entering an educational setting, Nate was by no means a blank slate (Dyson, 1984b; Heath, 1983). As an undergraduate and then as a graduate student in a curriculum and instruction (MAEd.) program, he had picked up some of the features of a literary journalistic prose style (Sims, 1984). He wrote with a well-defined persona, selecting active, colorful verbs and metaphoric constructions. Nate had done a considerable amount of writing in the 3 or 4 years before his entry into the Rhetoric Program, in the form of letters and memos to friends and colleagues, along with several conference papers. In these writings, Nate reflected on what he was learning from his classroom experiences teaching writing to students at an open admissions university in a small city in Missouri.

In Summer 1984, shortly before entering the rhetoric program, Nate participated in John Warnock's NEH Seminar, the Humanities Summer Seminar on "The Writing Process: A Humanistic Perspective." Warnock asked the members of the seminar to write informal responses for an hour each morning to what they were reading and discussing in the course of the 8 weeks. These writings were then shared within small groups. In some instances, an issue being mutually discussed by members of Nate's group led to a more formal statement. As one might expect, over the 8-week period a number of written "conversations" emerged among the seminar participants as well as a common vocabulary that can be observed in both the informal and more formal pieces that Nate wrote during this time. These conversations and the shared lexicon as well as the inquiry technique of using expressive writing for epistemic purposes lead us to call the Laramie Seminar a *discourse community*, although more ephemeral and loosely constituted than was the disciplinary community at CMU. The experience of writing in the Laramie community affected Nate deeply and gave him a firmly ingrained sense of himself as a writer. The following excerpt illustrates some of the features of his writing at this time. It is from a formal paper intended for an academic audience and is titled " 'Voice' in Reading and Writing: A Working Definition, Applications and Implication." In this paper, Nate argues that writers have two "voices," an "inner voice," and an "outer voice." The former he associates with Vygotsky's (1986) concept of inner speech, "coterminous," Nate argues, "with a writer's self ... taking the form of expressive writing ... the power behind free writing." In contrast, Nate claims that the outer voice is a construction, based on considerations of audience, purpose, and content. In the excerpt presented here, Nate enumerates the characteristics of the inner voice:

> A writer's inner voice is the inner speech that Vygotsky recognizes and is the fabric behind Murray's other self, the voice which rattles around in our head when we are cooking supper or silently reacting to a friend's tirade. It is the voice which fragments thinking, the voice of tangential ideas, of association, of caprice. It is the voice which allows for cognitive synapse, where disparate chunks of information are married or at least courted so that a writer begins to have something to say. The inner voice makes necessary the blank page. It calls for the codification of print so that the kaleidoscope stops turning for a moment.

In this excerpt, Nate's writing displays a number of linguistic and rhetorical features that are discrepant with the discourse conventions of social science expository prose that he will be expected to use later at Carnegie Mellon. First, there is a heavy use of sentential parallelism, so heavy in fact that, except for its syntactic complexity, it resembles that used by gospel preachers. All five sentences begin with the same subject, and four of the five end with embedded clauses. Second, the vocabulary ranges from informal (*rattles around*) to formal (*tangential, disparate*), from technical (*cognitive synapse*) to nontechnical (*cooking supper*). He mixes metaphors (*chunks* of information are *married* or *courted*) and uses other noncollocating terms like *fabric* and *kaleidoscope*. Finally, he strings out in listlike fashion rather than focusing hierarchically on a single main point. Familiar with the *process-oriented* composition pedagogy of Murray (1984) and Elbow (1981; cf. Faigley, 1986), Nate referred to this style as his voice. Like Murray (1984) and Graves (1983), Nate held the writer's voice to be as individual as a thumbprint. He was therefore taken aback early in his first semester at a professor's suggestion that his (and other graduate students') prose would come to reflect their thinking processes as research scientists:

> I always intended to be sensitized to the scientific canon, something I accept like father's lectures on handshakes, something I just need to do if for no other reason than you have to know something from the inside before you can ever fairly criticize it. I like to think analytically and I would hope that the bent toward research will satisfy an itch I've had for a long while. . . . But the line that chilled me was Young's conclusion that our training and experience will be reflected by our writing which will be the index of our assimilation of the scientific habit of mind. This is almost a Frankensteinian notion of what will happen to my mind. First I don't think that my writing will change. Of course I will learn patterns, but I have never been one to equate format with how someone composes. Form is etiquette. Handshakes. If I do change, and I agree that writing is a marvelous index, I wonder if I will be aware. . . . If anything in the last 8 years since I began to teach writing, I think I've moved dramatically away from academic writing and certainly from any traces of the scientific habit.

This excerpt, taken from one of his self-reports, shows Nate reflecting for the first time on the kinship between disciplinary-based thinking and writing. His initial response to this view is that formats and conventions are superficial—"etiquette, or handshakes," as he puts it. The last sentence of the excerpt hints at what was to be Nate's central writing conflict during his first year as a rhetoric doctoral student: the incompatibility between his approach to writing and the writing that was demanded of him in the program.

### Acquiring "Textual Competence"

One might best describe the shift that Nate was forced to make in graduate school as the transition from using a register for written discourse based on an informal oral repertoire to using a more formal register appropriate to academic discourse within a disciplinary community. The product of a dominant *expressive* movement in recent American writing pedagogy (see chap. 8), Nate was an articulate writer of informal prose (Chafe, 1982) who could control his text production processes when not burdened by such cognitively complex tasks as adopting an appropriate register (which included using rhetorical and stylistic conventions with which he was unfamiliar) and instantiating abstract concepts into prose (Flower & Hayes, 1984). Entering the Rhetoric Program, he discovered that he had to master both tasks within the genre of social science expository prose in order to write acceptable papers. This was no easy task for him. He reported that he listened more "to the words in my head than studying the words on the pages I was expected to emulate. Perhaps I acted like any student in a new environment, relying on what I knew best."

Acquiring *textual competence* (Brandt, 1983; cf. Hymes, 1971) within the Rhetoric Program necessitated that Nate draw on both *declarative* and *procedural knowledge* (Anderson, 1983). In using these terms, we refer to the distinction between a knowledge of facts ( i.e., "knowing that") and the application of facts to do a task (i.e., "knowing how"). For example, memorizing a recipe involves only declarative knowledge; executing that recipe, however, involves procedural knowledge because it requires one to translate facts into operations. Using Anderson's distinction enabled us to clarify Nate's difficulty in assimilating both the conversations and conventions of a new discipline. Procedural facility, or in Nate's case the translation of new information into text production, depended on prior mastery of a declarative, factual base from which to work.

During his early months in the program, Nate struggled to digest and manage unfamiliar material from his reading and at the same time reconcile a familiar informal style with what he thought were appropriate conventions of formal discourse. An analysis of his papers reveals several months of confusion during which his writing suffered from numerous stylistic problems: poor cohesion, disorganized paragraphs, lack of focus, and inappropriate vocabulary. For example, instead of using cohesion-promoting items such as logical connectives and discourse demonstratives, he relied heavily on first person pronouns (16.8 per 50 T–units or main clauses plus modifiers). This makes his prose seem very writer-based and makes it difficult for the reader to see how his ideas are linked together. The 25 expert expository writers in Sloan's (1984) study used explicit logical connectives in 29% of their T-units; Nate, by contrast, uses them in only 11.6%. Table 7.1 provides a comparison of these features for Nate's first semester writing (five academic papers) and his second and third semester writing (seven academic papers), indicating how he struggled at the beginning.

TABLE 7.1
Average Use of Three Linguistic Features per 50 T-units in Nate's Writings

| Semester | I's | | Connectives | | Discourse Demonstratives | |
|---|---|---|---|---|---|---|
| | M | SD | M | SD | M | SD |
| First (n = 5) | 16.8 | 12.3 | 5.8 | 1.6 | 4.8 | 1.9 |
| Second and third (n = 7) | 3.3 | 4.1 | 8.6 | 3.3 | 8.4 | 3.2 |

Although difficult to quantify, there are also obvious problems of information density and register in Nate's early writings. A good example of these problems can be found in a paper that Nate wrote for a course on "Computers in Education" during his first semester in the program. It begins as follows [sentence numbers added]:

> The Snoopy Tutorial looks at how writers compose when faced with definite constraints and at how those constraints, as they manifest in a text, can be lessened and finally solved through a tutor's intervention. (**1**) The exercise of a student writer composing a sentence which describes the action in a Snoopy cartoon and satisfying the content, order, and informational constraints in the directions produces examples of ways writers and tutors solve problems. (**2**) By studying a number of tutorial sessions, it is possible to locate the more highly problematic constraints and the corresponding strategies which lead to solutions. (**3**) This information could not only help the profession to understand the nature of specific writerly constraints but could also delineate those constraints approachable in a tutorial environment. (**4**)

The professor provided Nate with extensive written criticism, including the following general commentary:

> The work behind this report seems carefully done. The analysis goes far beyond and is more thorough than that done by other students on the assignment. Two problems with the report itself suggest that it is still what Linda Flower would call writer-based prose. First, the style is very dense, passive, sounds almost as if the writer is still wrestling with the ideas himself instead of trying to explain them to a reader. Second, the organization obscures the results.... All of the above characteristics are, I think, typical of reports written by those who are trying for the first time to wrestle a connection between observational and numeric data and a written verbal report.

That Nate is "wrestling with ideas" at the expense of organization and style illustrates how the acquisition of declarative knowledge precedes that of procedural knowledge. The absence of procedures for writing a "reader-friendly" research report is specified in the professor's editorial comments. In sentence 1, he crossed out the word *definite* and replaced it with *explicit*. He also circled the words *can be lessened* and *solved*, noting that "constraints are never lessened or solved—they are finally *adhered to* or *accommodated*." In sentence 4, he circled the word *profession* and wrote a question mark next to it, circled the -ly suffix on *writerly* without comment, circled the misspelling of *delineate*, and underlined *those constraints approachable* and wrote the comment "unclear." Much of this criticism, clearly, relates to Nate's misuse of terminology. But the professor's general comment of "very dense writing," written in the margin, probably refers as well to Nate's poor handling of given and new information distribution. Sentence 2, for example, has an extremely long (28-word) and complex subject noun phrase containing a good deal of textually new information. As is discussed in Langacker (1974) and Olsen and Huckin (1983), such heavy subjects often lead to problems of comprehension. The reader is forced to retain an unwieldy amount of information in short-term memory while searching for the main verb of the sentence.

Such negative feedback made Nate well aware of his stylistic shortcomings. He became frustrated in knowing that his writing was not good, that he had not cracked the code of academic writing. As he put it in a self-report:

> I feel like I'm butting heads finally with ACADEMIC WRITING—and it is monstrous and unfathomable. Young, Waller, and Flower write differently than me. I shouldn't lump them together because I know that they are quite different—and that what I see is only a final product—and that they have much more experience doing all kinds of writing—and that I should not compare myself with people—but I feel that they have access to the code and I do not.

Lacking the support for his writing that his colleagues in John Warnock's seminar and in Missouri had provided and faced with formal writing assignments such as critiques and research proposals and reports, Nate frequently "choked" when he tried to write. The following two excerpts illustrate the writer's difficulties and the way that he attempted to overcome them. These excerpts are from two pieces of writing that Nate did for an assignment in his research methods course. His professors had asked the class members to read and to write a critique of Mishler's (1979) "Meaning in Context: Is There Any Other Kind?", an essay that attacked the use of experimental methodology in educational research. The Mishler essay dealt with theoretical issues that would be largely unfamiliar to novice researchers. It is reasonable to assume that Nate had little specific background knowledge to bring to bear on his reading. Nevertheless, he did his best, discussing in his critique Mishler's essay from his perspective as a new graduate student and as a writing teacher:

> My questions about communication and instruction have carried me to an environment which espouses empirical research—research that at first glance suffers from the tunnel vision that Mishler condemns. I can see, if I look hard enough, research designs born from problem analyses that are horribly narrow, their results untranslatable. I can see this if that is what I want to find. I am a teacher–writer–researcher who has a history of discounting if not ridiculing universalities. I should agree with Mishler's main premise, that "features of human action are not amenable to scientific explanation" (p. 10). Because of my liberal, literary background, I should rejoice that someone with Mishler's authority and spirit has championed the cause for the creative spirit.

Nate's "voice" in this passage is strained, his prose convoluted. The rhetorical devices of parallel grammatical form (*I can see . . . I should*) and the growing expectation of rebuttal do not suffice for an explicit, hierarchical plan that a reader expects (Meyer, 1982). He does not appear to have a rhetorical strategy or purpose around which to organize his material. At the level of word choice, he seems to be striving for an academic register, but this attempt has produced a hypercorrect, overinflated diction. And the focus of the piece is not on the Mishler essay, as one might expect in a critique, but rather on Nate's personal response. These problems suggest that the writer was neither able to reframe the abstract propositional information in the Mishler essay to fit a situationally appropriate rhetorical purpose, nor able to marshal the necessary strategic knowledge of genre and register to meet the requirements of the assignment.

There are also problems with cohesion and coherence in this piece, as the following paragraph illustrates:

> I am not a social scientist nor a historian or philosopher of science so I cannot assail his criticisms of those disciplines. (**1**) In mine I see no evidence of the misuse of scientific experimentation. (**2**) Instead I see a bias against the possibility that theories produced borrowed methodologies offer something new, a different dialectical context to expedite new answers to problematic questions. (**3**) Mishler apparently is blind to a curious imbalance in language studies in English. (**4**) The vast majority of our truths are imitative of other disciplines or have been drawn from habit or authority, our authorities firmly in the anti-positivist camp. (**5**) A law that existed in the time that I was taking English classes was that you could learn to write by studying the writing of the masters. (**6**)

Each sentence seems to represent an independent thought, with little connection to the thoughts that precede or follow it. The first sentence, with its double negation, does not give a clear idea of what the rest of the paragraph is likely to be about. The second sentence apparently sets up a contrast with the first, but the part that is supposed to refer anaphorically and cohesively to the first sentence —"the misuse of scientific experimentation"—does not clearly do so. One has to infer the connection. In Sentence 3, we could reasonably expect the writer to "take sides" by supporting either Sentence 1 or Sentence 2, but he does neither; instead he seems to be going off in another direction, criticizing his own discipline on grounds other than a "misuse of scientific experimentation." Sentence 3 is overloaded with new information, and it is difficult to see how it relates to anything preceding it, either in the immediate paragraph or in preceding paragraphs. The focus of the sentence is on a *bias*, and one expects to find perhaps some continued discussion of this "bias" in Sentence 4. But in Sentence 4 the discussion veers off once again. Mishler is topicalized for the first time in the entire essay and the focus shifts to "a curious imbalance in language studies in English." We are not told what this "imbalance" is, and perhaps we expect the next sentence to help us out. But Sentence 5 provides no help; rather, there is yet another shift to a new topic ("the vast majority of our truths").

And so it goes. Instead of following a clear rhetorical pattern, the text seems to skip and jump from one thought to another. Only two of its six paragraphs can be said to be well written in a standard sense (good topic sentence, clear pattern of development, unity of focus). Instead of using thematic information in subject position to help maintain topical continuity from one sentence to the next, it often uses nonthematic "I" 's and *displaced* (Brown & Yule, 1983) or *new* referring expressions. In fact, one fourth of the sentences in this text violate the so-called *given-new contract* (Haviland & Clark, 1974).

A few days after handing in the Mishler critique, Nate wrote his professor a memo, titled "On Writing and Thinking in the Process of Research." In it he explained that he wanted to rewrite the critique because he knew it "was trash," but decided instead to:

> Explore why I choke on paper, and why the Mishler article is so important to me. Maybe the two are related. First Mishler. I read the article carefully, slowly, thoughtfully. Over the weekend before the critique was due I took his criticisms of empirical research and ran with them. I thought about my history of teaching and writing and the "truth" that I held so dear. As I tried to point out in my critique, I should be in Mishler's camp. For example, I have believed in the power of voice long before I began to wonder just what the phenomenon means. Like many teachers I trust what I tacitly understand. My curiosity and initiative brought me to this campus. [n.b., see first sentence of his formal paper and compare.] What I've found is another way of seeing [with] the very empirical tools that Mishler disdains.
>
> ... All of this is exciting for me. And troublesome. Mishler made me confront my re-tooling, my new orientation. I don't have the language to accurately capture what is going on.... Maybe it is too soon for me to critique Mishler ... I'm just beginning to understand the issues. This brings me to my writing in your course. Maybe I choke at the chance to critique Mishler because I try to say too much. You and Hayes are profound. My thoughts and the writing I've used to capture them are shallow.... I lost, if you will, my voice—or never had it from the start. ... I think it is more a question of trying to say too much too soon. The same grievous error plagues my writing as when my students write to please only the teacher. They write to become someone they really know nothing about.

This informal writing demonstrates Nate's active and constructive learning processes (cf. Dyson, 1984a, 1984b; Heath, 1983). Granted his memo was not a revision of the critique assignment, it is questionable whether Nate had sufficient theoretical knowledge of experimental research to address the questions that the Mishler essay raised. Instead, Nate dealt with his writing problem by creating a forum through which he could write expressively about his reading experience, rather than about the essay as a text. He then linked this experience with his views about the "scientific" research model he was learning, his professors as role models, and his diagnosis of his writing problems. Given his prior experiences writing to sympathetic readers in the NEH Seminar and in Missouri, it appears likely that he sought to replicate the communicative forum that had worked for him in those contexts.

## A Closer Look at Nate's Texts

Table 7.2 displays some of the major linguistic features of the two texts we have just discussed.

Perhaps the most striking linguistic similarity between these two texts is the high number of first person singular pronouns they contain. Indeed, there is so much foregrounding of the writer in these texts that one can reasonably consider them writer-based. A self-referential focus seems appropriate for the confessional nature of the memo, but it is altogether inappropriate for the kind of expository writing expected in the Mishler critique. In the 1 million-word Lancaster/Oslo-Bergen corpus of written British English, for example, it was found that the first person singular pronoun was used an average of only once per 1,000 words of scholarly prose but more than 5 times per 1,000 in miscellaneous informative prose and almost 15 times per 1,000 in fiction (Johansson, 1985). In a smaller corpus of 10,000 words from nine American composition theorists (see Table 7.4), we found that first person singular pronouns were used at the rate of only 2.7 per 1,000. Similarly, the average sentence length of 15.1 words per sentence in an informal memo seems quite normal, but 18.1 words per sentence in academic prose of this type is far below the average. The composition theorists whose writing we examined wrote sentences that were consistently longer than that, averaging 26.2 words per sentence.

In other respects, the two texts differ noticeably in linguistic features. First of all, the Mishler critique is filled with register errors, or sociolinguistically inappropriate vocabulary. For example, the word *horribly* in the sentence "I can see, if I look hard enough, research designs born from problem analyses that are horribly narrow," is almost certainly not the term that an expert writer of academic

TABLE 7.2
A Comparison of Nate's First Two Texts

| Criteria | Mishler Critique | Memo |
|---|---|---|
| Length in words | 950.0 | 860.0 |
| Number of sentences | 52.0 | 57.0 |
| Average sentence length | 18.3 | 15.1 |
| Number of "I's" (per 1,000) | 25.0 | 42.0 |
| Connectives (per 1,000) | 7.0 | 8.0 |
| Discourse demonstratives (per 1,000) | 10.0 | 6.0 |
| Register index (%) | 3.7 | 0.3 |
| Number of definite articles | 43.0 | 36.0 |
| Number of indefinite articles | 31.0 | 11.0 |
| Article ratio | 1.4 | 3.3 |

expository prose would use. It is too evocative, too hyperbolic for this kind of writing. The *register index* is a simple way of quantifying such vocabulary problems, denoting, for any particular text, the percentage of off-register words or phrases. Though raters working independently will seldom reach perfect agreement on off-register vocabulary, they are usually close enough in their overall assessment to make the evaluation a valid one. Our three raters were English professors with publications on composing theory in the standard journals of the field. In the case of Nate's Mishler critique, one rater found 25 register flaws, another found 35, and the third, 46. This yielded an average of 35 register flaws in 950 words of text, or approximately 3.7%. Words like *mindframe, horribly, looking glass*, and *ridiculing* were unanimous selections as being off-register.

In personal letter or memo writing, however, a broader range of lexical choices is allowed. And indeed, Nate's memo contains both informal Germanic words like *trash, choke*, and *swell up* and more formal Latinate terms like *magnum opus, phenomenon*, and *eloquent*. Such a mixture seems perfectly acceptable in this context. In fact, words like *horrible* and *blind*, which were judged inappropriate in the Mishler critique, appear also in the memo and seem quite appropriate there. Because this kind of writing is highly personal and not very conventionalized, an accurate assessment of its register index can be made only by the intended reader. This reader felt there were only four register errors (*ran with them, forsaken, grievous error*, and *plagues*).

The other major linguistic difference between these two texts has to do with cohesion and coherence. Subjectively, one feels that Nate's memo is far more cohesive and coherent than his critique. It is difficult to quantify this difference, especially when both texts contain such an excessive number of *I*'s in sentence subject position. The most common methods of analyzing cohesion and coherence rely on the fact that sentence subjects are usually carriers of topical information (e.g., Witte, 1983) or of given information (e.g., Vande Kopple, 1982). But first person pronouns used repeatedly in subject position represent given information in only a trivial sense and cannot be said to represent topical information at all. Hence, the standard methods are relatively ineffective when applied to such texts. What seems to work better as a measure of cohesion and coherence in cases like these is the ratio of definite articles to indefinite articles, as suggested in Johansson (1985). Definite articles usually mark given information, especially through anaphoric reference, whereas indefinite articles usually mark new information. Hence a high definite-to-indefinite article ratio tends to indicate a high degree of thematic continuity in a text. Furthermore, because articles occur in a variety of syntactic positions, not just sentence subject position, this measure avoids the problem of excessive first person pronoun usage just described. In the 10,000-word corpus of writings by nine composition theorists, we found the average article ratio to be 3.1:1 (see Table 7.4, which appears later in the chapter ). In Nate's memo the ratio comes very close to that (3.3:1), but in his critique it is a low 1.4:1. This finding constitutes evidence that his academic writing style at this early stage lacks the cohesion and coherence found in expert academic writing and also in his own less formal writing.

In writing the follow-up memo to his professor, Nate seems to have adopted a different, more effective rhetorical stance. Essentially, he seems to have recognized that his earlier critique suffered mainly from insufficient domain knowledge and that the only way he could remedy this shortcoming for the time being would be to change the universe of discourse to one where he had more domain knowledge. One way of doing this would be to focus less on the Mishler piece and more on his (Nate's) own personal history and present circumstances. Not only did this move put Nate on firmer ground in terms of domain knowledge, it also let him use a narrative form of presentation. Psycholinguistic research (e.g., Graesser, Hoffman, & Clark, 1980) has shown that it is easier to create coherence and cohesion with a narrative pattern than with any other, and this is certainly a case in point.

Therefore, in writing the memo to his professor, Nate took a more personalized approach than he had in his earlier critique. First, he used a letter format with personal first-name salutation and, thereafter, many uses of *we* and *you* in addition to *I*; in effect, he narrowed the communication situation to a two-person dialogue. Second, he used a predominantly narrative pattern for each of the major paragraphs as well as for the memo as a whole, inserting many time adverbs and verb tense alternations to help keep the reader on track. Third, apparently confident of the higher degree of shared knowledge existing between him and his professor, Nate used a much higher percentage of definite articles in relation to indefinite ones. Definite articles, unlike indefinite articles, typically indicate what the writer considers to be shared knowledge.

Many of the ideas discussed in the critique are repeated in the memo, but in a more comprehensible form. For example, corresponding to the critique excerpt just discussed is an excerpt from his memo, as follows:

> My curiosity and initiative brought me to this campus. What I've found is another way of seeing—the empirical tools that Mishler disdains. I have not been asked to give up anything that I learned before coming here. I still have my tacit truths, but I have been asked to entertain the possibility that science can show me how to think differently. Mishler doesn't seem to understand that, at least in the field I know, English, we are forever locked into context and that nothing is forsaken if we limit context. Nothing is lost if we use science to gain a different perspective. He also does not confront the barren and disjointed truths that have ruled for the last 80 years in English.

Instead of writing "a different dialectical context to expedite new answers to problematic questions," as he did in the critique, Nate simply refers to "another way of seeing," clarifying that further by suggesting that we "use science to gain a different perspective." As in the critique, there is a preponderance of *I*'s in this writing. But here they work. In personalizing his argument and making it less abstract, Nate has constructed an I-based scenario where the I versus Mishler opposition is topicalized, making a focus on the first person pronoun fully justified.

Nate was to repeat the strategy of writing informally to work out his ideas without having to juggle the constraints imposed by genre and register. He used this technique to reflect on what he was learning in his self-reports (in which such writing was encouraged) and in letters to friends; he also continued to write informal memos and notes to professors through much of the first year. As one might expect, Nate soon realized that these informal writings would not substitute for the required formal academic discourse. Nevertheless, the technique of using expressive writing to explore new ideas had considerable heuristic power for him during the period that he had to make the adjustment from using *oral* to *literate* strategies (Tannen, 1982) in his academic papers.

## Rats in Boxes: Increasing the Flow of Thought by Ignoring Constraints

The informal, expressive pieces Nate wrote provided him the opportunity to give free rein to his intellect. It appears that, by ignoring many of the constraints imposed by the genre and register conventions of the academic writing expected of him, he could more easily explore new ideas. In his first semester, as exemplified in the two Mishler pieces, he would do this by writing a *companion document* that embodied a complete switching of modes, that is to say, the informal epistolary genre instead of the formal academic one. By the second semester, however, he was able to perform the same kind of switch within the same document, relaxing some constraints but adhering to others.

An example of this selective relaxation of constraints appears in a piece of writing Nate did for Berkenkotter (the participant–observer researcher) during the second semester while taking an independent study course. This course, which enabled him to get credit for participating in the present case study, required him to write a series of short responses to the articles he was reading on case study and ethnographic research. One of these he titled "An Introduction to Ethnographic Research: Old Rats and New Boxes." The essay provides considerable information about Nate's reading and writing processes at a time in the program when he was acquiring, but had not yet mastered, new conventions.

Nate began the piece by writing an introduction in the register that he had adopted for academic critiques:

> Kenneth Kantor recently pointed out the impact ethnographic study is having on research in English Education (Kantor [et al.], 1981). Studies concerned with "hypothesis generation" and the dynamism of language in context proliferate. In their wake grows a more refined appreciation and articulation of the methods and purposes driving ethnographic research: extended, participatory roles for the researcher and converging measures of data collection and analysis. This critique attempts first to review and catalogue fundamental aspects of good ethnographic research.

On the second page, however, finding a metaphor for characterizing the difference between experimental and ethnographic research, he dropped the academic register:

> It is ... the context that distinguishes ethnography from experimental research ...
> experimental studies are chided for putting rats in boxes, a hunk of cheese hidden
> by a labyrinth of unfamiliar corridors and decisions. Ethnographers study rats in
> boxes as well—it is the box, however, that often demands their most scrupulous
> attention. ... As ethnographers we could take notes on the box—the shape, dis-
> tinctive patterns, physical characteristics and history—how other rats have solved
> the cheesy dilemma and [ask] what other uses for the box are there besides befud-
> dling rats? We could certainly watch and take notes as an outside observer, peering
> over the walls of the box as the rat negotiates the maze. As we watch over time,
> we begin to isolate patterns in our observations and in the rat's behavior, patterns
> that could lead to new hypotheses ...

Nate then extended the rat-in-the-box metaphor to take a humorous jab at
conflicting research approaches:

> As ethnographers we could balance our field notes with interviews of the rat at
> timely and spontaneous moments. Retrospective and introspective accounts by rats
> are suspect because of the inconsistency of recall, but these recollections have a
> higher currency because they occur more naturally inside the box and in closer
> proximity to the rat's cognitive processes. As our rat rounds a corner looking for
> the illusive limburger and hoping not to find a blank wall or an electric shock, the
> ethnographer might interrupt and ask:
>
>> What was your reaction to that last turn?
>> Do you know why you made it?
>> Have you made similar turns in the past?
>> Where to next?

Nate concluded the passage by using the metaphor to suggest a connection
between ethnographic and cognitive process research:

> Finally the ethnographer can look at what physical traces of cognitive activity the
> rat leaves behind. In boxes of language study—schools, disciplines, programs and
> classes—this means written texts, be they formal assignments, notes, rough drafts,
> memos, letters or self-reports.

The rat in the box metaphor was a serendipitous and strategic discovery that
gave Nate the opportunity to reflect on not only the Kantor article, but on ideas
and values that he was encountering in courses and through talk with peers and
faculty members. The metaphor appears to have been a flexible yet concrete
imagistic representation, allowing Nate to draw on and integrate material from
long-term memory.

In a self-report written immediately after he wrote the essay draft, Nate claimed
to have redirected his commentary from an initial "dead reader of deader critiques
to an outside audience ... who doesn't have any vested interest in the (meth-

odological) squabbles we know so well . . . interested in understanding what I'm trying to say and how I'm saying it." If Nate's subjective account accurately captures his thinking processes, he shifted audience representations, thereby creating a new rhetorical agenda for himself. He had done this before (in writing the memo to his rhetoric professor after doing the Mishler critique), and in that case he had adjusted his register, his sentence length, his use of discourse demonstratives, and his article ratio. In short, he had found it difficult to express himself in an academic style of writing and had reverted to his more accustomed, informal style. Here, however, he does not find it necessary to make such a total shift. In using the extended "rat-in-the-box" metaphor, he shifts into a casual register (*cheesy dilemma, befuddling rats, elusive limburger*) and uses a number of *we's* and *our's*, but in other respects—sentence length, discourse demonstratives and connectives, article ratio—he *does not* significantly change his style. This can be seen in Table 7.3, which compares that part of the extract occurring before the point where the rat-in-the-box metaphor is introduced and that part occurring after. Average sentence length, connectives and demonstratives, and article ratio are virtually the same in both parts of the text. However, there is a significant infusion of first person pronouns in the second part, and the register changes: All of the off-register words in the first part, as marked by the reader for whom the text was written, are perceived to be too formal or too belletristic, whereas 64% of the off-register words in the second part are perceived to be too casual.

In sum, at this stage in his development, Nate seemed to be comfortable enough with the academic style to stay in it even when, for inventional purposes, he elected to introduce an extended metaphor that was not appropriate to that style. He thus was able to pursue his intellectual development in this paper (by using a metaphor that helped him crystallize his thinking about the topic) without completely abandoning the linguistic conventions of his discipline. The "rat-in-the-box" metaphor caused him to use off-register vocabulary, certainly, but it did not detract otherwise from his attempts to use a basically academic style of writing.

TABLE 7.3
Nate's "Rat-in-the-Box" Text

| Criteria | First Part | Second Part | Total |
|---|---|---|---|
| Length in words | 324.0 | 699.0 | 1023.0 |
| Number of sentences | 16.0 | 34.0 | 50.0 |
| Average sentence length (words) | 20.3 | 20.6 | 20.5 |
| Number of first-person pronouns | 0.0 | 14.0 | 14.0 |
| Connectives and discourse demonstratives (per 1,000) | 21.6 | 21.5 | 22.0 |
| Off-register words | | | |
|   Too formal or belletristic | 13.0 | 8.0 | 21.0 |
|   Too casual | 0.0 | 14.0 | 14.0 |
| Article ratio | 1.8 | 1.7 | 1.7 |

## Writing as Legitimate Peripheral Participation in an Academic Discourse Community

By the end of his first year in the Rhetoric Program, Nate had gained increasing control over the language in his texts. His ability to manage information within prescribed conventions is evident in his papers from this period. He had also learned to better accommodate his register to the rhetorical context in which he wrote. But he had learned something else that was to serve him as a writer: He had become familiar with the central concerns and disciplinary issues with which Rhetoric Program faculty were concerned. An examination of a bibliographical essay that he wrote for Richard Young, the professor of his "Theories of Invention" course, will illustrate the ways in which Nate had learned to add his contribution to a formal "conversation" within the community of contemporary rhetoric scholars.

Nate's professor had been one of the initiators of this conversation, having written numerous articles on the emergence of rhetorical invention in composition studies (cf. Young, 1976, 1978, 1980) as well as co-authoring a well-known textbook on the use of tagmemic invention as a heuristic or discovery procedure (Young, Becker, & Pike, 1970). A number of Young's students (Katz, 1983; Lamb, 1974; Odell, 1970, 1974, 1978) and others (Nugent, 1980; Rabianski, 1980) had conducted empirical studies to evaluate the usefulness of tagmemic invention in the composition classroom. In effect, Young's work had created a following of scholars (e.g., Lauer, 1967, 1972) and researchers who debated in professional journals the value of using structured inquiry procedures as a catalyst to writing with depth and perception about a subject matter. Behind this debate were a number of significant pedagogical as well as theoretical questions: Can freshmen writers with limited intellectual experience and with limited discourse schemata emulate the imaginative processes observed in skilled adult writers? Is creativity in writing a process that can be facilitated by the use of conscious strategies? Can pedagogical practices be developed from theoretical constructs such as Kenneth Pike's theory (cited by Young, 1978) of universal rational thinking processes? How is the adequacy of a theory-driven practice to be ascertained?

The genre of the bibliographical essay is particularly well suited to helping young scholars develop a sense of the history of present issues in the discipline (a goal to which Young was committed). It also enabled Nate to "give shape and emphasis to [his] citations and commentaries" (Tate, 1976, p. ix). As one might imagine, much of this shape and emphasis was strongly affected by the interpretative framework of his professor's scholarly writings. Yet at the same time, Nate did not simply parrot what his professor had said, but added his contribution to an inquiry his professor had helped to initiate. We see Nate's use of this forum as one instance of his legitimate peripheral participation in the community of rhetoric and composition scholars that he was joining in the course of graduate study.

In a 1978 essay, "Paradigms and Problems: Needed Research in Rhetorical Invention," Young had invoked Thomas Kuhn's (1970) theory of scientific revolutions to suggest that (with qualifications) the discipline of composition studies was undergoing a "paradigmatic" shift between a "current-traditional" and a "new" rhetorical theory. To support this claim, Young argued:

> During the last fifteen years, two extremely important changes have occurred in the discipline: composition is now being examined as a process, and four substantial theories of invention have emerged, classical invention, Kenneth Burke's dramatistic method, D. Gordon Rohman's prewriting method, and Kenneth Pike's tagmemic invention. It is no accident that the shift in attention from composed product to the composing process is occurring at the same time as the reemergence of invention as a rhetorical discipline. Invention requires a process view of rhetoric; and if the composing process is to be taught, rather than left to the student to be learned, arts associated with the various stages of the process are necessary. (Young, 1978, p. 35)

After having summarized each of the "four substantial theories of invention," Young called for new research "directed toward determining the adequacy of the present paradigm and the proposed alternatives. . . . With the emergence of competing theories comes the necessity to judge and to decide" (p. 39).

Nate's essay appears to be a response to his professor's call for research directed at judging and deciding. To understand the ways in which this essay both reflects and adds to a disciplinary conversation, one must look at both the writer's word choice and at his rhetorical position. From the first perspective, one can observe many statements in the essay that reflect Nate's professor's conceptual framework. For example, the essay's title, "Structured Heuristics: Problems in the New Paradigm," echoes his professor's "Paradigms and Problems: Needed Research in Rhetorical Invention." The title also promises that the essay will define problems that have arisen in the wake of the emergence of the new paradigm that his professor's (1978) essay had identified. (Nate had not read *The Structure of Scientific Revolutions*, but he was familiar with his professor's Kuhnian appropriations.) One also hears an echo of Young's (1976) comment, "Invention usually begins with determining the *status,* or crucial issues to be argued" (p. 9) in Nate's purpose statement: "By classifying the criticism and isolating commonalties, I hope to arrive at the *stasis* or crucial issues in the debate in order to direct further evaluation and discussion of the role of structured heuristics in the teaching of composition."

Though complex and perhaps somewhat obscure, this language is much more reader-based than the formal prose that Nate was writing during his early months in the program. But although one hears many echoes of his professor's language and intellectual framework in Nate's commentary, the rhetorical position that he adopted in the essay indicates that he did not merely reiterate his professor's views. He did not, for example, share his professor's preference for teaching practices derived from theoretical constructs (Young, 1978, pp. 38–39). Nate's criterion for the evaluation of a teaching method was much more pragmatic:

> If rhetorical models and theories cannot be adequately transferred to composition instruction, they are useful only for aficionados and historians. . . . Criticisms and questions leveled at how a heuristic model succeeds or fails in the classroom are far more useful in that they are related to problems inherent in the challenge of teaching writing.

This preference for criticism based on practical, as opposed to philosophical (and therefore ideological), grounds suggests that Nate's rhetorical position was affected by his identity as a writing teacher. He furthermore identified his essay persona by noting "For this teacher . . ." This teacher persona, however, is not the same Nate who had been frightened months earlier by the suggestion that he would assimilate the "scientific habit of mind." On the contrary, Nate contended that "questions and complaints about the practicality of heuristic models and strategies should be answered—and carefully—with evidence." This comment clearly reveals a growing identification with the values of a writing research community.

Nate supported his claim by arguing that empirical research is a necessary adjunct to theory, a position narrower than that of his professor who had also called for historical and metarhetorical research to arbitrate issues arising from competing theories. After referring to several empirical studies conducted by his professor's students and by others who addressed issues raised by the professor's detractors, Nate both qualified and expanded on his position that the adequacy of structured heuristics (and, by implication, other practices based on theoretical models) must be determined by carefully controlled studies. He may have felt that he overstepped his bounds (that is, offended his professor who was a theoretician rather than a researcher) when he commented: "I do not mean to imply that current research has countered the attacks made on structured heuristics—or that teachers, scholars, and theorists should simply turn the question of adequacy over to researchers."

Despite this qualification, Nate argued eloquently in the following and concluding paragraph on the need for empirical research to resolve debates raised during changes in a dominating paradigm:

> If Thomas Kuhn's descriptions of paradigm shifts in scientific communities are accurate, it is fair to expect resistance to change and the display of deeply rooted loyalties to the current paradigm. With regard to invention we are beyond the stage of simply encountering anomalies or interesting phenomena; we know that students invent and (that) our interaction with their invention processes is essential and problematic. We have built and are still building new models that are an attempt to address contradictions and inconsistencies in theory and practice. "The resistance to the new paradigm will dissipate when its advocates can demonstrate that it will

solve problems . . ." (Hairston paraphrasing Kuhn). Demonstration is the key, and though the call (for) more research frequents all too many essays, in this case that call is most appropriate. The scant findings available speak all too clearly to criticisms raised and point directly at further study. The question of adequacy of structured heuristics, their place and purpose, is far too difficult and demanding to be answered by unsubstantiated argument. In this case, rhetoric alone is not the answer.

This passage weaves together Young's Kuhnian perspective with Nate's own conviction that "difficult and demanding" issues need to be addressed through research rather than the arguments in professional journals he had reviewed. His rhetorical aim here seems to be to achieve a consensus with his professor, yet at the same time make his point that theoretical claims must be substantiated by research.

On another level, Nate can be seen to be positioning himself within an academic conversation. We are tempted to add that he is positioning himself—quite actively—within a discourse, rather than assuming a positioned subjectivity. One can see in this essay the image of both Nate the classroom teacher and Nate the empirical researcher. His year in the Rhetoric Program had not changed his dedication to teaching, yet he had come to view issues in composition pedagogy from a perspective mediated by his training in research methodology. He had mastered the conventions of the bibliographical essay, and he wrote with the fluency of one who has become acquainted with one of many conversations in a disciplinary community.

This is not to say that Nate had fully assimilated the linguistic style of his professor or the other composition theorists and researchers whose work he was reading. He continued to use considerable hyperbole in his diction, with terms like *shake, attack, revolutionary, draws fire, threatens the political sovereignty of, champion, a deeply rooted distaste and fear, inhuman, warn, recoil from, potential danger, chastise fervently*, and *scorn*. As indicated by our register judges, such language is unlikely to be used by any of the rhetoricians or composition theorists whose writing Nate was reading and citing at the time. When he wrote, "Tagmemics with its roots in tagmemic linguistics and the social science problem-solving paradigm also draws fire for promising more than it can deliver and for threatening the political sovereignty of both students and scholars of language and literature," most scholars, we believe, would feel that he is exaggerating and thus being imprecise. But, whereas such imprecision occurred frequently in his earlier writing, now it occurred only occasionally: Only 1.3% of his words in this paper were marked by our judges as being off register, compared to 3.9% in the Mishler critique. Other signs of increasing linguistic competence can be seen in longer sentences, averaging 26.7 words, almost as long as those in his professor's own writing (28.4). His article ratio is up from 1.4:1 to 1.8:1, indicating greater thematic continuity. And, perhaps most importantly, he has stopped overusing the first person singular pronoun. In the two papers and one memo that he had written earlier for this professor, he had averaged 31 "I" 's per 1,000 words; here there is only one. Instead of foregrounding himself and his feelings and beliefs, he now seems to be concentrating primarily on the subject matter, employing conventions that communicate (semiotically) distance and objectivity.

## A Summary Overview of Nate's Linguistic Development

Perhaps the best indicator of this development of Nate's is the set of five papers he wrote for this one professor:

1. The Mishler critique, 11-5-84
2. The follow-up memo, 11-15-84
3. A paper on "How and Why Voice is Taught," 12-11-84
4. The bibliographic essay on structured heuristics, 5-23-85
5. A paper on "Expressive Writing in Academic Discourse Communities," 9-15-85

We analyzed in detail the first 1,000 words of each of these texts (1 and 2 were only 950 and 860 words long, respectively), paying special attention to those features that, impressionistically, appeared to be most salient: register, diction, coherence and cohesion (including thematic continuity), average sentence length, given–new information distribution, and first person subject pronouns. Ten other texts of the same genre that Nate had cited favorably in his own writing were similarly analyzed to see if there is a *stylistic template* for this kind of writing that Nate could emulate. Ten thousand words is, of course, too small a sample to make generalizations about the entire field of composition theory, and the 9 writers of these 10 texts are certainly not representative of the field as a whole. But because Nate's thinking about the field was clearly being influenced by these particular texts and others like them, it seems reasonable to assume that if he were going to change his linguistic style in any way, these texts would be representative of the role models on which he might draw. And, indeed, although there is of course some variation from author to author, these writers do seem to conform to certain stylistic norms for this genre. Table 7.4 gives the relevant data.

If we analyze Nate's own writing in terms of these stylistic norms, we find that in some respects it is developing fairly steadily in the direction of these norms, although in other respects it is not. The figures are given in Table 7.5. Except for Text 2, the memo, Nate's writing style displays a consistent increase in syntactic complexity, as shown in average sentence length, to the point where he is actually producing longer and more complex sentences than the composition theorists he admires. His predilection for first person pronouns, no doubt a product of his expressive-writing background, disappears beginning with Text 4. And his register index shows a spectacular decrease in hyperbole, colloquialisms, and inflated diction: in his last two texts he is using one fourth as many off-register

TABLE 7.4
Some Stylistic Features of Nate's Reading in Composition Theory

| Author | Average Sentence Length | Connectives | Discourse Demonstratives | I's | Article Ratio | Register Index (%) |
|---|---|---|---|---|---|---|
| Bizzell (1982) | 25.1 | 12 | 11 | 0 | 3.9 | 0.4 |
| Hairston (1984) | 29.4 | 17 | 10 | 3 | 3.6 | 0.4 |
| Hillocks (1982) | 25.7 | 11 | 4 | 0 | 2.5 | 0.1 |
| Kantor (1975) | 26.3 | 10 | 7 | 2 | 5.4 | 0.3 |
| Kinneavy (1971) | 26.0 | 9 | 7 | 0 | 2.6 | 1.5 |
| Kroll (1981) | 21.7 | 13 | 8 | 4 | 2.3 | 0.2 |
| Odell (1978) | 25.7 | 18 | 17 | 10 | 1.7 | 0.2 |
| Shafer (1981) | 25.6 | 12 | 11 | 5 | 3.5 | 0.6 |
| Young (1971) | 27.6 | 6 | 7 | 0 | 3.3 | 0.3 |
| Young (1978) | 28.9 | 5 | 3 | 3 | 2.5 | 0.1 |
| Average | 26.3 | 11.3 | 8.5 | 2.7 | 3.1 | 0.4 |

words as in his first text, indicating that he is adapting his discourse to the norms described earlier. Part of this improvement in register is due to his abandoning his use of hyperbole in Text 5. Until then, as pointed out earlier, he had often used colorful terms like *horribly, at the mercy of,* and *inhuman.* But in Text 5 he tones his diction down and relies on more standard social science terminology like *encounter resistance, are minimized,* and *was found less effective than.*

On the other hand, he does not appear to have made much improvement in coherence and cohesion. His use of sentential connectives drops off slightly, as does his use of what we are here calling discourse demonstratives, that is, those demonstrative adjectives and pronouns that refer to information in sentences other than the one in which they are used. The composition specialists who used relatively few connectives and discourse demonstratives apparently compensated by using a large number of definite articles. Kantor, for example, used only 10 connectives and 7 discourse demonstratives but 92 definite articles, more than any of the other eight writers. And Young used 79 and 76 in his two 1,000-word

TABLE 7.5
Some Stylistic Features of Nate's Writing for His Rhetoric Professor
(1,000-Word Samples)

| Text | Average Sentence Length | Connectives | Discourse Demonstratives | I's | Article Ratio | Register Index (%) |
|---|---|---|---|---|---|---|
| 1 | 18.3 | 7 | 10 | 25 | 1.4 | 3.7 |
| 2 | 15.1 | 8 | 6 | 42 | 3.3 | 0.3 |
| 3 | 19.1 | 9 | 6 | 27 | 2.3 | 2.6 |
| 4 | 26.7 | 5 | 3 | 1 | 1.8 | 1.3 |
| 5 | 34.3 | 7 | 5 | 1 | 1.3 | 1.1 |

samples, topped only by Kantor's 92 and by Hairston's 80. But Nate did not compensate. He simply uses few connectives, few discourse demonstratives, and few definite articles. And his article ratio, instead of increasing toward the 3.1 average of his models, increases momentarily and then tails off. This means that he is using relatively few definite articles compared to indefinite articles, which indicates that he is not referring to *given* information as often as experts do and thus not maintaining thematic continuity. Only in Text 2, written in an informal epistolary style, and in Text 3, which uses a straightforward experimental-report style, is he able to maintain consistent thematic continuity. In the other three texts there is simply too much new information (often marked by the indefinite article) being presented at one time.

## DISCUSSION

The findings from this study suggest that Nate made substantial progress in developing a command over the conventions of the academic writing that was required of him in the rhetoric program. His writing increased in syntactic complexity, the use of hyperbole had diminished by the writing of Text 4 and was absent in Text 5, his paragraphs followed more conventional expository patterns, and his sentence subjects referred to the subject matter under discussion, not just to himself. Despite his growing ability to generate such patterns, however, he appears to have been juggling too many conceptual and linguistic constraints to consistently produce cohesive ties; therefore his writing relied heavily on his reader's ability to make logical connections. In summary, Nate's texts, even at the end of the first year, reveal problems in thematic continuity, suggesting that he still needed to develop ways of creating coherent and cohesive texts. Specifically, he needed to learn how to be more explicit in the way he ties sentences together, by using more connectives and more demonstratives and by relying more heavily on mutual knowledge (Thomas, 1986). The latter development, which would be indicated, for example, by an increased use of definite articles, may occur naturally as he gains more knowledge of the field and is able to represent his audience more accurately.

Although Nate had not developed the procedural schemata necessary for creating cohesive texts, the case study information, as well as many of the features in his texts, show that his declarative or substantive knowledge increased significantly by the end of his first year. Nate's essay, "Structured Heuristics: Problems in the New Paradigm," indicates that the writer had a command over the issues that his professor had raised in print. In this essay Nate developed a rhetorical framework, instantiating material from his reading as brief gists that served to support the points he wished to make. The qualitative findings also suggest that, as a learner, Nate used various strategic procedures for reframing new information to make it personally meaningful. When unable to write clearly using the conventions of the academic critique, he temporarily abandoned these conventions and drew on familiar (expressive) discourse schemata to get his ideas down on paper. Elsewhere he created the scenario of the vulnerable rat in the ethnographer's box to both instantiate information from and comment critically on recent reading. These kinds of responses on his part lead us to infer that Nate was an active and constructive reader and writer who could employ various strategies to gain a mastery over new material.

Nate's learning processes were idiosyncratic, and generalizations must therefore be limited; nevertheless, we believe that many teachers and researchers will recognize characteristic difficulties that confront learners entering new educational and rhetorical communities. In Nate's case, it appears that the kind of advanced literacy associated with learning a field of knowledge, or with entering a discipline or vocation, hinged on the learner's ability to integrate subject matter knowledge with a knowledge of situationally appropriate linguistic and rhetorical conventions (Purves & Purves, 1986). Nate appears to have developed the former from reading and coursework more readily than the latter. His use of informal writing as a learning tool seems to have served him well in the former respect, but it may have slowed his progress as an academic writer. Freed from the constraints of genre and register, writing informally and expressively appears to have enabled Nate to assimilate new material quickly. Elbow's (1985) description of the *ephemeral*, playful characteristics of expressive discourse seems appropriate applied to Nate's informal writings; the personal and self-focused characteristics of this writing seem to have served Nate as a learner.

These observations can be explained in large part by reference to long-attested differences between oral and written language production. Horowitz and his colleagues, for example, in controlled experiments measuring the number of idea units produced in the two modes of expression, found that their subjects generated "more ideas" in speech than in writing (Horowitz & Berkowitz, 1964, p. 617). They attributed this difference to the fact that speaking is mechanically and psychologically easier than writing and to the fact that in speaking there is a tendency to avoid silence. Informal, expressive writing shares a number of characteristics with informal speech, and Nate's use of such writing for inventional purposes can then be seen as a natural, instinctive, and predictably fruitful move.

At the same time, it seems that dependence on an oral-based, informal style of writing can interfere with the development of the procedural knowledge needed to construct text structures appropriate to formal expository discourse. As Chafe (1982), Akinnaso (1982), and others noted, formal expository writing differs from informal speech in many linguistic parameters, including longer sentences, more abstractions, more subordination and other forms of syntactic elaboration, more definite articles, fewer self-reference words, more Latinate vocabulary, and more hierarchical paragraph structure. The linguistic analysis we did on Nate's texts show clearly that he had difficulty switching from the one mode to the other. Although informal, expressive writing appears to help writers explore new ideas, it also may deter them from expressing these ideas in the highly explicit, cohesive, hierarchical style expected in formal expository prose. (In retrospect, we should note that by the time Nate had been in the program for a few years he was able to quite adroitly shift between informal and formal registers depending on the goals for a piece of writing and the reader's expectations.)

Chafe also observed that, in informal speech, speakers focus on their thoughts and feelings. Expressive writers also focus on their involvement or experience with the object at hand, a psychological perspective that places the writer at the center of the discourse. This subjective perspective, as Britton, Burgess, Martin, McLeod, and Rosen (1975) and many others have shown, has a heuristic function, helping learners to think about experience and observation in their own terms. Yet the personal point of view may in itself present difficulties when it becomes necessary for writers to abandon it. As a writer in the Rhetoric Program, Nate found it necessary to adopt a *writer as observer* (rather than *writer as knower*) stance toward his material in order to keep his reader's eye on his research rather than himself. Making this change in perspective, and adopting appropriate rhetorical and linguistic conventions to create detachment from (rather than involvement with) subject and audience appear to have been a continuing source of difficulty, although he began to alter the surface features in his prose fairly early in the year, as the analyses of Texts 1–5 (Table 7.5) indicate.

## CONCLUSION

Looking at Nate's development as a writer in the Rhetoric Program from theoretical perspectives in cognitive psychology and sociolinguistics provides two different but complimentary frameworks for two final comments. From the perspective of cognitive psychology, the changes that we observed in Nate's texts during his first year demonstrate the asymmetrical way in which the writer built declarative and procedural schemata. As Anderson (1983) suggested, the growth of declarative knowledge outstrips that of procedural knowledge, but the latter is derived from the former. Nate's difficulties with cohesion and coherence persisted long after he gained a relative mastery over the material that he was studying in his courses, the empirical research methods he was learning in the program. The acquisition of procedural knowledge, when viewed over time as in this case study, appears to be a lengthy and difficult process.

This process, we submit, is affected significantly by sociocultural factors. From a sociolinguistic perspective, Hudson (1980), paraphrasing Le Page, Christie, Jurdant, Weekes, and Tabouret-Keller (1974), noted that:

> There is ample evidence that society is structured, from a sociolinguistic point of view, in terms of a multi-dimensional space. . . . One need only think of the rather obvious ways in which people can be classified more or less independently ac-

cording to the dimensions of age, region of origin, social class (or profession) and sex, to see an example of a four-dimensional space, each dimension of which is relevant to language. Once a person has constructed a model of how this multi-dimensional space looks from his point of view, he then has to choose where to locate himself in it. Language is only one part of the picture, of course, but a particularly important part because it gives the speaker a very clearly structured set of symbols which he can use in locating himself in the world. If we think of a child in an area where there are two different groups of children of roughly his age, and he belongs clearly to one of them, then he will most probably model his speech largely on that of others in the group he has joined, because that is the pattern he has chosen. In other words, at each utterance his speech can be seen as an ACT OF IDENTITY in a multi-dimensional space. (pp. 13–14)

Nate's "multi-dimensional space" included both the teaching and expressive writing communities he had belonged to for many years and the more empirical research-oriented community of rhetoricians and composition theorists he was trying to enter. In turn, the *community of practice* that was the Rhetoric Program at Carnegie Mellon in the mid-1980s is part of a larger, exceedingly diverse, national community of teachers, scholars, and researchers of many theoretical and methodological persuasions.

What can we conclude about Nate's development as a researcher and scholar during his first year in his doctoral apprenticeship, when we stand back to consider the forms of legitimate peripheral participation in which he engaged (and that we chronicle in this chapter)? (See also John Ackerman's Postscript, pp. 145–150.) His heavy use of first person pronouns, hyperbole, and other features associated with expressive writing at the beginning of the year may be seen as acts of identity indicating his allegiance to the former groups, his teaching associates and fellow writers from John Warnock's seminar. As the year progressed, however, his writing displayed more and more features of social science expository prose, indicating a desire on Nate's part to be considered a member of the latter group as well. Just as every person belongs simultaneously to many different discourse communities, this adoption of language characteristic of one community does not mean that he was rejecting the other. Indeed, we have shown that Nate's expertise with self-expressive writing in certain respects facilitated his entry into the empirical research community—especially when we consider his writing memos to his mentor as an act of legitimate peripheral participation—which in this case enabled us to see the active, constructive character of his learning processes. Nate continued to write informally to members of the former group. Meanwhile, however, he had learned to add his voice to the conversations of the latter group and even wrote articles for publication with some of his mentor–teachers.

This study described the rather unorthodox processes through which one writer began to achieve a mastery of the conventions and conversation for literate communication within a specific disciplinary framework. It focused on the writer at that period in his career when he was preparing for entry into professional communities existing beyond his immediate environment. What seems most salient in this tale is the very active role that the writer took in his learning process. This was no conversion, no subjugation of an identity into a subject slot in a hegemonic social structure. Rather, to borrow from Lave and Wegner (1991), the social structure (that is virtual) within the community of practice, "its power relations, and its conditions for legitimacy define possibilities for learning" (p. 98).

# POSTSCRIPT:
# THE ASSIMILATION AND
# TACTICS OF NATE

John M. Ackerman
University of Utah

Ten years have now passed since my first year of graduate school at Carnegie Mellon, the time and events upon which "Conventions, Conversations, and the Writer" was based. Carol, Tom, and I created "Nate" to disguise my identity at that time and later as my program of study and professional life unfolded. As I will discuss, we were nervous about revealing the co-identity of researcher and research subject; we needed some of the conventional distance between researcher and participant in social science writing to analytically discuss 1 year out of someone's intellectual life. As I now reread, the narrative underlying this research report speaks back, and I appreciate again the ethos of Nate in his struggle to gain academic and professional fluency. Although our research is primarily an analysis of textual practice, the struggle of a writer to produce those texts is apparent. What is graduate school for many students but a struggle for identity, in a contested professional space defined by genre activity, quarrels over epistemology and method, and a search for affiliation? For me, graduate school was all of that plus an intense personal process of rendering oneself anew. I am proud of what I accomplished that year, and I prefer not to repeat the process.

Having studied Nate from the vantage points of personal narrative and research subject, I am aware of the inherent difficulties in sociolinguistic accounts of genre activity, because of the interpretive leap from textual analysis to intellectual identity, and especially so when the writer in the study has a voice in the analysis. It is one thing to equate rhetorical process with product, in the way that a text can be read for the presence or absence of planning or of an appropriate register. It is something else to attempt to locate writers according to their affiliations, epistemological preferences, or ideology. Yet, it is the latter analysis (perhaps aided by the first) that teaches us how to respond to diversity—whether it appears in the cultural diversity of our students or the diversity of method in someone's or some profession's communicative acts.

In the opening chapter of this book, Carol and Tom construe that Nate "assimilated the rationalist/realist epistemology that constitutes empiricist inquiry in the social sciences" (p. 22) to mean that Nate learned the tools of this trade to complement and extend the repertoire of fluencies brought into the graduate school arena. They suggest in the concluding statements of "Conventions, Conversations, and the Writer" that professional enculturation is most accurately portrayed as a process of acquiring multiple fluencies and *legitimate peripheral participation* in communities. As many of my peers at Carnegie Mellon succeeded in doing, I perfected the codes and conventions of social science writing well enough to complete a dissertation but also as a bridge to other kinds of genres and certainly to many other professional conversations. The professional conversation at Carnegie Mellon was far from monolithic when we were in the middle of our enculturation, and when those focused years of study splintered and compounded in the years after graduation.

Others who theorize community literacy practices, and some who have critiqued our research specifically, view the assimilation of a dominant discourse less as a struggle for agency within a "multi-dimensional space" and more as the adoption of one or more ideological positions, with tacit rejection of others. Bizzell's (1992; see also Schilb's, 1988) reading of "Conventions, Conversations, and the Writer" (Berkenkotter, Huckin, & Ackerman, 1988) as well as a later essay that extends that research (Berkenkotter, Huckin, & Ackerman, 1991), deftly nudges our analysis beyond (still acknowledging) agency and community participation to a critique of writing practice as ideology. Although I agreed and agree now with the basic premise of this type of commentary—that studies of discourse communities should concern themselves with conflict and power— Bizzell's reading of Nate's political identity as a writer never rang true for me, perhaps because it suggested a more passive construction of the process of assimilation: Nate was absorbed by the discourse around him.

Here are Bizzell's (1992) conclusions with regard to three papers Nate wrote over the first 18 months of his degree program:

> Berkenkotter et al. provide information to suggest that the change Nate underwent is more far-reaching than a change in his style, that entering a discourse community required him to change his thinking about composition studies in radical ways. . . . The change in Nate's style is accompanied by a change in his sense of what should be studied, as reflected in the title of the paper he wrote after eighteen months in the Carnegie Mellon program: "Toward a Generative Computer Environment: A Protocol Study." (pp. 230–231)

I believe that this commentary on our study reveals as much about the commentator as it accurately portrays Nate's positioning within a discourse and professional culture. The paper Bizzell chose to represent as symbolic was one of a dozen or so that I wrote in graduate school and the first and last paper I ever wrote on computer environments. It was not, therefore, indicative of any position I took then or now on what should be studied or through what methodological lens. Bizzell continued in her commentary to suggest that a student's interest in voice, computers, cognition, and protocols could not be mere coincidence. Nate's world view is inferred from the composite of those interests and is labeled *expressivist*, a fully academic writing style and position in composition and rhetoric. Nate seems to have tripped, unwittingly, over a prior ideological critique, except that Nate within this construction is too perfect an example of Bizzell's earlier criticism of process teaching and research. Bizzell (1982a) argued that expressivist writing and teaching is related to cognitive research because it shares a preoccupation with the individual and the interior mind. With this inference drawn about Nate, however, Bizzell has left behind any trace of grounded interpretation, revealing more accurately, as Berkenkotter (1991) described, *her* own position along the fault line of composition studies. We are left with virtual Nate, a free floating subjectivity that can be interjected into a pre-existent scholarly conversation.

Of course, I have the advantage of historical hindsight, and thus I am not being fair to the game of hermeneutic criticism. Once "Nate" became a published identity, he was fair game for alternative interpretations. And from the moment of invention, that is from the moment that Carol's and my collaborative inquiry turned toward publication, "Nate" became a fictional character for our uses as well. Our methods were collaborative and conversational: We talked, shared time in classes, and read and discussed articles; and I shared my assigned writings and kept a weekly log of my thoughts. But when these methods, which dovetailed the daily activity of my degree program with Carol's research interests, shifted from data collected to data analyzed, "Nate" became an abstraction of all that we had witnessed together and separately.

I can tell you that it is no fun having your epistemology and ideology represented in public, but the more serious issue in sociolinguistic studies of genres and community membership is the degree to which our critical interpretations of textual practice obscure other kinds of genre activity that may not be so easily found either in formal, public texts or in ongoing critical debate. The real action, I would say, is beneath those pages.

The exterior qualities of the three papers that I wrote mask, to some degree, the ongoing epistemological quest of a student who, like all other students in graduate school, simultaneously tries to satisfy the demands and constraints of each professor and class while at the same time seeks a separate scholarly identity. Studies of the enculturation of graduate students, especially those in the humanities, are unique in that the tacit expectation of graduate programs is (still) to produce a relatively autonomous scholar. The dissertation genre as well as other assignments exert a centripetal force not only to conform to stable language conventions but to stable identity conventions as well. But far more difficult to trace are the counter forces at work in genre activity in discourse communities. Bakhtin's "primary" genres seem to carry more of the momentary, circumstantial, and personally relevant qualities, which would account for why and how students can write both within and against common, public genres. But even Bakhtin described these primary genres as "absorbed" and "digested" by the more constant "secondary" genres. Primary genres seem to have no life beyond the life inscribed by secondary genres, no autonomous life possible in the everyday.

How can studies of enculturation account for the ongoing everyday activity of shaping sense, of piecing together an intellectual project, of sustaining scholarly inquiry, of asking the same question over and over using whatever generic shell or linguistic tools are available? I am now posing questions that go beyond the intent of the study reported. This generative aspect of genre activity is captured in part with structuration theory, which, as Carol and Tom point out, represents genre activity as both constituting stable social structures and generating "situated, artful practice" (p. 20) reflexively.

 However, graduate students are not in a reciprocal political relationship with the social structure around them, and I recall the generative aspects of my graduate school writing as partly the necessary tactics of making do with someone else's conventional practice that at times I admired and other times I resisted (as I suspect all students do). De Certeau (1984) uses the term *tactic* to refer to the actions and devices of the less powerful in cultural spaces, and as I look back on those three writings, they are as much examples of the subterranean activities of graduate school as they are prime examples of conforming to the strictures of professional life. The papers that Carol, Tom, and I studied were a pilot survey in a first-semester methods course, a research proposal in a second-semester course on process-tracing research, and a term project in a course in the Psychology Department on human problem solving and artificial intelligence. As researchers, we concluded that the progression of papers revealed Nate's growing skill at constructing an intertext as he assimilated a literature, lexicon, and level of authorship within the research community of his choosing (Berkenkotter et al., 1991).

Autobiographically, I would portray these three papers as more circumstantially relevant, as exercises in "getting by" in the day-to-day expectations of a given class (and thus social configuration). I am not saying that Nate was disingenuous as a writer. The three papers are themselves fairly common genres that travel far beyond the terrain of Carnegie Mellon: a survey, a proposal, and a research report. I remember taking each assignment seriously as the survey was practice with an empirical tool, the proposal was presented as an opportunity to risk a research agenda based on a pilot study (the first for most of us), and the third paper was particularly difficult because all of what I knew about research, writing, and the field of composition and rhetoric had to be lodged in someone else's discourse and methodology. The third paper was public in the way the first two were not, and the method of choice was computer modeling in a course taught by Herbert Simon, a Nobel Prize winning economist and psychologist. This course was a quintessential moment for me as a student, partly because of my shortcomings. I realized that I was in the presence of a brilliant thinker, but I simultaneously realized the limits of using if–then logic chaining to model human creativity. Of course, as a student I still had to produce a text for a course (grade: B–).

Bizzell was right in assuming that my course paper on generative computer environments was a watershed event, but she would have no way of knowing in which direction. Simon's course was one of my favorites because it taught me another epistemology, one that I could tactically learn from on the way to declining it as a dominating method and belief system.

Carol and Tom are helping language researchers to broaden their notion of genre to include centrifugal as well as centripetal forces, to use Bakhtin's distinction. Without a doubt, had we the opportunity to repeat our study of Nate and face the genre activity of writing up our account, we would pose the struggle of Nate differently, because the genre of sociolinguistic report has itself evolved. For example, I predict that we would not have withheld Nate's authorial identity (revealed in print in Berkenkotter, 1991). I recall the evening in my tiny home in North Braddock (a working class borough in Pittsburgh) when the three of us were compiling, composing, and revising the first report for publication. We were in the midst of collaboration, and from my kitchen I could hear whoops of inspiration and productivity as Carol and Tom wrote upstairs. Later on that weekend, the task of writing the "methods" section of our first research report surfaced. We had decided to try for *Research in the Teaching of English* because it was to us at that time the premier journal for such research. Although we did debate whether to reveal the dual identities of Nate to the editors, reviewers, and readership of *RTE*, we decided to separate the two because (I paraphrase) our field had not yet published hybrid, collaborative research relationships, and thus to reveal our method was to take an unwise risk.

Rosaldo (1989; see also Stoller, 1989) and numerous feminists (e.g., Collins, 1990; hooks, 1990; Minh-ha, 1989) speak for those researchers engaged in qualitative research and cultural analysis who question (if not outright reject) codifying people's self and culture through either their interpretive "gaze" or by reproducing a stable, objective truth through the conventional discourse of their field. Rosaldo suggests a "plausible criterion" for judging the descriptions of social behavior by asking a simple question: "How valid would we find ethnographic discourse about others if it were used to describe ourselves?" (p. 49). I am not suggesting (through proximity) that Nate was a victim or that his career at Carnegie Mellon was a social injustice on the scale of the appropriated identities of the culturally disenfranchised. Rosaldo does help to politicize studies of writing activity by examining the language researchers use to publish their interpretations of others, by pointing out in his own field, "a gap between the technical idiom of ethnography and the language of everyday life" (p. 51).

For Rosaldo, "At issue is not the real truth versus the ethnographic lie" (1989, p. 50). And, at issue is not the real Nate *versus* the interpretive or empirical lie either. Sociolinguistic studies of genre activity as part of larger processes of enculturation can reveal the subtexts, conflicts, compromises, and negotiations in addition to those more centripetal forces in conventional language use. As I have tried to show, I believe it is one thing to discuss genre in the literary, hermeneutical style of Bakhtin and quite another to perform genre analysis on textual artifacts that are deemed representative of personal and cultural activity. If my retrospective account of the writing of Nate has a single point to make, it is that critical or empirical studies of genre will reveal as much about the genre activities of the authors of that research as the subjects of their writing. And this is a good thing.

As I reread the account of my intellectual life, I admire again the work of Carol and Tom, and the strange beauty of social scientific portrayal. As we reach for the authenticity proposed by Rosaldo, within the spectrum of inclusion, multivocality, and reflexivity, the genre activity of writing to capture someone else's life and times will reveal itself as completely interpretive and partial.

# 8

# SUFFER THE LITTLE CHILDREN: LEARNING THE CURRICULUM GENRES OF SCHOOL AND UNIVERSITY

*Issues, content or ideas are realized in language; they do not have identity apart from language patterns, any more than the skills of concern have an identity apart from the behavioural patterns in which they find expression.*
—Christie (1985, pp. 25–26)

Within any social setting such as a school classroom, a laboratory, or a corporate conference room, events, as we understand them, are configured within time and space. Our notions of how to act in each of these contexts take the form of socially typified responses: what we are supposed to do *at this moment, in this setting*. Following Miller (1984) and Bazerman (1988), we have described these typified responses to events that recur over time and across space as genres. Learning to speak and to write—like other forms of mediated cognition—is thus a process of learning the available patterns for communication, patterns that are imbricated in the activities of social life. When children enter the school system, they experience the activities that constitute classroom life as contiguous units, or structures, stretching over space and time. Situationally appropriate discourse conventions can therefore be seen to be learned in the context of spatially–temporally configured units. For example, *show and tell* talk, a primary speech genre, occurs during *sharing time* in the *sharing circle*, but not normally elsewhere or at other times (see Fig. 8.1). Thus, children's development of school-based genre knowledge is the development of spatially and temporally organized scripts or schemata. And a child's or adolescent's knowledge of "how to get on" in such contexts can be characterized as *situated literacy*.

In this chapter we consider that special class of genres known as *curriculum, pedagogical,* or *classroom* genres (Christie, 1985, 1987; Kress, 1982, 1987,

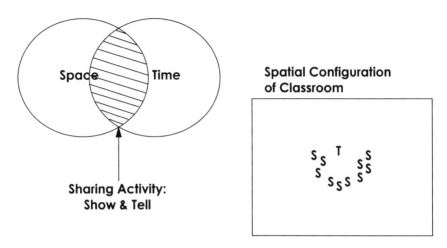

FIG. 8.1.   A child's knowledge of classroom genres learned in space/time contexts:
What we are supposed to do at this moment in this setting.

1989). Although the disciplinary genesis of the pedagogical genres are to be found in various fields of the natural and social sciences and the humanities, they are essentially what Bakhtin (1986) called primary speech genres, embedded in local settings and activities. These *primary* genres are both oral (e.g., triadic dialogue, teacher monologue, see Lemke, 1990) and written (book report, report on science experiment, poem or dialogue for English class). Because of the institutionalized, didactic character of formal schooling, mastery of these genres does not occur through a process of *legitimate peripheral participation* as it does within the *communities of practice* described by Lave and Wegner (1991), at least not until graduate or professional school (see chap. 7, this volume). Thus, many learners, whose home and community language learning environments would make them amenable to the kinds of apprenticeship that Lave and Wegner discussed, are less prepared to handle the genres of didactic instruction than are so-called "mainstream" children. For these learners, how much genre knowledge needs to be made explicit and in what ways? Is it even possible to make such knowledge explicit, given that the linguistic/rhetorical features of genre are embedded in content instruction in different domains such as science class? (See Halliday & Martin, 1993; Lemke, 1990, for discussions of scientific genre conventions as they are conveyed through classroom talk and students' reading.)

   In this chapter we are concerned with the place of genre instruction in the context of classroom instruction. We focus on the issues of what factors prevent the explicit teaching of genre conventions, and whether or not the pedagogical genres should be explicitly taught within the curricula in which they occur (science lesson, literature lesson, history lesson). These issues are at the center of an intense debate in Australia and the United Kingdom; however, they have not attracted attention in the United States except perhaps among applied linguists (for an exception, see Comprone, 1993). The various positions in this controversy are represented in a 1987 collection of essays, *The Place of Genre in Learning: Current Debates*.

## THE DEBATE IN AUSTRALIA AND THE U.K. OVER THE EXPLICIT TEACHING OF GENRE

Generally, language arts and composition teachers in the United States do not spend much time teaching genre conventions of the disciplines, although Swales (1990) and other ESL specialists have integrated the teaching of scientific genres into courses for nonnative speakers. We might attribute this lack of interest in the explicit teaching of generic conventions to a number of factors:

1. the influence of James Britton and his colleagues' (1975) research on children's and adolescents' development of writing abilities.
2. the expressivist pedagogical movement that developed in its wake.
3. the writing-to-learn movement (also based on Britton et al.'s work) that has taken root in American pedagogical practice as the result of the numerous spin-offs of the Bay Area Writing Project and Writing-Across-the-Curriculum workshops.

Furthermore, many college-level composition teachers negatively associate the explicit teaching of genres with the prescriptive *rhetorical modes* approach that had students reading "exemplary" essays by linguistically and rhetorically mature writers. These essays, which supposedly exemplified generic forms or rhetorical *modes* such as *comparison and contrast, descriptive, narrative, pro-and-con*, were used as models for student writing.

Although we are not advocating a return to that pedagogy or to those text types, we would like to raise a number of vexing questions: To what extent and in what ways should teachers make students cognizant of the patterns of discourse that constitute instructional genres in various domains? What are the sociocognitive implications of teachers ignoring the genre conventions that children and adolescents must master in public schools and universities in order to demonstrate communicative competence?

These questions are complex because the character of instructional genres changes radically throughout the course of students' school experience as they progress from elementary school through college. As Ackerman (1993) recently noted, students are very gradually socialized into disciplinary genres because of the integrated curricula of the primary grades. During the middle and high school years, specialized subject areas are differentiated, but not explicitly linked to the manufacture of knowledge until the college years when "the voices of the academic disciplines are loud. . . . The undergraduate degree is . . . a part of a social conversion, an immense social experiment whereby students learn by 'approximations' of the languages of institutionalized power" (pp. 342–343). However, even though the connection between academic discourse and knowledge production is not made explicit until the college years, children are exposed to many of its grammatical, syntactical, and lexical features in elementary school through their reading and in the course of classroom talk. Lemke (1990), and Halliday and Martin (1993) described the lexical and syntactic features of scientific academic discourse present in instructional conversation and the didactic texts that children read from the earliest grades on.

From the perspective of functional linguistics, Martin, Christie, and Rothery (1987) made a strong case for explicitly teaching academic genres. Martin et al. described genres as "semiotic systems [that] evolve in such a way that they introduce a kind of stability into a culture at the same time [being] flexible enough to participate in social change. In this respect they are like language itself" (p. 59). These linguists are concerned about the ways in which teachers in the elementary grades communicate a knowledge of genre to children. They argue that in the United Kingdom and Australia non-White, nonmiddle-class children are seriously disenfranchised when teachers ignore the explicit teaching of classroom genres, observing that children are often overly dependent on narrative at the expense of learning other expository forms more suitable for reports of scientific experiments, analyses of historical events, and so forth. The functional linguistic framework that informs their view can be seen in Christie's (1985) paper, "Language and Schooling." In that paper, Christie argued that a major cause of many primary and elementary school children's inability to learn written genres other than narrative is that teachers do not make explicit their tacit and seemingly unreflexive knowledge of classroom genres. Such knowledge constitutes the *hidden curriculum* of the language arts classroom.

Doing well in school, Christie (1985) observed, "is largely a language matter—a matter, that is, of capacity to interpret and manipulate the various patterns of discourse characteristic of the many kinds of knowledge, information, and ideas schools value" (p. 21). Paradoxically our use of language is of such a pervasive character and:

> So intimately a part of the total patterns of interaction in which people engage in schools, that it simply slips from the forefront of teachers' attention. Language is much more readily lost among mother tongue specialists than among second language specialists, for the very good reason that the latter are obliged to give some conscious attention to the language their students must learn. Most mother tongue teachers—whether specialists in the teaching of school subject English or specialists in the teaching of other school subjects—focus not upon language, but upon what they think of as the 'issues,' 'ideas,' or 'content' to be dealt with, or the mental skills to be developed in their students. Yet issues, content or ideas are realized in language; they do not have identity apart from language patterns, anymore than

the skills of concern have an identity apart from the behavioural patterns in which they find expression (pp. 25–26).

For White, middle-class children, a teachers' lack of awareness of language patterns (or what we are calling genre conventions) is not a problem because the patterns of interaction and the language system into which they were socialized corresponds with what they will encounter as they move through the various school curricula. But when the patterns of interaction and language system of home and community are at variance with that of school culture, children's receptivity to classroom genres is hindered, unless children aspire to participate in the teacher's language system. Christie's view of the importance of paying attention to how children acquire genre knowledge in *different* domains or content areas is shared by Kress (1982, 1987, 1989, 1993) and Martin and Rothery (1987, 1993). Their position is very much at odds with the expressivist view of language learning represented in two other essays by Dixon (1987) and by Sawyer and Watson (1987), which appear in *The Place of Genre in Learning*.

Dixon appears to be very close to Britton et al. (1975) in his view that children can best process their learning in different content areas by utilizing in their writing "the resources gathered in speaking" (Britton et al., 1975, p. 16).[1] Like Britton and his colleagues, Dixon saw writing from the developmental perspective that foregrounds the individual child's psychosocial maturation as a matter of drawing on the resources of speech. According to this view, what is most important is that teachers secure for children the opportunity to develop their understanding of new concepts through whatever conventions are most "natural" to them (Dixon, 1967, pp. 34–45). The conventions of spoken language adopted in children's written texts are therefore held to be the instrumental tools for cognitive development. And, conversely, the various curriculum genres constitute "mind-forg'd manacles" or "algorithmic patterns" (1987, pp. 9–10). Children should not be held accountable for learning them, but rather should be free to choose whatever combination of generic conventions best serves them in conceptualizing what they are learning through formal instruction.

Sawyer and Watson concur with Dixon. They also are concerned that explicitly teaching genre conventions might have a negative effect on students' development of writing abilities. They question the kinds of prescriptive teaching practices that might result if the explicit teaching of genre were to be integrated into the writing curriculum:

---

[1]Dixon's very influential book, *Growth through English: A Report Based on the Dartmouth Seminar, 1966* was published in 1967, 8 years before the publication of Britton et al.'s (1975) *The Development of Writing Abilities (11–18)*. Although Britton et al. did not cite Dixon's book, they shared many of the same ideas about the need for children and adolescents to use talk and the resources gathered from talk in their writing. Writing is seen as a means for personal development and intellectual growth rather than the medium through which students demonstrate communicative competence.

Does "direct teaching" mean "explicit drilling in form"? . . . Certainly it seems to suggest direct instruction of the sort characterized by 'teacher-presents-model-students-follow-model'. . . . Teachers ought to be aware that what is being re-opened is the whole question of whether conscious knowledge of structure makes for more effective performance in writing . . . a question that should, one would have thought been laid to rest by the research into the relationship of explicit grammatical knowledge to writing. (1987, pp. 48–49)

## THE CLASSROOM SEMIOTICS OF A SCIENCE LESSON IN AUSTRALIA

Many of the authors of the essays that appear in *The Place of Genre in Learning* responded to issues Christie raised in her 1985 paper. To clarify the substance of these issues we describe in some detail in the next few pages the fine-grained linguistic/semiotic analysis Christie presented in that essay. To drive home her point that teachers have not been aware of the importance of explicitly teaching the curriculum genres, Christie devoted considerable space to describing the language environment of an elementary school classroom in which 6-year-old children were learning about the development of chicken embryos. The semiotic environment of the classroom consisted of multiple, interrelated social meanings. For example, in this classroom was an incubator in which fertilized eggs were hatching. The children were thus able to witness the process of birth as they viewed baby chicks pecking their way out of the eggs. They were also reading a lesson in a children's science textbook, *Egg to Chick*, that illustrated the development of a chicken through its various stages. In describing the fertilized egg, the author had written, "The blood (in the egg) is full of food from the yolk. The tiny chicken begins to grow. It is called an embryo. All animals are called embryos when they first begin to grow." Christie observed that the author of this passage created *scientific* meanings by using statements in the universal present tense to describe experiential processes: "the blood is full," "the chick begins to grow," and so forth. Such statements, which are presented as factual, verifiable generalizations, are a characteristic feature of scientific discourse, she argued.

In this context of scientific discourse and meanings, the teacher asked her students to *write a story* describing, in their own words, the information in a series of pictures she gave them depicting the life cycle of a chicken from egg to hatched chick, and captioned "How a Chicken Grows." The following texts were produced by four of the class members in response to the teacher's assignment:

Joel:   Once upon a time a hen lay a egg inside the egg a chicken was being born the chick eats the yolk it makes (a) little hole now the chick is making a big crack.

Simone:   This is how a chicken grows first a Mother hen lays eggs then the chicken inside gets bigger then the chicken starts to crack a dotted line around the shell then the chick pushes out and when the chicken is out it was all wet and when it has dryd it getts yellow and fluffy. The end.

Susy:    The mother hen is keeping the chicken warm under her feathers on the egg and chicken drinking the yolk and it is pecking [t]he shell and thek chick has petk in a circle and naw is getting dray and feathers and yellow to and now he is troing to walk but he kant and naw he has got feathers.

Joseph:    an . hen . lad. a. egg and. The ., murd sat . on . the . egg and evri . day . it got big. are . and The cickn . peckt and .at . lust . it cam at . it to twnione days (A hen laid an egg and the mother sat on the egg and every day it got bigger and the chicken pecked and at last it came out. It took twenty-one days.)

Christie noted that none of these four students succeeded in following the teacher's instruction to write a story. Instead, each of the children, influenced by the semiotic cues in the setting and by their discursive activities, mixed features of scientific and narrative exposition. For example, although Joel's text starts out in a narrative vein ("Once upon a time . . ."), it soon shifts to the universal present tense of scientific description ("the chick eats the yolk"). Simone's text, though concluding with a stock narrative phrase ("The end"), features present-tense descriptions throughout. Susy's text resembles a narrative in its unfolding of events, but its stream-of-consciousness use of present progressive verbs is not so much that of true narrative as the mere descriptive labeling of a series of pictures. Joseph's text, according to Christie, comes closest to true narrative in its use of past tense verbs to describe a chronological sequence of events, but lacks the story complication expected of narratives.

Christie (1985) concluded that all four of the children's' texts turned out to be ambiguous, "blurred genres"—a concatenation of narrative and descriptive/expository elements. The children mixed their conventions, she argued, because:

> It was confusing [for the teacher] to ask the children to write "a little story" about chickens. The experiences with which they were to deal, and the meanings they were involved in making, were of a scientific kind; they were not the meanings of narrative. Had the teacher had a more explicit sense of the kind of generic structure required she could have focused discussion upon it, and enabled the children to master it the more effectively (p. 37).

Christie's argument here is that written communication always takes place in a semiotic *context of situation*,[2] and that students in responding to the semiotic cues

---

[2]Halliday (1978), following Malinowski (1935), argued that children's socialization occurs through their language learning and use within what he calls the "context of situation." Briefly, the context of situation refers to the meaning potential that is associated with various situation types, such as "players instructing a novice in a game," "mother reading a bedtime story to child," or "customer ordering goods over the telephone" (p. 29). Children learn that certain language behaviors are appropriate in certain situation types. Halliday's concept of situation type is very close to Schutz's concept of social typification and, therefore, to our notion of genre.

of the classroom, make choices that are contingent on the meanings and resources in the setting. In this classroom, with its preoccupation with the life cycle of chickens, there were multiple visual and verbal semiotics that one commonly associates with the forms of inquiry/knowledge associated with scientific culture.

In her essay in *The Place of Genre in Learning* Christie (1987) commented retrospectively about the texts that had been the subject of the 1985 paper. She observed, "the writer's choices are not arbitrary, but selective, and used for the construction of the scientific meanings which this context actually requires" (pp. 26–27). Elementary (or infant school) teachers need to be trained to be sensitive to how children develop knowledge of genre conventions from specific instructional contexts (e.g., science lesson, history lesson, etc.). Both the content and form of what children write are strongly influenced by the semiotic cues that they receive within these *contexts of situation*—in other words, cues embedded in classroom activities, and in instructional conversation. Teachers, therefore, need to understand that the imperative, "write a story," will be perceived by children as a default command overriding other cues in the setting.

Kress (1987) concurred with Christie in his essay in *The Place of Genre in Learning*, observing that the critical issue is not whether children do or do not have the freedom to experiment with different generic conventions, but rather whether or not children's innovations can succeed within the broader culture:

> The children [described in Christie's (1985) essay] seemed to feel free—and to be able—to try a range of forms to cope with this task, including the invention of a new genre. All involve generic innovation: using a generic form which is not usually used, for the expression of a particular discourse or for the report of an event which conventionally has a specific genre associated with it, is one kind of innovation, one kind of creativity. However neither these nor Joel's innovation are likely to succeed, because the child-writers are the least "authorized" writers in the culture, and their innovations can be quite disregarded. In other words, we are now in the arena of social power, the power in this instance to vary culturally established textual rules.
>
>     . . . . unless there is a change in the social structures—and in the kinds of social occasions in which texts are produced—the new generic forms are unlikely to succeed. This is why childish innovations fail: not because they do not constitute perfectly plausible solutions to textual/cognitive problems, but because they are supported neither by a stable social occasion, nor by "authority." (pp. 41–42)

Kress' comments here constitute a serious challenge to the U.S. writing pedagogy that has developed in the wake of the 1966 Dartmouth conference.[3] Many teachers and pedagogical theorists share the view that the emancipatory pedagogies such as expressivism, and more recently, critical theory or cultural studies

---

[3]For a discussion of the legacy of that conference, see Harris (1991); for an analysis of the limitations of the "writing-as-learning" approach to curricular reform in American writing pedagogy, and a critique of related empirical research on writing-to-learn, see Ackerman (1993).

pedagogy, provide the key for teachers committed to social justice (see, for example, the essays in Berlin & Vivion, 1992). Although Kress himself is known for his work in critical discourse analysis (a branch of discourse analysis growing out of critical theory), he differs from those holding a critical theory or cultural studies perspective by insisting that the power to *bend* these rules is more in the hands of major scientists or well-established scholars than it is in those of children or college students, "Genres are cultural constructs, they are as culture determines. Challenging genres is therefore challenging culture.... [Dixon] and I are in a position to risk and perhaps to achieve that. However it seems to me entirely inappropriate to ask those least able to carry that burden" (1987, p. 44).[4]

## PEDAGOGICAL IMPLICATIONS

With hindsight we can see that Britton and his colleagues' research was very timely in that it provided a rationale for a student-centered pedagogy based on a developmental epistemological model. This is the view of learning that Dixon (1967) articulated so eloquently in the well received *Growth Through English*. Such a model, however, as Martin, Christie, and Rothery (1987) pointed out, may have had insidious effects on written language instruction owing to the fact that:

> The whole movement toward child-centered education has foundered on the idea that children can understand and undertake history, geography and other subject areas "in their own words." That this is a necessary starting point, no one would deny, especially not those interested in genre-based approaches to writing development. But that children should be stranded there, writing stories for example as their only genre in infant and primary school is impossible to accept. It cuts them off absolutely from any real understanding of what the humanities, social sciences and sciences are about and denies them the tools those disciplines have developed to understand the world. Those tools are fundamentally linguistic ones—the genres and varieties of abstract and technical language associated with each discipline. Education cannot make access a viable goal unless it deconstructs the language involved and the ways in which such language can be taught. (p. 64)

Kress (1987), from a similar, but more overtly political perspective, worried that the:

> overly strong emphasis on individual creativity quite overlooks the fact that children come to school with very different linguistic/generic preparation from home. To the child from the literate middle-class home the teacher's exhortation to express

---

[4]Both Myers (1990) and Bazerman (1993b) wrote case studies of genre anomalies that examine the textual strategies through which superstar scientists such as Crick (Myers) and Gould and Lewontin (Bazerman) reconstitute a rhetorical situation by radically altering the genre conventions. These two studies suggest that it is only the most prestigious members of a culture that may take the liberty of "bending the genre," so to speak.

her/himself is no threat—she or he will implement the generic forms acquired at home. A child from the inner-city slums of Sydney cannot respond in the same way. (p. 43)

Research by the linguists discussed in this essay as well as that of Heath (1983), Dyson (1987, 1988, 1990), and Daiute (1989, 1990) showed children's learning of curriculum or school genres to be interwoven in the specific contexts of situation that recur in the classroom: sharing time, history/geography lesson, language arts time, and so forth. Each of these contexts of situation may be distinguished from others by different patterns of discourse that children are responsible for learning and for employing as they advance through the various curricula. We contend that teachers must be aware of what information they need to provide for students from a variety of backgrounds so that the youngsters may effectively use those various patterns. According to this view, a prompt such as "write a story" given in a context of situation in which the activities and texts support meanings of a scientific character has the effect of cueing children to language behaviors that are situationally inappropriate.

The gist of the arguments that Christie (1987), Kress (1987), and Martin, Christie, and Rothery (1987) made in *The Place of Genre in Learning* is that the overemphasis on the development of the individual child has stranded many children from becoming communicatively competent in patterns of discourse other than narrative. This problem is especially egregious for children whose home and community cultures do not foster such values as self-disclosure and "intimate intellectual relationships with teachers and peers" (Ackerman, 1993, p. 351). Furthermore teachers from the elementary school through the university need to be aware that children's first experience of instructional genres takes place in the context of activity sequences occurring during sharing time, history/geography lesson, language arts time, and so forth. Each of these spatially and temporally bound contexts of situation may be distinguished from others by distinctive patterns of discourse.

Although we concur with Dixon (1987) and with Sawyer and Watson (1987) on the importance of individual creativity, we cannot agree with their contention that genres are simply "mind-forged manacles." On the contrary, we would argue that genres are essential elements of language just as are words, syntactic structures, and sound patterns. In order to express one's individual thoughts, one must use available patterns for speech, that is to say, genres, in one way or another. Virtually every communicative interchange between people, whether in speech or in writing, involves generic structure; in any language there are large numbers of established genres from which to choose. Furthermore, far from being rigid templates, genres can be modified according to the rhetorical circumstances. If teachers use only a few of these genres and require their students to slavishly conform to them, then they are simply using an impoverished pedagogy. It does not follow from this practice, however, that genres in general are manacles. Indeed, we would argue that given the ubiquity of genres in all kinds of speech and writing, students are manacled only when teachers fail to expose them to a broad range and appropriate use of curriculum genres. This, we fear, is the case when rhetoric and composition faculty and the graduate teaching assistants they train ignore or repudiate the patterns of discourse in the sciences and social sciences on the basis of their perceived hegemony and institutionalized authority. (See Bazerman, 1993a, for a critique of this position.)

For the foregoing reasons, we find the essays of Christie, Kress, and of Martin, Christie, and Rothery in *The Place of Genre in Learning* to raise provocative questions concerning the role that the various pedagogical genres play in students' concept learning in different domains and, concomitantly, the role that concept learning in different domains plays in students' development of genre knowledge. For example, what do children and adolescents need to know in the way of concept/genre knowledge to be communicatively competent in writing about historical events?[5] What do they need to know to construct a connected series of statements or reasons intended to establish a position with regard to such events, and hence to refute the opposite? What do they need to know to write about biological processes, such as the stages through which chicken embryos

---

[5]Freedman (1993) recently made the argument that genre knowledge is tacitly acquired rather than explicitly learned. Using an argument curiously similar to that of Martin, Christie, and Rothery (1987) and Halliday and Martin (1993), although emanating from the opposite premises, she argued that a language learner's response to cues in the context of situation seems to be the fundamental factor. To support this observation she describes a recent study she conducted of Canadian university undergraduates enrolled in an introductory law course. Freedman argued that the college students she observed developed their understanding of a distinctive academic (though not professional) subgenre of legal discourse as they worked their way through course assignments, and through the talk and social interaction in the lecture hall and seminar room:

> In the law study I was impressed by the richness and thickness of the texture of the context woven by the instructors and by the degree to which the writing elicited was a response to this context. This enabling context was established through the lectures, through the readings assigned, through the questions posed in the seminars to the students, and through the talk and social interaction in general in the lecture hall and seminar room. The assignment evolved naturally out of disciplinary conversation, and in responding to it, the students were able to draw on the appropriate cues so that on the one hand they all produced the same distinctive academic subgenre (writing for law) and on the other hand through this writing, they enacted the ways of thinking and the ways of identifying, delimiting, construing, and approaching phenomena characteristic of this discipline. (1993, p. 239; see also Freedman, Adam, & Smart, 1994).

Freedman's observations of the situated learning occurring in the introductory law course she observed are significant, we feel, in light of the importance of the context of situation in written language learning that Christie and others noted. And there is an important related point to be made here: What has been observed in such studies of writing in different domains or content areas is shaped in numerous ways through classroom interaction and reading. As Freedman noted, "it is in this way, rather than through attempts at explicit formation of rules, that formal instruction elicits the learning of new genres" (p. 239).

develop? Do teachers—by ignoring explicit instruction in the patterns of discourse that accompany formal learning in different domains—exclude those children and adolescents whose ways with words make them the most vulnerable to economic and social inequities?

The view of child and adolescent language learning that underlies these questions is compatible with Vygotsky's _social-interactional_ view of concept development in children, which differs considerably from the Piagetian focus on the individual as starting point,[6] which we see as underlying the arguments made by Dixon and by Sawyer and Watson. The Piagetian focus, which foregrounds individual development (although Piaget acknowledged the importance of social inputs) informs _both_ expressivist and critical pedagogical approaches. Although both Piaget and Vygotsky took into account social and natural processes in cognitive development, Piaget as Rogoff (1990) noted, "focused on the individual, sometimes interacting with others on logical problems with social origin, and Vygotsky focused on children participating with other people in a social order" (p. 37). In contrast to Piaget's sequential formulation of intellectual development as existing on a continuum between everyday spontaneous concepts and the nonspontaneous concepts (of formal instruction) which supplant the former as the child matures, Vygotsky viewed the relationship between children's spontaneous concepts and the nonspontaneous formal concepts of instruction as being complex and interactive.[7] He observed scientific, nonspontaneous concepts to be "_no less natural_ for a child than everyday ones, because the former reflect an important aspect of the child's life—systematic education and interaction with adults" (Kozulin, 1990, p. 168, italics added; see also Vygotsky, 1987).

Although Britton and his colleagues acknowledged the influence of both Vygotsky and Piaget in their 1975 study of writing in the secondary school, their argument that children possess a natural, unstructured language that is gradually

---

[6]For a discussion of differences between Piaget's and Vygotsky's conceptions of the relationship of the social world to the individual, see Rogoff (1990, pp. 33–37).

[7]What is critical here, in terms of the argument we are making, is that Vygotsky held that the learning of what he called _scientific_ concepts originated:

> in the highly structured and specialized activity of classroom instruction and are characterized by hierarchical, logical organization. The concepts themselves do not necessarily relate to scientific issues—they may represent historical, linguistic, or practical knowledge—but their organization is "scientific" in the sense of formal, logical and decontextualized structures. Everyday concepts, on the other hand, emerge spontaneously from the child's own reflections on immediate, everyday experiences; they are experientially rich but unsystematic and highly contextual. In this sense they are not concepts but rather complexes. . . . Vygotsky argued that "scientific" concepts are no less natural for a child than everyday ones, because the former reflect an important aspect of the child's life—systematic education and interaction with adults. (Kozulin, 1990, p. 168)

Following Vygotsky (1986, cf. 1987), we make a distinction between formal concepts and empirical, "everyday" concepts anchored in a child's experience outside of school.

replaced through formal instruction by the more abstract depersonalized forms of written communication is remarkably similar to the Piagetian conception of child development. In contrast, in the Vygotskian paradigm, instruction and development are held to be inextricably interwoven, dialogical processes. This view of the interrelationship between instruction and development can be seen as underlying Vygotsky's construct of the *zone of proximal development*. At one end of this developmental range is what a child is able to achieve intellectually by herself when performing a task or solving a problem. At the other end is the child's potential development in the context of *assisted performance*, that is to say what the child is able to achieve when guided by an adult or knowledgeable peer (see Cole, 1985; Moll, 1990; Rogoff, 1990). Cognitive change is, therefore, not an individual matter; it is social and interactive. Vygotsky and the linguists whose work we have discussed in this chapter share a common ground in that all emphasized the socially situated nature of the learning of concepts from different domains, and the embeddedness of concepts/genres in school activity.

We described in this chapter a genre-based, sociocognitive perspective on language instruction developed by the functional/systemic linguists discussed earlier. This perspective has, we believe, much in common with the recent work in educational psychology on Vygotskian approaches to classroom instruction. Together, these two strands of inquiry have implications for a serious rethinking of written language instruction at all levels. However, a caveat is in order: It may be that a *genre approach* to the teaching of writing does not fit many language arts and composition teachers' conception of their role, given their training, ideological loyalties, and professional allegiances. If this is the case, rethinking the training of language arts and composition teachers as well as the current curricula in language arts and university writing courses may be what is called for, should enough teachers and scholars see a need to bring about systemic, programmatic change.

# A

# CHRONOLOGY OF DAVIS DRAFTS
# AND CORRESPONDENCE

17 May, 1989: "Elevation of fibrinogen levels due to injection of *Candida albicans* or recombinant tumor necrosis factor (TNFα) in the mouse: Protection with RNF antibodies" sent to editor of *Infection and Immunity* (*IAI*).

16 June, 1989: Manuscript returned with reviews. Editor did not accept manuscript noting that his main concern was that the paper is "incomplete, lacking data on TNF" (see Davis, 29 January, 1990, letter to editor of *IAI*). In an interview, Davis indicated that the reviews were unfavorable.

23 August, 1989: "Elevation" sent to *Journal of Medical and Veterinary Mycology* (*JMVM*).

29 November, 1989: Manuscript returned from editor of *JMVM* with referees' comments. Editor did not accept manuscript; however, he noted that he would reconsider a substantially revised paper.

29 January, 1990: Davis sent to editor of *IAI* a revised manuscript with new title, "TNF is induced in mice by *Candida albicans*: Role of TNF in fibrinogen increase."

13 February, 1990: Editor of *IAI* sent reviewers' comments to Davis.

12 April, 1990: Davis returned revised manuscript to *IAI* editor with an accompanying letter in which she responded point by point to reviewers' comments.

18 May, 1990: *IAI* editor sent second set of comments by reviewer 1 (reviewer 2 had signed off). Editor noted in letter that "we seem close to acceptance now." This is almost, to the date, 1 year after Davis sent first draft to *IAI*.

30 May, 1990: Davis sent revision to *IAI* editor, including in the cover letter a numbered list of changes she had made on manuscript.

8 June, 1990: "TNF is induced in mice by *Candida albicans*: Role of TNF in fibrinogen increase" is accepted for publication in *IAI*.

# B

# Theme Statement for the 1992 CCCC Convention

## (Gere, 1991)

### CONTEXTS, COMMUNITIES, AND CONSTRAINTS: SITES OF COMPOSING AND COMMUNICATING

Annual conventions of CCCC reflect the continuing growth and vitality of our organization as well as our areas of endeavor. Typically attended by approximately one-half of the CCCC membership, conventions provide opportunities to share and develop ideas, to renew friendships and meet colleagues, to examine materials and learn about new developments, and to survey our intellectual sphere.

This sphere has been variously described as a discipline, a proto-discipline, a field, and an area of study. Clearly interdisciplinary, uniting theory and practice, implicating and implicated by multiple institutions including those we call schools, composition and communication elude definition. The theme for the 1992 CCCC Convention assumes that composition and communication can best be described as sites where multiple forces participate in mutually defining and shifting relationships. Rather than concentrating on defining boundaries, this theme urges attention to the contexts in which we teach and do research; to the overlapping communities with which we, our students, and our colleagues identify; and to the constraints that create positive and negative tensions in our professional lives.

Labels such as basic writing, business communication, first-year composition, technical communication, and writing center suggest various contexts. This convention invites interrogation of these labels, examining the meanings attached to them and how those meanings are changing. We might also think about how material conditions—including texts, course packs, facilities, media, and technology—interact with other forces to shape contexts of teaching. What does it mean to write with computers, both within and beyond the classroom? How can we describe the interactions of gender with writing instruction? The term "social context" is frequently appended to words like reading, writing, and speaking. How do we interpret these combinations and what implications do they have for our work? How does collaborative writing/learning shape and how is it shaped by the contexts of instruction?

The multiple and overlapping communities to which we belong pose questions about various kinds of relationships. What can we say, for example, about institutional relations among universities, two-year colleges, secondary schools, and the communities in which they exist? How might we describe the relationships among administrators, faculty, and graduate students? How does the history of rhetoric shape and how is it shaped by current theories and practices? How do we characterize the communities represented by the term critical theory, and how do they interact with other communities? How do the various discourse communities to which we belong, whether within or across so-called disciplines, constitute themselves? What implications do these discourse communities have for the programs, instruction, and theory grouped under the term writing across the curriculum? How might we describe the interrelationships of composition and literature, and how are these relationships changing? The concept of professionalism has received considerable attention within our organization in recent years. What meanings do we attach to this concept and how are those meanings enacted within our various communities? The communities constituted by race and class frequently shape and are shaped by the development, politics, and practices of literacy. How can we describe these relationships?

Rather than limitations or boundaries, constraints refer to the interactions of forces that shape our professional lives. Issues such as assessment, intellectual property (including plagiarism), feminist theory, genres of writing (especially the privileging of some discursive forms at the expense of others), ideology, innovative teaching practices, portfolio evaluation, and working conditions of instructors (especially those who are part-time/temporary) suggest contested meaning. These contests emerge because we care so deeply about the meanings we attach to these terms. Composition has been described as a form of cultural studies. What meanings and implications do we attach to this? How do we describe the interactions evoked by diversity in all its forms? What contests emerge in ESL classes, in teacher-training programs, in theories of knowledge and learning, in theories of composing, in rhetorical theories, in teaching outside schools, in research on composing, in the history of instructional practices, in the relationships between research and practice, and in curriculum development?

This convention offers a space where these and other contested meanings can be explored. It encourages as diverse a range of proposals as the membership wishes to create. Together let us explore the contexts, communities, and constraints that constitute the sites of our engagement.

Anne Ruggles Gere
1992 Program Chair

# C

# METHOD

## DATA COLLECTION

One of the authors shared an office with graduate students during the 1984–1985 academic year and attended classes required of students in the Rhetoric Program. She wrote field notes from her observations and conducted 60- to 90-minute audiotaped interviews with faculty members and with graduate students at various stages in the program. The field notes and interviews provided background information about the educational setting, including the history of the Rhetoric Program, faculty members' research programs, and doctoral candidates' dissertation projects. The notes and interviews also supplied considerable information about the theoretical foundations of the research methodology that doctoral students learned. At the beginning of the academic year, two first-year students agreed to serve as case study subjects. They wrote weekly self-reports of their experiences in the program and met with the researcher to discuss the contents of these reports. They also gave the authors copies of all papers they wrote in their courses. One student dropped out of the study at the beginning of the second semester. The remaining student, Nate, served as the subject for our research.

About one fourth of the audiotaped interviews were transcribed and copies were made to provide part of a database (Yin, 1984) for the study, along with copies of the field notes and the subject's self-reports and texts.

## DATA ANALYSIS

By using multiple sources of evidence and a combination of research perspectives and techniques when analyzing the data, we sought to achieve methodological triangulation (Denzin, 1970) and thereby increase the construct validity of the study (Yin, 1984). Both qualitative and quantitative analyses of the data were performed. The field notes, self-reports, and interview transcripts were read several times by two of the researchers (Berkenkotter and Ackerman). This material was then condensed into *gists* (brief summaries chronologically ordered) and *themes*. These reduction procedures enabled us to extrapolate from a large amount of written narrative a chronology of Nate's experiences in the Rhetoric Program, as depicted by both Nate and the researchers.

The third researcher (Huckin), working independently of the other two and without looking at any of their material, analyzed Nate's texts linguistically to see if they revealed any developmental changes. The total corpus consisted of 12 academic papers, and approximately 31,500 words. The analyses were designed to identify the most revealing linguistic features and patterns of these texts. This meant taking a *problem-driven*, rather than a *theory-driven*, approach, choosing techniques on the basis of their applicability to the case at hand rather than on the basis of their perceived importance to linguistic theory (Evensen, 1985). This researcher followed a five-step procedure. First, in the interest of ecological validity, he read each of the texts holistically, forming and recording the kinds of impressionistic judgments about such features as cohesion, coherence, and diction that any careful reader, linguist or nonlinguist, might make. Then he analyzed these impressions linguistically, selecting the first 50 T-units from each text and using quantitative methods wherever possible. At this point he decided to control for the audience variable by focusing on a subset of five texts that Nate had written for the same reader, Richard E. Young: The first 1,000 words from each text were subjected to fine-grained analysis. Then, using the same stylistic parameters, he analyzed the writing of Professor Young and of eight other composition theorists whom Nate had cited favorably in his writings. This allowed him to compare Nate's style with that of these more experienced writers and to see if Nate had indeed been learning how to communicate in the language of his discipline.

The initial phase of the linguistic analysis showed that the most problematic text-features of Nate's early writings in the Rhetoric Program were: (a) excessive use of the first person singular subject pronoun, (b) insufficient cohesion and coherence, and (c) inappropriate diction. In order to analyze these features more closely the following linguistic measures were used:

1. Number of "I" 's per 50 T-units or 1,000 words of text.
2. Number of connectives (e.g., and, but, however, thus) per 50 T-units or 1,000 words of text. Sloan's (1984) list of connectives was used as a basic reference, and the investigator counted only those connectives used to link T-units, not those used to link phrases.
3. Number of discourse demonstratives per 50 T-units or 1,000 words of text. Discourse demonstratives were defined as any instance of *this, these, those,*

or *that* used to help tie two T-units together. A demonstrative referring only to entities within the same T-unit would not therefore count as a discourse demonstrative.

4. Average sentence length, as measured in words per sentence. This is a generally reliable indicator of syntactic complexity which, in turn, is an important indicator of textual cohesion. Relative clauses, adverbial clauses, and other forms of syntactic subordination tie ideas together without using connectives or discourse demonstratives.

5. Ratio of definite articles to indefinite articles. Definite articles typically mark given information, whereas indefinite articles typically mark new information. Hence, as discussed in Johansson (1985), this ratio is a good way of measuring thematic continuity. The investigator chose this method over more traditional topic-oriented methods based on Functional Sentence Perspective because the texts (both by Nate and by the nine composition theorists) being examined often did not have clearly identifiable sentence topics.

6. Percentage of off-register words and phrases. To identify sociolinguistically inappropriate vocabulary, the investigator asked three rhetoricians to read Nate's texts and those of the comparison group and, as stated in the provided instructions, to "mark any words or phrases that strike you as being off-register, i.e., either too casual or too formal or too belletristic for social science research writing." The register index represents an averaging of these scores.

# References

Ackerman, J. (1993). The promise of writing to learn. *Written Communication, 10*(3), 334–370.

Akinnaso, F. N. (1982). On the differences between spoken and written language. *Language & Speech, 25*, 97–125.

Amsterdamska, O., & Leydesdorff, L. (1989). Citations: Indicators of significance? *Scientometrics, 15*, 449–471.

Anderson, J. R. (1983). *The architecture of cognition.* Cambridge, MA: Harvard University Press.

Austin, J. L. (1975). *How to do things with words.* (J. O. Urmson & M. Sbisa, Eds.), Cambridge, MA: Harvard University Press.

Bakhtin, M. (1981). *The dialogic imagination: Four essays by M. M. Bakhtin* (C. Emerson & M. Holquist, Trans.; M. Holquist, Ed.). Austin: University of Texas Press.

Bakhtin, M. (1986). *Speech genres and other late essays* (V. W. McGee, Trans.; C. Emerson & M. ⁊ Holquist, Eds). Austin: University of Texas Press.

Bartholomae, D. (1985). Inventing the university. In M. Rose (Ed.), *When a writer can't write* (pp. 134–165). New York: Guilford.

Bazerman, C. (1985). Physicists reading physics: Schema-laden purposes and purpose-laden schema. *Written Communication, 2*(1), 3–23.

Bazerman, C. (1988). *Shaping written knowledge: The genre and activity of the experimental article in science.* Madison: University of Wisconsin Press.

Bazerman, C. (1993a). From cultural criticism to disciplinary participation: Living with powerful words. In A. Herrington & C. Moran (Eds.), *Writing teaching, and learning in the disciplines* (pp. 61–68). New York: Modern Language Association.

Bazerman, C. (1993b). Intertextual self-fashioning: Gould and Lewontin's representation of the literature. In J. Selzer (Ed.), *Understanding scientific prose.* Madison: University of Wisconsin Press.

Bazerman, C. (1994). *Constructing experience.* Carbondale: Southern Illinois University Press.

Bazerman, C., & Paradis, J. (1991). Introduction. In C. Bazerman & J. Paradis (Eds.), *Textual dynamics of the professions.* Madison: University of Wisconsin Press.

Bennett, T. (1990). *Outside literature.* London: Routledge.

Benson, P. (1985). Writing visually: Design considerations in technical publications. *Technical Communication, 32*(4), 35–39.

Bergvall, V. (1992, April). *Different or dominant? The role of gender in the academic conversation.* Paper presented at the annual meeting of the American Educational Research Association, San Francisco, CA.

Berkenkotter, C. (1990). Evolution of a scholarly forum: *Reader, 1977–1988.* In G. Kirsch & D. Roen (Eds.), *A sense of audience in written communication* (pp. 191–215). Newbury Park, CA: Sage.

Berkenkotter, C. (1991). Paradigm debates, turf wars, and the conduct of sociocognitive inquiry in composition. *College Composition and Communication, 42*(2), 151–169.

Berkenkotter, C., & Huckin, T. N. (1993a). You are what you cite: Novelty and intertextuality in a biologist's experimental article. In N. R. Blyler & C. Thralls (Eds.), *Professional communication: The social perspective* (pp. 109–127). Newbury Park, CA: Sage.

Berkenkotter, C., & Huckin, T. (1993b). Rethinking genre from a sociocognitive perspective. *Written Communication, 10*(4), 475–509.

Berkenkotter C., Huckin, T. N., & Ackerman, J. (1988). Conventions, conversations, and the writer: Case study of a student in a rhetoric Ph.D. program. *Research in the Teaching of English, 22,* 9–44.

Berkenkotter, C., Huckin, T. N., & Ackerman, J. (1991). Social contexts and socially constructed texts: The initiation of a graduate student into a writing research community. In C. Bazerman & J. Paradis (Eds.), *Textual dynamics of the professions: Historical and contemporary studies of writing in academic and other professional communities* (pp. 191–215). Madison: University of Wisconsin Press.

Berlin, J. A., & Vivion, M. J. (Eds.). (1992). *Cultural studies in the English classroom.* Portsmouth, NH: Boynton/Cook.

Beutler, B., Milsark, T. W., & Cerami, A. L. (1985). Passive immunization against cachectin/tumor necrosis factor protects mice from lethal effect of endotoxin. *Science, 229,* 869–887.

Bitzer, L. (1968). The rhetorical situation. *Philosophy and Rhetoric, 1,* 1–14.

Bizzell, P. (1982a). Cognition, convention, and certainty: What we need to know about writing. *PRE/TEXT, 3,* 213–243.

Bizzell, P. (1982b). College composition: Initiation into the academic discourse community [Review of *Four worlds of writing* and *Writing in the arts and sciences*]. *Curriculum Inquiry, 12*(2), 191–207.

Bizzell, P. (1992). *Academic discourse and critical consciousness.* Pittsburgh: University of Pittsburgh Press.

Blakeslee, A. (1994). The rhetorical construction of novelty: Presenting claims in a letters forum. *Science, Technology, and Human Values, 19*(1), 88–100.

Bleich, D. (1975a). The subjective character of critical interpretation. *College English, 36,* 739–755.

Bleich, D. (1975b). *Readings and feelings: An introduction to subjective criticism.* Urbana, IL: National Council of Teachers of English.

Bleich, D. (1976a). Pedagogical directions in subjective criticism. *College English, 37,* 454–487.

Bleich, D. (1976b). The subjective paradigm. *New Literary History, 7,* 313–334.

Bleich, D. (1978). *Subjective criticism.* Baltimore: Johns Hopkins University Press.

Bleich, D. (1979, June). [Reply to reader's responses to *Subjective Criticism*]. *Reader: A newsletter of reader-oriented criticism and teaching* (pp. 25–30). (Available from Elizabeth A. Flynn, Humanities Dept., Michigan Technological University)

Boden, D., & Zimmerman, D. H. (1991). *Talk and social structure: Studies in ethnomethodology and conversation analysis.* Berkeley: University of California Press.

Bourdieu, P. (1987). *Choses dites* [Things said]. Paris: Les Edtions de Minuit.

Brandt, D. (1983). Writer, context, and text (Doctoral dissertation, Indiana University). *Dissertation Abstracts International, 43*(9), 2855A.

Brandt, D. (1990). *Literature as involvement: The acts of writers, readers and texts.* Carbondale: Southern Illinois University Press.

Britton, J., Burgess, T., Martin, N., McLeod, A., & Rosen, H. (1975). *The development of writing abilities, 11–18.* London: Macmillan.

Brown, G., & Yule, G. (1983). *Discourse analysis.* Cambridge, UK: Cambridge University Press.

Brown, J. S., Collins, A., & Duguid, P. (1989). Situated cognition and the culture of learning. *Educational Researcher, 18,* 32–42.

Bruner, J. (1991). The narrative construction of reality. *Critical Inquiry, 18,* 1–21.

Bryant, C. G. A., & Jary, D. (Eds.). (1991). *Giddens' theory of structuration: A critical appreciation.* London: Routledge.

Campbell, D. T., & Stanley, J. C. (1966). *Experimental and quasi-experimental designs for research.* Boston: Houghton Mifflin.

Campbell, K. K., & Jamieson, K. H. (1978). Form and genre in rhetorical criticism: An introduction. In K. K. Campbell & K. H. Jamieson (Eds.), *Form and genre: Shaping rhetorical action* (pp. 9–32). Falls Church, VA: Speech Communication Association.

Carter, M. (1988). *Stasis* and *kairos:* Principles of social construction in classical rhetoric. *Rhetoric Review, 7,* 97–112.

Cazden, C. (1986). Classroom discourse. In M. Wittrock (Ed.), *Handbook of research on teaching* (pp. 432–463). New York: Macmillan.

Cazden, C. (1989, March). *Vygotsky and Bakhtin: From word to utterance and voice.* Paper presented at the annual conference of the American Educational Research Association, San Francisco, CA.

Chafe, W. L. (1982). Integration and involvement in speaking, writing, and oral literature. In D. Tannen (Ed.), *Spoken and written language: Exploring orality and literacy* (pp. 35–53). Norwood, NJ: Ablex.

Christie, F. (1985). Language and schooling. In S. Tchudi (Ed.), *Language, schooling, and society.* Upper Montclair, NJ: Boynton/Cook.

Christie, F. (1987). Genres as choice. In I. Reid (Ed.), *The place of genre in learning: Current debates.* Geelong, Australia: Centre for Studies in Literacy Education, Deakin University Press.

Chubin, D., & Hackett, E. (1990). *Peerless science: Peer review and U.S. science policy.* Albany, NY: SUNY Press.

Clay, M. M., & Cazden, C. B. (1990). A Vygotskian interpretation of Reading Recovery. In L. C. Moll (Ed.), *Vygotsky and education: Instructional implications and applications of sociohistorical psychology* (pp. 206–222). Cambridge, MA: Cambridge University Press.

Clifford, J. (1983). On ethnographic authority. *Representations, 1,* 118–146.

Clifford, J. (1988). Introduction: On first reading Rosenblatt. *Reader: Essays in reader-oriented theory, criticism, and pedagogy, 20,* 1–6.

Clifford, J., & Marcus, G. E. (Eds.). (1986). *Writing culture: The poetics and politics of ethnography.* ✓ Berkeley: University of California Press.

Cole, M. (1985). The zone of proximal development: Where culture and cognition create each other. In J. V. Wertsch (Ed.), *Culture, communication and cognition: Vygotskian perspectives.* Cambridge, MA: Cambridge University Press.

Cole, M. (1990). Cognitive development and formal schooling: The evidence from cross-cultural research. In L. C. Moll (Ed.), *Vygotsky and education: Instructional implications and applications of sociohistorical psychology* (pp. 89–110). Cambridge, MA: Cambridge University Press.

Collins, A., Brown, J. S., & Newman, S. E. (1989). Cognitive apprenticeship: Teaching the craft of reading, writing, and mathematics. In L. B. Resnik (Ed.), *Knowing, learning and instruction: Essays in honor of Robert Glaser* (pp. 453–494). Hillsdale, NJ: Erlbaum.

Collins, P. H. (1990). *Black feminist thought: Knowledge, consciousness, and the politics of empowerment.* New York: Routledge.

Comprone, J. (1993). Generic constraints and expressive motives: Rhetorical perspectives on textual dialogues. In N. R. Blyler & C. Thralls (Eds.), *Professional communication: The social perspective* (pp. 92–108). Newbury Park, CA: Sage.

Contractor, N. S., & Eisenberg, E. M. (1990). Communication networks and new media in organizations. In J. Fulk & C. W. Steinfield (Eds), *Organizations and communication technology* (pp. 143–172). Newbury Park, CA: Sage.

Cozzens, S. E. (1985). Comparing the sciences: Citation content analysis of papers from neuropharmacology and the sociology of science. *Social Studies of Science, 15*, 127–53.

Cozzens, S. E. (1989). What do citations count? The rhetoric-first model. *Scientometrics, 15*, 437–447.

Crane, D. (1972). *Invisible colleges.* Chicago: University of Chicago Press.

Crosman, R. (Ed.). (1977a, January). [Introduction to the newsletter]. *Reader: a newsletter of reader-oriented criticism and teaching*, (1), 1–2. (Available from Elizabeth A. Flynn, Humanities Dept., Michigan Technological University)

Crosman, R. (Ed.). (1977b, April). [Advice to readers on submitting informal responses]. *Reader: a newsletter of reader-oriented criticism and teaching*, (2), 5. (Available from Elizabeth A. Flynn, Humanities Dept., Michigan Technological University)

Crosman, R. (1979, June). [Response to David Bleich's *Subjective criticism*] *Reader: a newsletter of reader-oriented criticism and teaching* (6), 5–6.

Daiute, C. (1989). Play as thought: Thinking strategies of young children. *Harvard Educational Review, 59*, 1–23.

Daiute, C. (1990). The role of play in writing development. *Research in the Teaching of English, 24*, 4–45.

De Certeau, M. (1984). *Practice of everyday life.* Berkeley, CA: University of California Press.

Denzin, N. (1990). *The research act.* Chicago: Aldine.

Derrida, J. (1981). The law of genre. In W. J. T. Mitchell (Ed.), *On narrative* (pp. 51–77). Chicago: University of Chicago Press.

Devitt, A. (1991). Intertextuality in tax accounting: Generic, referential, and functional. In C. Bazerman & J. Paradis (Eds.), *Textual dynamics of the professions: Historical and contemporary studies of writing in professional communities* (pp. 336–357). Madison: University of Wisconsin Press.

Dixon, J. (1967). *Growth through English.* London: National Association for the Teaching of English and Oxford University Press.

Dixon, J. (1987). The question of genres. In I. Reid (Ed.), *The place of genre in learning: Current debates* (pp. 9–21). Geelong, Australia: Centre for Studies in Literacy Education, Deakin University.

Dorr-Bremme, D. (1990). Contextualization cues in the classroom: Discourse regulation and social control functions. *Language and Society, 19*, 379–402.

Dyson, A. H. (1984a). Emerging alphabetic literacy in school contexts: Toward defining the gap between school curriculum and child mind. *Written Communication, 1*, 5–55.

Dyson, A. H. (1984b). Learning to write/Learning to do school: Emergent writers' interpretations of school literacy tasks. *Research in the Teaching of English, 18*, 233–264.

Dyson, A. H. (1987). The value of "time off task": Young children's spontaneous talk and deliberate text. *Harvard Educational Review, 57*(4), 396–420.

Dyson, A. H. (1988). Negotiating among multiple worlds: The space-time dimension of young children's composing. *Research in the Teaching of English, 22*(4), 355–391.

Dyson, A. H. (1990). The word and the world: Reconceptualizing written language development; or Do rainbows mean a lot to little girls? *Research in the Teaching of English, 25*(1), 97–119.

Elbow, P. (1981). *Writing with power.* New York: Oxford University Press.

Elbow, P. (1985). The shifting relationship between speech and writing. *College Composition and Communication, 36*, 283–303.

Engstrom, Y. (1987). *Learning by expanding.* Helsinki: Orienta-Konsultit Oy.

Erickson, F., & Schultz, J. (1982). *The counselor as gatekeeper: Social interaction in interviews.* New York: Academic Press.

Evensen, L. S. (1985). A note on the relationship between theory and application. *Text, 5*(4), 269–279.

Fahnestock, J., & Secor, M. (1991). The rhetoric of literary criticism. In C. Bazerman & J. Paradis (Eds.), *Textual dynamics of the professions* (pp. 76–96). Madison: University of Wisconsin Press.

Faigley, L. (1986). Competing theories of process: A critique and a proposal. *College English, 48,* 527–542.

Faigley, L., & Witte, S. (1983). Topical focus in technical writing. In P. V. Anderson, R. J. Brockman, & C. Miller (Eds.), *New essays in technical and scientific communication: Research, theory, practice* (pp. 59–68). Farmingdale, NY: Baywood.

Fairclough, N. (1992). *Discourse and social change.* London: Polity.

Fairclough, N. (1993). Critical discourse analysis and the marketization of public discourse: The universities. *Discourse and Society, 4*(2), 133–168.

Featherstone, M. (1991). *Consumer culture and postmodernism.* London: Sage.

Ferrara, K., Brunner, H., & Whittemore, G. (1991). Interactive written discourse as an emergent register. *Written Communication, 8*(1), 8–34.

Fish, S. (1971). *Surprised by sin: The reader in Paradise Lost.* Berkeley: University of California Press.

Fish, S. (1973a). *Self-consuming artifacts.* Berkeley: University of California Press.

Fish S. (1973b). What is stylistics and why are they saying such terrible things about it? In S. Chatman (Ed.), *Approaches to poetics* (pp. 109–152). New York: Columbia University Press.

Fish, S. (1976). Critical response III: Interpreting "Interpreting the *Variorum.*" *Critical Inquiry, 3,* 191–196.

Fish, S. (1980). *Is there a text in this class? The authority of interpretive communities.* Cambridge, MA: Harvard University Press.

Fisher, W. (1987). *Human communication as narration: Toward a philosophy of reason.* Columbia: University of South Carolina Press.

Fleck, L. (1981). *Genesis and development of a scientific fact.* Chicago: University of Chicago Press.

Flower, L., & Hayes, J. R. (1984). Images, plans, and prose: The representation of meaning in writing. *Written Communication, 1,* 120–160.

Flynn, E. (1983). A note from the editor. *Reader: Essays in Reader-oriented Theory, Criticism, and Pedagogy, 9,* i–iii.

Flynn, E. (1986). A note from the editor. *Reader: Essays in Reader-oriented Theory, Criticism, and Pedagogy, 16,* i–ii.

Freadman, A. (1987). Anyone for tennis? In I. Reid (Ed.), *The place of genre in learning: Current debates* (pp. 91–124). Geelong, Australia: Deakin University Press.

Freedman, A. (1993). Show and tell? The role of explicit teaching in the learning of new genres. *Research in the Teaching of English, 27,* 222–251.

Freedman, A., Adam, C., & Smart, G. (1994). Wearing suits to class: Simulating genres and simulations as genre. *Written Communication, 11,* 193–226.

Gallimore, R., & Tharp, R. (1990). Teaching mind in society: Teaching, schooling, and literate discourse. In L. C. Moll (Ed.), *Vygotsky and education: Instructional implications and applications of sociohistorical psychology* (pp. 175–205). Cambridge, MA: Cambridge University Press.

Garfinkel, H. (1967). *Studies in ethnomethodology.* Englewood Cliffs, NJ: Prentice-Hall.

Geertz, C. (1973). *The interpretation of cultures.* New York: Basic Books.

Geertz, C. (1983). *Local knowledge: Further essays in interpretive anthropology.* New York: Basic Books.

Giddens, A. (1979). *Central problems in social theory: Action, structure and contradiction in social analysis.* London: Macmillan.

Giddens, A. (1984). *The constitution of society: Outline of the theory of structuration.* Berkeley: University of California Press.

Gilbert, G. N. (1977). Referencing as persuasion. *Social Studies of Science, 7,* 113–122.

Gilbert, G. N., & Mulkay, M. (1980). Contexts of scientific discourse: Social accounting in experimental papers. In K. D. Knorr, R. Krohn, & R. Whitley (Eds.), *The social process of scientific investigation* (pp. 269–294). Amsterdam: D. Reidel.

Gilbert, G. N., & Mulkay, M. (1984). *Opening pandora's box: A sociological analysis of scientists' discourse.* Cambridge: Cambridge University Press.

Giltrow, J. (1992, April). *Genre and the pragmatic concept of background knowledge*. Paper presented at the International "Rethinking Genre" Conference, Carleton University, Ottawa, Canada.

Glaser, B. G., & Strauss, A. L. (1967). *The discovery of grounded theory: Strategies for qualitative research*. New York: Aldine de Gruyter.

Goodwin, C. (1979). The interactive construction of a sentence in everyday conversation. In G. Psalthas (Ed.), *Everyday language: Studies in ethnomethodology* (pp. 97–122). New York: Irvington.

Graesser, A., Hoffman, N., & Clark, L. (1980). Structural components of reading time. *Journal of Verbal Learning and Verbal Behavior, 19*, 135–151.

Graves, D. H. (1983). *Writing: Teachers and children at work*. Exeter, NH: Heinemann.

Gross, A. (1990). *The rhetoric of science*. Cambridge, MA: Harvard University Press.

Halliday, M. A. K. (1978). *Language as social semiotic*. London: Edward Arnold.

Halliday, M. A. K., & Martin, J. R. (1993). *Writing science: Literacy and discursive power*. Pittsburgh: University of Pittsburgh Press.

Halloran, M. (1984). The birth of molecular biology: An essay in the rhetorical criticism of scientific discourse. *Rhetoric Review, 3*, 70–83.

Hansen, K. (1988). Rhetoric and epistemology in the social sciences: A contrast of two representative texts. In D. Jolliffe (Ed.), *Writing in academic disciplines* (pp. 167–210). Norwood, NJ: Ablex.

Harrell, J., & Linkugel, W. A. (1978). On rhetorical genre: An organizing perspective. *Philosophy and Rhetoric, 11*, 262–281.

Harris, J. (1991). After Dartmouth: Growth and conflict in English. *College English, 53*(4), 631–647.

Haviland, S. E., & Clark, H. H. (1974). What's new? Acquiring new information as a process in comprehension. *Journal of Verbal Learning and Verbal Behavior, 13*, 512–521.

Heath, S. B. (1983). *Ways with words: Language, life, and work in communities and classrooms*. Cambridge, UK: Cambridge University Press.

Hedrick, D. (1977, April). [Letter to the editor]. *Reader: a newsletter of reader-oriented criticism and teaching*, (3), 3.

Herndl, C. G., Fennell, B. A., & Miller, C. R. (1991). Understanding failures in organizational discourse: The accident at Three Mile Island and the shuttle Challenger disaster. In C. Bazerman & J. Paradis (Eds.), *Textual dynamics of the professions: Historical and contemporary studies of writing in professional communities* (pp. 279–305). Madison: University of Wisconsin Press.

Herrington, A. (1989). The first twenty years of *Research in the Teaching of English* and the growth of a research community in composition studies. *Research in the Teaching of English, 22*, 117–138.

Holland, N. (1973). *Poems in persons: An introduction to the psychoanalysis of literature*. New York: Norton.

Holland, N. (1975a). *The dynamics of literary response*. New York: Norton.

Holland, N. (1975b). *Five readers reading*. New Haven, CT: Yale University Press.

Holland, N. (1975c). Unity identity text self. *Publications of the Modern Language Association, 90*, 813–822.

Holquist, M. (1986). Introduction. In M. M. Bakhtin, *Speech genres and other late essays* (V. W. McGee, Trans.; C. Emerson and M. Holquist, Eds., pp. ix–xxii). Austin, TX: University of Texas Press.

Hooks, B. (1990). *Yearning: Race, gender, and cultural politics*. Boston, MA: South End.

Hopkins, A., & Dudley-Evans, T. (1988). A genre-based investigation of the Discussion sections in articles and dissertations. *English for Specific Purposes, 7*(2), 113–121.

Hopper, P. (1988). Emergent grammar and the *a priori* postulate. In D. Tannen (Ed.), *Linguistics in context: Connecting observation and understanding* (pp. 117–134). Norwood, NJ: Ablex.

Horowitz, M., & Berkowitz, A. (1964). Structural advantage of the mechanism of spoken expression as a factor in differences in spoken and written expression. *Perceptual and Motor Skills, 19*, 619–625.

Huckin, T. (1987, March). *Surprise value in scientific discourse*. Paper presented at the 38th annual meeting of the Conference on College Composition and Communication. Atlanta, GA.

Huckin, T. (1992, March). *Genre knowledge and the ad hoc discourse community*. Paper presented at the 43rd annual meeting of the Conference on College Composition and Communication, Cincinnati, OH.

Huckin, T., Haynes, M., & Coady, J. (1993). *Second language reading and vocabulary learning.* Norwood, NJ: Ablex.

Hudson, R. A. (1980). *Sociolinguistics.* Cambridge, UK: Cambridge University Press.

Hunt, R. R., & Vipond, D. V. (1985). Crash-testing a transactional model of literary learning. *Reader: Essays in Reader-oriented Theory, Criticism and Pedagogy, 14,* 23–39.

Hymes, D. (1971). Competence and performance in linguistic theory. In R. Huxley & E. Ingram (Eds.), *Language acquisition: Models and methods* (pp. 3–28). London: Academic Press.

Iser, W. (1971). Indeterminacy and the reader's response in prose fiction. In J. H. Miller (Ed.), *Aspects of narrative* (pp. 1–45). New York: Columbia University Press.

Iser, W. (1974). *The implied reader.* Baltimore: Johns Hopkins University Press.

Iser, W. (1975). The reality of fiction: A functionalist approach to literature. *New Literary History, 7,* 7–38.

Iser, W. (1978). *The act of reading: A theory of aesthetic response.* Baltimore: Johns Hopkins University Press.

Johansson, S. (1985). Word frequency and text type: Some observations based on the LOB corpus of British English texts. *Computers and the Humanities, 19,* 23–36.

Kantor, K. J., Kirby, D. R., & Goetz, J. P. (1981). Research in context: Ethnographic studies in English education. *Research in the Teaching of English, 15,* 293–310.

Katz, S. (1983). Teaching the tagmemic discovery procedure: A case study of a writing course. (Doctoral dissertation, Carnegie-Mellon University). *Dissertation Abstracts International, 45*(05), 1320A.

Kaufer, D. S., & Geisler, C. (1989). Novelty in academic writing. *Written Communication, 6,* 286–311.

Kinneavy, J. (1983). Writing across the curriculum. *Profession 83* (pp. 13–20). New York: Modern Language Association.

Kozulin, A. (1990). *Vygotsky's psychology: A bibliography of ideas.* Cambridge, MA: Harvard University Press.

Kress, G. (1982). *Learning to write.* London: Routledge & Kegan Paul.

Kress, G. (1987). Genre in a social theory of language: A reply to John Dixon. In I. Reid (Ed.), *The place of genre in learning: Current debates.* Geelong, Australia: Deakin University Press.

Kress, G. (1989). *Linguistic processes in sociocultural practice.* Oxford: Oxford University Press.

Kress, G. (1993a). Against arbitrariness: The social production of the sign as a foundational issue in critical discourse analysis. *Discourse & Society, 4,* 169–192.

Kress, G. (1993b). Genre as a social process. In B. Cope & M. Kalantzis (Eds.), *The powers of literacy: A genre approach to teaching writing* (pp. 22–37). Pittsburgh, PA: University of Pittsburgh Press.

Kuhn, T. S. (1970). *The structure of scientific revolutions* (2nd ed.). Chicago: University of Chicago Press.

Lakatos, I. (1970). Falsification and the methodology of scientific research programs. In I. Lakatos & A. Musgrave (Eds.), *Criticism and the growth of knowledge* (pp. 91–196). Cambridge, UK: Cambridge University Press.

Lamb, C. E. (1974). On suffering change: Toward a theory of instruction in the art of invention. (Doctoral dissertation, University of Michigan, Ann Arbor.) *Dissertation Abstracts International, 35*(05), 2654A.

Langacker, R. (1974). Movement rules in functional perspective. *Language, 50,* 629–664.

Latour, B. (1987). *Science in action.* Cambridge, MA: Harvard University Press.

Latour, B., & Woolgar, S. (1986). *Laboratory life: The social construction of scientific facts.* Princeton, NJ: Princeton University Press.

Lauer, J. M. (1967). Invention in contemporary rhetoric: Heuristic procedures. (Doctoral dissertation, University of Michigan, Ann Arbor.) *Dissertation Abstracts International, 28,* 5060A.

Lauer, J. M. (1972). The problem of problem-solving. *College Composition and Communication, 23,* 208–210.

Lave, J. (1977). Tailor-made experiments and evaluating the intellectual consequences of apprenticeship training. *The Quarterly Newsletter of the Institute for Comparative Human Development, 1,* 1–3.

Lave, J. (1988a). *Cognition in practice.* Boston, MA: Cambridge University Press.

Lave, J. (1988b). *The culture of acquisition and the practice of understanding* (IRL Report No. 88–00087). Palo Alto: CA: Institute for Research on Learning.

Lave, J., & Wegner, E. (1991). *Situated learning: Legitimate peripheral participation.* Cambridge, MA: Cambridge University Press.

Lemke, J. (1990). *Talking science: Language, learning, and values.* Norwood, NJ: Ablex.

LePage, R. B., Christie, P., Jurdant, B., Weekes, A. J., & Tabouret-Keller, A. (1974). Further report on the sociolinguistic survey of multilingual communities: Survey of Cayo District, British Honduras. *Language in Society, 3,* 1–32.

Lewontin, R. C. (1991). Facts and the factitious in natural sciences. *Critical Inquiry, 18,* 140–154.

Leydesdorff, L., & Amsterdamska, O. (1990). Dimensions of citation analysis. *Science, Technology, and Human Values, 15,* 305–335.

Lincoln, Y. S., & Guba, E. G. (1985). *Naturalistic inquiry.* Beverly Hills, CA: Sage Publications.

Lloyd, J. E. (1985, June 26). Selling scholarship down the river: The pernicious aspects of peer review. *The Chronicle of Higher Education,* p. 64.

MacDonald, S. P. (1987). Problem definition in academic writing. *College English, 49,* 315–330.

MacDonald, S. P. (1989). Data-driven and conceptually driven academic discourse. *Written Communication, 6,* 411–435.

MacDonald, S. P. (1992). A method for analyzing sentence-level differences in disciplinary knowledge-making. *Written Communication, 9,* 435–464.

Malinowski, B. (1935). *Coral gardens and their magic, Vol. 2.* London: Allen & Unwin. Reprinted as *The language of magic and gardening* (Indiana University Studies in the History and Theory of Linguistics), Bloomington: Indiana University Press, 1967.

Manning, P. K. (1989). *Symbolic communication.* Cambridge, MA: MIT Press.

Marshall, M. J., & Barritt, L. S. (1990). Choices made, worlds created: The rhetoric of *AERJ. American Educational Research Journal, 27,* 589–609.

Martin, J. R., Christie, F., & Rothery, J. (1987). Social processes in education: A reply to Sawyer and Watson (and others). In I. Reid (Ed.), *The place of genre in learning: Current debates.* Geelong, Australia: Deakin University Press.

Martin, J. R., & Rothery, J. (1993). Grammar: Making meaning in writing. In B. Cope & M. Kalantzis (Eds.), *The powers of literacy: A genre approach to teaching writing.* Pittsburgh, PA: University of Pittsburgh Press.

McCormick, K. (1988). "First steps" in "Wandering Rocks": Students' differences, literary transactions, and pleasures. *Reader: Essays in Reader-oriented Theory, Criticism, and Pedagogy, 20,* 48–67.

McHoul, A. (1978). The organization of turns at formal talk in the classroom. *Language and Society, 7,* 183–213.

Medawar, P. B. (1964, August 1). Is the scientific paper fradulent? *Saturday Review,* pp. 42–43.

Mehan, H. (1991). The school's work of sorting students. In D. Boden & D. H. Zimmerman (Eds.), *Talk and social structure: Studies in ethnomethodology and conversation analysis* (pp. 71–90). Berkeley: University of California Press.

Meyer, B. J. F. (1982). Reading research and the composition teacher: The importance of plans. *College Composition and Communication, 33,* 37–49.

Miller, C. R. (1984). Genre as social action. *Quarterly Journal of Speech, 70,* 151–167.

Miller, C. R. (1992). *Kairos* in the rhetoric of science. In S. Witte, N. Nakadake, & R. Cherry (Eds.), *A rhetoric of doing: Essays honoring James L. Kinneavy* (pp. 310–327). Carbondale: Southern Illinois Press.

Miller C. R., & Selzer, J. (1985). Special topics of argument in engineering reports. In L. Odell & D. Goswami (Eds.), *Writing in nonacademic settings* (pp. 309–341). New York: Guilford.

Minh-ha, T. T. (1989). *Woman native other.* Bloomington: Indiana University Press.

Mishler, E. G. (1979). Meaning in context: Is there any other kind? *Harvard Educational Review, 39,* 1–19.

Mistacco, V. (1977). Seminar. The *Reader* in modern French fiction. *Reader: a newsletter of reader-oriented criticism and teaching,* (4), 7–9.

Moll, L. C. (1990). Introduction. In L. C. Moll (Ed.), *Vygotsky and education: Instructional implications and applications of sociohistorical psychology* (pp. 1–27). Cambridge, UK: Cambridge University Press.

Murray, D. (1984). *Write to learn.* New York: Holt, Rinehart, & Winston.

Myers, G. (1990). *Writing biology: Texts in the social construction of scientific knowledge.* Madison: University of Wisconsin Press.

Nugent, S. (1980). *A comparative analysis of two methods of invention.* Unpublished doctoral dissertation, Indiana University of Pennsylvania, Indiana.

Nystrand, M. (1986). Reciprocity as a principle of discourse. *The structure of written communication: Studies in reciprocity between writers and readers* (pp. 39–58). Orlando, FL: Academic Press.

Nystrand, M., & Wiemelt, J. (1991). When is a text explicit? Formalist and dialogical conceptions, *Text, 11,* 25–41.

Odell, L. (1970). *Discovery procedures for contemporary rhetoric.* Unpublished doctoral dissertation, University of Michigan, Ann Arbor.

Odell, L. (1974). Measuring the effect of instruction in pre-writing. *Research in the Teaching of English, 8,* 223–240.

Odell, L. (1978). Another look at tagmemic rhetoric: A response to James Kinney. *College Composition and Communication, 29,* 146–152.

Olsen, L. A., & Huckin, T. N. (1983). *Principles of communication for science and technology.* New York: McGraw-Hill.

Ong, W. J. (1982). *Orality and literacy: The technologizing of the word.* London: Methuen.

Ongstad, S. (1992, April). *The definition of genre and the didactics of genre.* Paper presented at the International "Rethinking Genre" Conference, Carleton University, Ottawa, Canada.

Perelman, C., & Olbrechts-Tyteca, L. (1969). *The new rhetoric: A treatise on argumentation.* Notre Dame, IN: University of Notre Dame Press.

Pinker, S. (1984). *Language learnability and language development.* Cambridge, MA: Harvard University Press.

Poole, M. S., & DeSanctis, G. (1990). Understanding the use of group decision support systems: The theory of adaptive structuration. In J. Fulk & C. W. Steinfield (Eds.), *Organizations and communication technology* (pp. 195–219). Newbury Park, CA: Sage.

Potter, J., & Wetherell, M. (1987). *Discourse and social psychology: Beyond attitudes and behavior.* London: Sage.

Purves, A. C., & Purves, W. C. (1986). Viewpoints: Cultures, text models, and the activity of writing. *Research in the Teaching of English, 20,* 174–197.

Rabianski, N. (1980). *Systematic or unsystematic invention instruction: Which is more effective for a student writer?* Unpublished manuscript, State University of New York at Buffalo, Buffalo, NY.

Rabinowitz, P. (1977, April). [Letter to the editor]. *Reader: a newsletter of reader-oriented criticism and teaching,* p.2. (Available from Elizabeth A. Flynn, Humanities Dept., Michigan Technological University)

Rafoth, B. A. (1990). The concept of discourse community: Descriptive and explanatory adequacy. In G. Kirsch & D. H. Roen (Eds.), *A sense of audience in written communication* (pp. 140–152). Newbury Park, CA: Sage.

Raymond, J. (1993). I Dropping and Androgyny: The Authorial I in Scholarly Writing. *College Composition and Communication, 44,* 478–483.

Reid, I. (Ed.). (1988). *The place of genre in learning: Current debates.* Geelong, Australia: Deakin University Press.

Riipi, L., & Carlson, E. (1990). Tumor necrosis factor (TNF) is induced in mice by Candida Albicans: Role of TNF in fibrinogen increase. Infection and Immunity, 58, 5019–5029.

Rogoff, B. (1990). Apprenticeship in thinking: Cognitive development in social context. New York: Oxford University Press.

Rogoff, B., & Lave, J. (Eds.). (1984). Everyday cognition: Its development in social context. Cambridge, MA: Harvard University Press.

Rosaldo, R. (1989). Culture & truth: The remaking of social analysis. Boston: Beacon.

Rosenblatt, L. M. (1978). The reader, the text, the poem: The transactional theory of the literary work. Carbondale: Southern Illinois University Press.

Ryan, M. L. (1981). Introduction: On the why, what and how of generic taxonomy. Poetics, 10, 109–126.

Rymer, J. (1988). The scientific composing process: How eminent scientists write articles. In D. Jolliffe (Ed.), Writing in the academic disciplines (pp. 211–250). Norwood, NJ: Ablex.

Sawyer, W., & Watson, K. (1987). Questions of genre. In I. Reid (Ed.), The place of genre in learning: Current debates (pp. 46–57). Geelong, Australia: Deakin University Press.

Scanlon, R. (n.d.). Program notes to the American Repertory Theater production of The Writing Game. Cambridge, MA.

Schilb, J. (1988). Ideology and composition scholarship. Journal of Advanced Composition, 8, 22–29.

Schryer, C. (1993). Records as genre. Written Communication, 10, 200–234.

Schutz, A., & Luckmann, T. (1973). The structures of the life-world (R. M. Zaner & H. T. Engelhardt, Jr., Trans.). Evanston, IL: Northwestern University Press. (Original work published 1975)

Scribner, S. (1984). Studying working intelligence. In B. Rogoff & J. Lave (Eds.), Everyday cognition: Its development in social context (pp. 9–44). Cambridge, MA: Harvard University Press.

Searle, J. R. (1969). Speech acts: An essay in the philosophy of language. Cambridge, UK: Cambridge University Press.

Searle, J. R. (1979). Expression and meaning: Studies in the theory of speech acts. Cambridge, UK: Cambridge University Press.

Simons, H. W. (1978). "Genre-alizing" about rhetoric: A scientific approach. In K. K. Campbell & K. H. Jamison (Eds.), Form and genre: Shaping rhetorical action (pp. 33–50). Falls Church, VA: Speech Communication Association.

Sims, N. (1984). The literary journalists. New York: Ballantine.

Sloan, G. (1984). The frequency of transitional markers in discursive prose. College English, 46, 158–179.

Small, H. G. (1977). A co-citational model of a scientific specialty: A longitudinal study of citation research. Social Studies of Science, 7, 139–166.

Small, H. G. (1978). Cited documents as concept symbols. Social Studies of Science, 8, 327–340.

Stoller, P. (1989). The taste of ethnographic things. Philadelphia: University of Pennsylvania Press.

Suleiman, S. (1978). What is reader-oriented criticism? Reader: A Newsletter of Reader-oriented Criticism and Teaching. (Available from Elizabeth A. Flynn, Humanities Dept., Michigan Technological University), 4, 3–6.

Suleiman, S., & Crosman, I. (Eds.) (1980). The reader in the text: Essays on audience and interpretation. Princeton, NJ: Princeton University Press.

Swales, J. M. (1986). Citation analysis and discourse analysis. Applied Linguistics, 7, 39–56.

Swales, J. M. (1990). Genre analysis: English in academic and research settings. Cambridge, UK: Cambridge University Press.

Swales, J. M. (1993). Genre and engagement. Revue Belge de Philologie et d'Histoire, 71, 687–698.

Swales, J. M., & Najjar, H. (1987). The writing of research articles: Where to put the bottom line? Written Communication, 4, 175–191.

Tannen, D. (1982). Oral and literate strategies in spoken and written narratives. Language, 58, 1–21.

Tate, G. (Ed.). (1976). *Teaching composition: 10 bibliographical essays*. Fort Worth, TX: Texas Christian University Press.

Thomas, G. (1986). Mutual knowledge: A theoretical basis for analyzing audience. *College English, 48*(6), 580–594.

Todorov, T. (1976). The origin of genres. *New Literary History, 8,* 159–170.

Tompkins, J. (1977, April). [Letter to the editor]. *Reader: a newsletter of reader-oriented criticism and teaching,* (2), p. 2. (Available from Elizabeth A. Flynn, Humanities Dept., Michigan Technological University)

Tompkins, J. (Ed.). (1980). *Reader-response criticism: From formalism to post-structuralism.* Baltimore, MD: Johns Hopkins University Press.

Toulmin, S. (1958). *The uses of argument.* Cambridge, UK: Cambridge University Press.

Troyka, L. (1980). Pulse of the profession. *College Composition and Communication, 31,* 227–231.

Van Dijk, T. (1986). News schemata. In C. Cooper & S. Greenbaum (Eds.), *Studying writing: Linguistic approaches* (pp. 155–185). Beverly Hills, CA: Sage.

Vande Kopple, W. J. (1982). Functional sentence perspective, composition, and reading. *College Composition and Communication, 33,* 50–63.

Van Eemeren, F. H., & Grootendorst, R. (1983). *Speech acts in argumentative discussions.* Dordrecht, Netherlands: Foris.

van Maanen, J. (1988). *Tales of the field: On writing ethnography.* Chicago: University of Chicago Press.

Vygotsky, L. S. (1978). *Mind in society: The development of higher psychological processes* (M. Cole, V. J. Steiner, S. Scribner, & E. Souberman, Eds.). Cambridge, MA: Harvard University Press.

Vygotsky, L. S. (1986). *Thought and language* (A. Kozulin, Trans. and Ed.). Cambridge, MA: MIT Press.

Vygotsky, L. S. (1987). The development of scientific concepts in childhood. In R. W. Rieber & A. S. Carton (Eds.), *The collected works of L. S. Vygotsky: Vol. 1. Problems of general psychology* (N. Minick, Trans.). New York: Plenum.

Wernick, A. (1991). *Promotional culture.* London: Sage.

Wertsch, J. V. (Ed.). (1981). *The concept of activity in Soviet psychology.* Armonk, NY: M. E. Sharpe.

Wertsch, J. V. (1991). *Voices of the mind: A sociocultural approach to mediated action.* Cambridge, MA: Harvard University Press.

Wilson, T. P. (1991). Social structure and the sequential organization of interaction. In D. Boden & D. H. Zimmerman (Eds.), *Talk and social structure: Studies in ethnomethodology and conversation analysis* (pp. 22–43). Berkeley: University of California Press.

Witte, S. (1983). Topical structure and revision. *College Composition and Communication, 34,* 313–341.

Yates, J. A., & Orlikowski, W. J. (1992). Genres of organizational communication: A structurational approach. *Academy of Management Review, 17,* 299–326.

Yin, R. K. (1984). *Case study research: Design and methods.* Beverly Hills, CA: Sage.

Young, R. (1976). Invention: A topographical survey. In G. Tate (Ed.), *Teaching composition: 10 bibliographical essays* (pp. 1–43). Fort Worth, TX: Texas Christian University Press.

Young, R. (1978). Paradigms and problems: Needed research in rhetorical invention. In C. R. Cooper & L. Odell (Eds.), *Research on composing: Points of departure* (pp. 29–47). Urbana, IL: National Council of Teachers of English.

Young, R. (1980). Arts, crafts, gifts and knacks: Some disharmonies in the new rhetoric. In A. Freedman & I. Pringle (Eds.), *Reinventing the rhetorical tradition* (pp. 53–60). Conway, AR: L & S Books.

Young, R., Becker, A., & Pike, K. (1970). *Rhetoric: Discovery and change*. New York: Harcourt, Brace & World.

Zuckerman, H., & Merton, R. K. (1973). Institutionalized patterns of evaluation in science. In R. K. Merton, *The sociology of science: Theoretical and empirical investigations* (N. W. Storer, Ed.). Chicago: University of Chicago Press.

Zuckerman, S. H., & Bendele, A. M. (1989). Regulation of serum tumor necrosis factor in glucocorticoid-sensitive and -resistant rodent endotoxin shock models. *Infection and Immunity, 57*, 3009–3013.

# Author Index

183

# SUBJECT INDEX

## A

Abstractness, 98–99
Abstracts, 30–32, 34–35, 42, 97–116
Academic culture, 10
Academic discourse, 43
Activity theory, Russian, 3, 12
Apprenticeship, 7, 10, 13, 22–24, 117–144
Archival features, 39
Argument, Toulmin, 52, 56–57
Argumentation, 47–60, 65–66, 70–74
Articles, definite vs. indefinite, 128–130, 133, 137, 139–140
Audience, 2–3, 14–16, 24, 55, 58–59, 82, 124, 142–143

## B

Bending the genre, 159–160
Biology, 28–77
Blurred genres, 11, 157

## C

Carnegie Mellon University Rhetoric Program, 119–120, 123–149
Centrifugal vs. centripetal forces, 116, 149
Certification of knowledge, 76

Citation indices, 43, 92–93, 96
Citation, *see* Referencing
Cognition, situated, 3–4, 7–8, 10, 12–13, 28, 43, 117, 151–163
Cognitive psychology, 92, 119, 142
Coherence, textual, 126, 129, 139
Cohesion, textual, 123, 126, 129, 139–140
Collaborative inquiry, 147, 149
*College English,* 102
Communicative competence, 155, 160–161
Communities, discourse, *see* Discourse communities
Community ownership, 4, 115; *see also* Discourse communities
Composing processes, 28, 42
Composition and rhetoric, 97–144, 147, 161
Conference on College Composition and Communication, 97–116
Conference proposals, *see* Abstracts
Connectives, logical, 124, 128, 133, 139
Consumer culture, *see* Promotionalism
Context of situation, 157–158, 160–161
Contextualization, 47
    cues, 8
Conversation analysis, 10–11, 19
Credibility, authorial, *see* Ethos
Criticism, literary, 80–81, 83, 94–95, 109–112
    reader-oriented, 80–96
Cultural
    capital, 82

**187**